Future 21

Directions for America
in the 21st Century

Future 21

Directions for America in the 21st Century

EDITED BY

Paul M. Weyrich

AND

Connaught Marshner

Devin-Adair, Publishers
Greenwich, Connecticut

EXCELLENCE, SINCE 1911

Devin-Adair, Publishers, is America's foremost publisher of quality conservative books. Founded in 1911, the company has championed the cause of the Thinking Right and historically has published the work of major conservative writers. In recent years Devin-Adair has increased its emphasis in this area and today is considered the leading publishing firm of the right.

The company also has a long-standing reputation for works of significance in the fields of ecology, Irish literature, health and nutrition. It publishes superbly illustrated nature and travel books on the Eastern seaboard through its Chatham Press subsidiary.

Devin-Adair's newest emphasis is in the area of books, programs and software relating to the personal computer.

Devin-Adair operates the Veritas Book Club for conservative readers, the Ecological Book Club for nature and health audiences, and the Irish-American Book Society.

Copyright © 1984 by Paul M. Weyrich and Connaught Coyne Marshner

All rights reserved. No portion of this book may be reproduced or transmitted in any form or by any means, electronic or mechanical, including photocopy, recording, or any information and retrieval system, without the written permission of Devin-Adair, Publishers, 6 North Water Street, Greenwich, Connecticut 06830.

Manufactured in the United States of America.

Library of Congress Cataloging in Publication Data
Main entry under title:

Future 21.

   1. United States—Politics and government—1981–   —
Addresses, essays, lectures.   2. United States—Economic
policy—1981–   —Addresses, essays, lectures.
3. United States—Social policy—1980–   —Addresses,
essays, lectures.   4. Conservatism—United States—
Addresses, essays, lectures.   I. Weyrich, Paul M., 1942–
II. Marshner, Connaught Coyne, 1951–   III. Title:
Future twenty-one.
JK271.F87   1984   361.6'1'0973   84-1738
ISBN 0-8159-5523-5

Contents

Introduction	vii
I Economic Issues	1
1 *Growth in the 21st Century: Full Employment, Four Percent Interest Rates, A Balanced Budget and the Gold Standard* Lewis Lehrman	3
2 *Toward a New Nationalism: The Second Sacking of the West* Patrick J. Buchanan	26
II Defense and Foreign Policy Issues	41
3 *Strategic Defense: Toward Assured Survival* Lt. Gen. Daniel O. Graham, USA (Ret.)	43
4 *Space: The New Frontier* Congressman Newt Gingrich and James A. M. Muncy	61
5 *The U.S. and the UN: Time for Reappraisal* Burton Yale Pines	70
6 *Third World Policy to Strengthen Freedom* Major Gen. John K. Singlaub, USA (Ret.)	90
7 *Foreign Policy and the Conservative Blueprint* Charles A. Moser	103
III Social Issues	117
8 *Right and Wrong and America's Survival: An Ethical System for the Future* Connaught Marshner	119
9 *Decadence and Reform: Toward a Conservative Educational Agenda for the 21st Century* Allan C. Carlson	134

10 *Family Protection: The Imperative of the Future*
Connaught Marshner   148

11 *Making Ends Meet:
A Strategy for American Health Care Reform*
Ronald F. Docksai   167

12 *Zwap, Zing, Broing, Or, Computers Are Not Just Toys*
John C. Grunden   176

IV Institutional Issues   183

13 *Bureaucracy: An Inherent Evil?*
Paul M. Weyrich   185

14 *Judicial Reform: Improving the American System*
Patrick B. McGuigan   197

15 *The Reform of Democratic Institutions:
The National Initiative*
Paul M. Weyrich   222

Conclusion   230

Contributors   234

Index   242

Introduction

Unless you, yourself, are a conservative, you probably tend to see the conservative as one in a series of stereotypes.

The images take a number of forms: There is the highly educated eccentric, secreted in his own private world, disdaining or oblivious to the hot and weary struggles of the poor. Another image is that of the capitalist—as Thomas Nast might have drawn him—filthy with riches, hard of heart and cold of eye, muttering over and over, "What's good for business is good for America," as he stomps on a defenseless union maid.

Recently, another stereotype has emerged. Conservatives may now be envisioned as dowdy, middle-aged women, eyes glowing with self-righteousness as they stridently scream that abortion is murder and link arms with thick-skulled preachers who want to force their morals down everyone's throats. And detractors always include in their portrayals of conservatives the semi-jock who likes violence for its own sake, who carries a rifle because it reinforces his macho self-image, and who slavers after a commie under every bed, longing to push the button and nuke 'em all.

These "conservative" pigeonholes are not to be found in the pages of *Future 21*. The authors include academicians and businessmen, military men and right-to-lifers. The book itself is a redefinition of the issues of concern to conservatives, thereby, we believe, by extension of concern to all Americans. A few of the familiar issues are here: a strategy for defeating (not containing, note) the Soviets; a call for denying the United Nations some of its lifeblood sucked from the U.S. Treasury. This is a forward-looking book: Space and computers, both futuristic, are critical to a conservative opportunity society. Traditional ethics and values, as understood by beliefs older than 1776, are part of this conservative agenda.

Not every conservative will agree with all the propositions contained in these essays. Direct democracy, as advocated by Paul Weyrich, is not a standard conservative belief. Similarly, Patrick McGuigan's call for control of the federal judiciary will not please those who think conservatism means never changing the established institutions.

If conservatism is going to be of consequence in the 21st century, it must broaden its base. Coalition building is the tactic of the future; re-shaping the agenda is the strategy of today. In that spirit, then, is this book offered as a contribution to the general effort.

—Connaught Marshner

I
Economic Issues

1

Growth in the 21st Century: Full Employment, Four Percent Interest Rates, A Balanced Budget and the Gold Standard

Lewis E. Lehrman

Preface

We live in an age of financial disorder. Inflation and unemployment are its hallmarks. Punctuated by brief and painful moments of austerity, recession, and deflation, the world of work hurtles without compass toward a rendezvous with monetary catastrophe. Trapped between ever-rising prices and ever-higher unemployment, the American dream eludes the grasp of much of our generation. Full employment, four percent interest rates, a home, the chance of a college education for all our children must be restored and they can be. But only if we create rapid economic growth *and* end inflation *now*.

Usually defined by economists as too much money chasing too few goods, inflation is really the depreciation of money by government authorities. Inflation is the process of destruction of the monetary standard—in our case, the dollar. But a stable monetary standard is essential in a free economy. It is in fact the indispensable standard of commercial value.

Stable money is bound up with economic growth and the stability of civilization itself. Just as the depreciation of moral and legal standards eventually brings about revolution, so the depreciation of the monetary standard, the commercial yardstick of civilization, brings chaos and disorder. In our era, as in times gone by, social disorder is marked by false paper money and scarcity of work.

For a generation we have witnessed the debasement of historic

American standards of value—not only in the world of commerce, but also in our public life, our schools, our families, our art, and our science. Whether this destructive course continues will determine the fate of our country. It is clear that the unique American constitutional order hangs in the balance.

I. Real Money and The Federal Reserve System

When stable political institutions are overturned, the result is revolution. Inflation and deflation are price revolutions in the world of commercial institutions. And history shows that a price revolution often precedes a political revolution. Lenin in Russia, Hitler in Germany, and Mao in China—just three examples—came to power after periods of great inflation.

Our postwar age of inflation ended America's high productivity, low interest rates, and low unemployment rates. In the past three years real interest rates in the West, to paraphrase Helmut Schmidt, the former West German Chancellor, have been the highest since the birth of Christ. Under President Reagan, we have made progress. But today, we endure a permanent financial crisis throughout the world because men and women no longer trust their money.

Politicians have destroyed the monetary standard. The moral order of money has decomposed. We no longer trust the value of the American dollar—not even now, when inflation abates for a moment. That is because the dollar is no longer an honest measure of the value of work. The dollar has also ceased to be the stable standard of economic worth throughout the world.

In 1971, President Nixon cut the paper dollar's final link to the gold standard. Since then, our currency has been nothing but printed pieces of green paper or impulses on a computer tape, manipulated by a government-created monopoly bank called the Federal Reserve System. What the managers of the Post Office have done to our mail, the currency of communications, the Fed, a government monopoly, has done to the currency of commerce, the dollar. Our economy is sick: the disease is the debasement of our money. High interest rates and high unemployment are merely the symptoms.

Working people understandably refuse to hold the volatile paper dollar for long periods. When it depreciates, they spend it quickly for a house, a car, an antique, a rare coin—anything *real*. When it appreciates for short periods, as in 1982, they lend their paper and credit dollars for equally short periods to the highest bidder, usually the U.S. government or money market funds, neither of which creates new technologies, builds factories, or hires unemployed workers.

Why have producers and consumers alike lost faith in the dollar, our commercial standard of value? Because the U.S. government and the Federal Reserve, along with their wards, the so-called private banks, have created more dollars than market participants want to hold. Even when the dollar rises against foreign currencies its value still declines at home. While the foreign exchange rate of the dollar hit new ten-year highs on world currency markets in early November 1982, its domestic purchasing power was still 5–6 percent below that of November 1981. Even during recession, falling demand and periods of high unemployment the dollar depreciates at home.

The paper and deposit dollars Americans are required to hold were, and are, often issued to pay for colossal budget deficits, created by special-interest government which dominates the Congress in Washington. The process by which our government finances a part of its deficits with *new* credit money is an indirect one. Indeed, it is a hidden process largely carried out in the banking system. Essentially, the Federal Reserve System buys government bonds in the market and pays for them not with real money but with new credit (or deposit) money only the Fed has the power to create. These bonds were originally issued to the market by the Treasury to pay for the government deficit. Only later do they become the basis of new money issued by the Fed.

By purchasing government bills and bonds the Fed simply issues new credit in the banking system to finance *indirectly* the government deficit. Economists call this process open market operations, or government debt monetization. The new money pouring from the Fed also provides reserves to the banking system in order to create new commercial bank credit which is added to the credit provided by true national savings. Indeed, the new bank credit is often issued to bail out insolvent banks and foreign debtors. The proposed 50 percent quota increase for the IMF today was a concrete example. It is simply a hidden tax, a transfer of billions of dollars of purchasing power from working Americans to foreign governments and troubled big city banks.

Conversely, during short periods of government created dollar scarcity and recession, such as 1981–82, the Fed literally denied credit to homebuyers, farmers, and small business by purchasing fewer government bonds on credit, in order to correct for previous periods of inflationary credit excess. During such periods of bank credit restriction by the Fed, the Treasury goes into the market and takes up most of the real savings. Small borrowers are squeezed out. Dollar scarcity, recession, small business bankruptcies, mortgage foreclosures and unacceptable levels of unemployment result.

In truth, Fed manipulation of our money and credit, by means of open market operations in government debt, causes both inflation *and* deflation. This instability and disorder will continue until free Americans decide what the dollar standard is to be. Is the dollar to be a manipulated piece of worthless paper brought into being by the monetization of government debt? Or is it to be a monetary standard of substance, of lasting value? Is it to be ruled by the principle of integrity? Or is it to be manipulated by a guardian elite at the Federal Reserve Board?

The lesson of commercial life is clear for all who would learn it. Real labor must be paid in true money. False money destroys incentive. The Fed can create false money. But the Fed cannot create real wealth. Only hard work creates wealth.

What the Fed and the politicians have forgotten is the sacred link between the value of the dollar and the value of work. Economics does not lie outside the dominion of the moral order. Nor do economics and monetary policy dwell outside the rule of law. The link between money and work is a constitutional bond. The link between work and money is a covenant which joined the nation at its birth. Indeed, it was part of the "dominion covenant," recorded in Genesis, present at the onset of civilization.

II. Real Money and Honest Work

To labor freely and to create wealth gives rise to the right to ownership. The right of ownership establishes an essential attribute of public order. Ownership is an indispensable condition of freedom of person. Without the right of ownership, "might" alone determines "right" among individuals who, without property rights, forcibly dispute ownership of the articles of wealth of the world. Therefore, in the world of work true personhood can only arise with lawful rights to claim wealth. Originating in honest work, real money is simply the free right to claim wealth, the products of human labor. These rights help to establish public order. Without public order, freedom disappears. True money and freedom of person are, therefore, inextricably linked.

In America honest money was the birthright of all who lived under our written Constitution; ownership established the right of free men and women of disposal over their property, so long as the laws and regulations of the land were observed. Ownership led free people to trade the things they had for those they desired. Trade brought about the free market.

It is no accident that America, a continental nation living under a free constitutional order, became the greatest open market in world history. Ours was the fulfillment of thousands of years of struggle for the free market order.

In very early times, on the market, men and women directly exchanged the products of their work. This is barter economy. Later, they exchanged their goods indirectly for money—and then traded the money for goods. This is money-exchange economy. But in either case, human work, resulting in useful products, is the unique endowment of both primitive and modern economies.

A worker labors many hours to create a product. If he exchanges the product of his work for irredeemable Federal Reserve notes today, he receives for his costs of production a paper dollar that costs almost nothing to produce. But if he exchanges a valuable service or product of his hands for, say, a gold dollar, the making of which entails real costs of production, he receives in exchange for the sacrifice of his work the product of labor offered by other craftsmen. All workers and producers intuitively desire to trade proportional real product values of honest work—both in quality and quantity. On the open market producers learned to use real money, the products of miners and minters, to exchange the lawful rights of ownership to the real value of their work product.

The American Constitution embodies these truths in two monetary clauses. First, the Constitution prohibits the states from making anything but "gold and silver coin" a legal tender, i.e., lawful money. Second, Congress is given the exclusive power "to coin money." The word "coin" is explicit. But just as decisive, during the constitutional debates of 1787–1789, the founders clearly ruled out the power of the Federal government to create (or "emit") irredeemable government bills of credit, or, as we call such bills today, inconvertible paper money. The irredeemable Federal Reserve note is therefore false money.

Authentic American money is standard gold or silver coin. Or it may also be properly issued paper claims convertible by law into standard weights of gold and silver coin. Only the gold or silver dollar is real money according to the Constitution.

But the paper dollar, the so-called Federal Reserve Note, with which Americans are now paid, is not now convertible to gold and silver coin. Constitutionally, it is not lawful money. Nor is it real money. Virtually no work is required of the government to produce credit money at the Fed. There is virtually zero cost to mass-printing the paper dollar bill. Government paper money has no underlying value because it costs almost nothing to make. That is why, in 50 years, the value of the paper dollar has fallen almost 90 percent. The dollar now declines inexorably toward its real costs of production, which are virtually nothing.

Since August 15, 1971, the paper dollar has not even been *indirectly* linked to anything of real value. Yet the paper dollar is what the government declares "legal tender." That is, the U.S. government requires Americans to accept valueless paper money in payment of all debts, public and private. In exchange for real work, real values, and real debts, Americans are required to accept government produced paper money—unless a contract specifies otherwise.

No wonder American factories grow idle. The fluctuating value of manipulated paper money reduces the incentive to lend at long term and to produce new goods, because the money value of future rewards for those who work and lend is so uncertain and likely to fall. But new technologies, new factories, new businesses, and new jobs can only be built with savings lent at long term. When the value of money is manipulated by the sovereign, investors freely go on strike and workers involuntarily lay down their tools.

In America, long term saving is no longer a security and a providence for an uncertain future. Long term saving is dead. So, therefore, is long term lending. As a result, free Americans have involuntarily become unproductive, short term speculators to save themselves. In a world of monetary disorder, gamblers replace savers. Deprived of long term savings, the capital markets atrophy. Real interest rates rise. Long term economic growth and stable prices disappear.

Who will work, save, lend and invest for long periods in exchange for paper money issued and depreciated by the government? Fewer and fewer Americans. But the future depends upon those who will save and lend for long periods to others who create new enterprises and new jobs. Without faith in the future purchasing power of money, the wellsprings of economic growth dry up. The overriding issue of our times is, therefore, how we reestablish trust in a government which, by destroying the monetary standard, destroys the future. Can such a government long endure?

A hyperactive government which manipulates our currency and credit has converted America from the promised land of work, family and future, from a nation of savers and investors, into a vast gaming table, a nation of speculators who fear the future. Indeed, the whole commercial world has now come to resemble a vast Las Vegas, a global casino wherein the speculative players of Wall Street wait upon the big dealers at the Federal Reserve and foreign central banks to issue and withdraw, as if by magic, the empty monetary tokens of their trade.

Almost two hundred years ago, during America's first great inflation of the Revolutionary War period, Thomas Jefferson wrote, "We are now taught to believe that magical tricks upon paper can produce as solid wealth as hard labor in the earth." The author of the Declaration of Independence and the founder of the Democratic Party ruled out the paper money experiment. Gold and silver coin, "specie" money, he wrote, "is the most perfect medium . . . because having intrinsic and universal value, it can never die in our hands. Paper money is liable to be abused, has been, is, and forever will be abused, in every country in which it is permitted."

Inflation, high interest rates and economic stagnation are monetary problems. They are caused by diseased money, which is the political issue of our times. Until this political issue is resolved no budget policy, no tax policy, no regulatory policy, no jobs policy, no economic growth policy, no interest rate policy, no defense policy will establish conditions leading to lasting prosperity, full employment and stable prices.

Five financial forces now conspire to destroy the President's noble economic ideals: anarchy in the international monetary system, ever-rising federal spending, the "permanent" federal deficit, the Treasury demand for credit to finance the deficit, and the arbitrary creation and destruction of money and credit by the Federal Reserve System. Together, these forces will continue to cause extreme price and exchange rate volatility, high real interest rates, and global economic stagnation.

It is true that economic recovery is now underway. But the story is not yet fully told. Either this shall be one more stop-go cycle, or we shall use this opportunity to create a lasting prosperity.

III. Real Money and Long Term Capital Markets

Consider the U.S. credit markets today. *Total* net government credit demand (Federal and local, direct and guaranteed) was approximately $250–300 billion in 1983. But personal savings, the source of non-bank credit for investment, were, at most, $150 billion that year. Total net national savings, not including depreciation, could be as much as approximately $250 billion. If all savings from depreciation are re-invested, we maintain the level of our capital stock. Thus, total government demand for credit almost equals net national savings, not including depreciation. The market for savings, or financial capital, is utterly dominated by ubiquitous government. The impact of this huge government demand for credit has stunned enterprise and dazed the capital markets.

When the demand for credit exceeds the supply of savings, the real price for credit must rise—especially if the Fed is following an austerity policy. And, of course, real interest rates, the price of credit, rise under such circumstances, despite high unemployment and use of industrial capacity. The level of real U.S. interest rates reduces normal investment incentives and perversely, like a magnet, draws savings from all over the world, further impoverishing developing countries starved for capital investment.

Throughout the world economy the public sector demand for credit almost equals, and in places exceeds, the total amount of private savings. As government consumes almost all true market savings that create *market credit,* business investment languishes worldwide. The world economy therefore depends on the willingness of central banks like the Federal Reserve to create *new bank credit.*

It is government spending and borrowing at present levels, joined to central bank money market manipulation and currency depreciation all over the world, that has immobilized the long term capital markets.

True, the short term capital markets have recently opened up—but mostly to larger companies. This occurred in the second half of 1982 as the demand for credit fell, as U. S. manufacturing production collapsed to 67 percent of capacity, bankruptcies proliferated, and unemployment rose to over 10 percent. But was it really necessary for the Fed, by means of credit austerity in 1981 and early 1982, to demolish healthy, if fragile, parts of American business? Do we really have to put our workers on the breadlines in order to reduce the demand for private credit while the U. S. government and foreign debtors preempt it all? Must we really create recession and unemployment in order to end inflation? Must the increasing wealth of the permanent government in Washington be purchased by imposing austerity on American working people? Must this human agony be the price paid so that the U.S. Treasury and the politicians can continue to borrow and spend our savings on special interest subsidies at home and abroad, while the hope of sustained non-inflationary economic growth recedes over the horizon? If the government commandeers our shrunken national savings, and if the worldwide government sector absorbs most of global savings, what kind of credit can be left over for entrepreneurs and working people in the commercial world?

The choice must not be austerity and unemployment on the one hand, or paper and credit money inflation on the other. Yet, under present monetary conditions that is our choice.

The issue is clear. Sustained economic growth and a rising demand for labor develop from *long term investment* of savings in new and productive industry. But government borrows almost all the savings. Thus, in the absence of sufficient private savings to satisfy both public and private sector demands, the Fed feels compelled to create new bank credit. This new Fed credit not only subsidizes the government and the banks; it is also necessary in order to stimulate the commercial sector from the lethargy imposed by austerity.

The resulting economic equation is inescapable. Government demand for goods, financed by new credit (offset by no supply of goods), plus private demand for goods leads to *total market demand for goods in excess of total supply* during the same market period. Continuous permanent excess demand causes permanent inflation. Economic and social disorder are the certain results.

To paraphrase Samuel Johnson's remark of two hundred years ago, the reigning error of mankind is that some men and most governments today are not content with the conditions on which the goods and blessings of life are granted. In a free and moral society all who are able must supply before they demand. For to consume before one produces entails a subsidy. But a subsidy can be obtained freely, as in a charity, or by force, as in a government exacted transfer of wealth. Since the government has a monopoly of force, organized special interests who seek subsidies instead of work, who seek to consume before they produce, try to commandeer the government. With control of the government, they can tax, create money, and subsidize their supplicants.

Big business, big labor, big government and big banks have made subsidies the stuff of American politics for two generations. But subsidies insulate enterprises from the consequences of their own actions. Subsidies jam the natural adjustment mechanism that leads free men and women to stable conduct and thus to stable institutions. As our government has proved, subsidies lead to follies. While the Department of Health and Human Services inveighs against the health hazards of smoking, Congress subsidizes the tobacco growers. Herbert Spencer once wrote that the ultimate consequence of insulating men from their follies was to fill the world with fools.

Previous government and Fed policies have sowed financial chaos. The time has come, therefore, for lasting monetary reform and an enduring expansion.

IV. Neo-Keynesian, Monetarist, or Classical Monetary Policy: Which Is It To Be?

Our economic disorders are not unique.

Financial instability greeted Margaret Thatcher in 1979 when she was elected Prime Minister of England. She purchased declining inflation with a 14 percent unemployment rate. Does it really have to be this way?

In 1958, economic chaos, inflation, and war destroyed the Fourth

Republic in France. But President Charles de Gaulle and his financial advisor, Jacques Rueff, understood the causes of the French financial collapse: huge defense spending on the Algerian War, government budget deficits (financed indirectly by the Bank of France), a central bank manipulated currency, and an overregulated economy. In creating the Fifth Republic, Rueff and de Gaulle established a new monetary standard, the gold franc, reformed the currency, balanced the current budget, and began the deregulation of the economy. France under de Gaulle also withdrew from Algeria and established peace. The result for France was national independence and a decade of extraordinary economic growth, greater even than that of Germany.

Here in the United States, decades of *Keynesian*[1] economic policies of government spending and credit expansion failed under Lyndon Johnson, Richard Nixon, and Jimmy Carter. Prime Minister Thatcher's *monetarist*[2] policies came to naught in England because they depended too much on central bank manipulation of the money supply and on austerity. They have been abandoned. Well-intentioned monetarist policies, officially adopted by the Reagan Administration and the Federal Reserve, have done no better in the United States. Falling inflation rates in the U. S. were brought about through government imposed credit restriction and unemployment. In the U. S., too, monetarist policies have now been abandoned. Because of the fear of depression and a worldwide financial collapse, Paul Volcker, Chairman of the Fed, modified his "practical monetarism," and between June and November of 1982, as unemployment reached 10.8 percent, the highest since 1940, charted a new expansionist credit policy for the Federal Reserve System.

Those of us who believed in the goals of the so-called Reagan revolution had to force ourselves to face up the consequences of Reagan's first two years. We called for boom and got something very close to bust. We called for a balanced budget and got record-shattering deficits. We called for a restoration of capital markets so business could borrow money for long periods at reasonable interest rates and we got a devastating credit crunch.

Why? There are many possible explanations, but in my view the

---

[1] Economic policies inspired by John Maynard Keynes, English economist, who advocated government spending and credit policies to end recession, and government imposed austerity to end inflation.

[2] Monetarist policies rely on government central bank manipulation of the money supply, a doctrine identified with economist Milton Friedman. Monetarism is the most recent form of the Quantity Theory of Money which holds that price stability and steady economic growth can be brought about by planned and regular increases in the quantity of money.

missing link is a policy we once called for but quickly forgot. Let me quote the 1980 Republican platform: "One of the most urgent tasks ... will be the restoration of a dependable monetary standard." The restoration of the true American monetary standard—a *gold* standard, the symbol of classical monetary policy—was held up as an alternative to the conventional economics of the past generation which had shattered the great American postwar prosperity.

All of Ronald Reagan's 1980 campaign rhetoric repudiated thirty years of Keynesian credit and fiscal manipulators. His campaign for economic renewal also called for an *end* to the budget deficit in 1983. It was argued at the time that only rapid economic expansion could create sufficient new tax revenues to balance the budget. Instead, double-digit real interest rates made such an expansion impossible. Fed policy ended the recovery from the 1980 recession, overwhelmed the 1981 tax cut, and sent the economy reeling in 1982 for the second recession in as many years. This back-to-back double recession in two consecutive calendar years is unique in the recorded history of American business cycles.

In terms of real growth figures, Presidents Carter and Reagan presided over a three-year recession. It ended only after a three-year Fed monetarist experiment, begun by Paul Volcker on October 6, 1979, collapsed. At that time, Chairman Volcker announced that Fed monetary policy by interest rate manipulation had been reformulated. Instead of targeting *interest rates,* a neo-Keynesian prescription, the Fed, he said, would henceforth target a *monetary quantity;* that is, a specific quantity of bank reserves held to be consistent with a certain rate of growth of the quantity of money in circulation (Mlb). This reform was branded as a monetarist revolution. In force for three years, the monetarist policy of the Fed, with the goal of fixing the quantity of money, was abandoned by Chairman Volcker on July 1, 1982. The decision came on an 8–4 vote of the Fed Open Market Committee under rising pressure from Congress and international debt problems. Eleven percent unemployment and a world banking crisis forced an end to Fed austerity.

The underlying truth is the Federal Reserve cannot fix the quantity of money in circulation. Nor, over the long run, can it fix interest rates, the monetary base, or the level of bank reserves. In attempting to accomplish these things the Fed has wrecked the long term capital markets of America. If a free country like ours must have a monopoly central bank, then it must be governed by the rule of a monetary constitution. Ours is a nation of laws, not of men.

The most efficient monetary rules would require the Fed to re-mobilize the discount rate, to prohibit the purchase by the Fed of government debt, and to join this central bank reform to a more general monetary reform—the establishment of a real gold standard. These rules would lead to reasonable price stability and sustained economic growth.

It is true that classical monetary policy, a real gold standard, is unfashionable among the political, bureaucratic, and academic elites. But so was Ronald Reagan. He won without them—because he was right. And so, too, will the gold standard—because its efficacy is based upon its ineffable simplicity and practicality. Ironically, that is a prime reason why the sophisticated experts reject it. To them a convertible currency is too straightforward a solution for the problems of economic stagnation and inflation. Mathematicians and economists are taught in graduate school that economics and economic statistics are very complex subjects. They conclude, therefore, that economic policies and their bureaucracies must be equally complex.

A marvel of the gold standard is that, in the absence of world war and trade war, it worked reasonably well in the past. It is also true *no* free economic institution can long survive global war and protectionism. Most important, a virtue of gold money is that it can be understood and trusted by working people. Under the rules of a real gold standard, free people alone control the quantity of money in circulation. A gold based currency is in fact democratic money. It is a populist institution beyond the reach of a guardian elite. If we adopt the gold standard the central government and the Federal Reserve System will no longer be able to manipulate the value and supply of the American dollar.

Curiously, it was in a conservative administration that the Fed was pressed by Reagan's White House neo-Keynesians *not* to reform our diseased money, but to once again expand central bank credit as quickly as possible. The new Fed credit was to accommodate not only U. S. government borrowing requirements, but also the reckless big city banks and the insolvent Third World countries—not to mention legitimate needs to private industry.

Change had to come. The gratuitous austerity imposed by the monetarism of the Fed during 1981 and 1982 rankled a free people too much. This was especially because the U.S. government had increased its own lavish spending in 1982 by 11–12 percent while the wages of workers rose only 5 percent.

On the horizon lurk another speculative bubble, foreign exchange crises, commodity booms, precious metal hysteria, more budget crises and world monetary disorder. True, the Fed will have bailed out the money-center banks and the bankrupt Third World, monetarism will be a thing of the past, the immediate unemployment crisis will be over, nominal interest rates will have fallen under the weight of Fed credit policy. All these things are certainly better than the feckless austerity and recession of 1981–1982.

We have not, however, launched a sustained economic recovery necessarily based upon a sound currency and a stable price level. Nor will we bring about low long term interest rates with a stop-go monetarist policy such as that employed by Paul Volcker in the early years of the Reagan Administration.

Under present monetary policies the hoped-for Reagan recovery, too, will pass, leaving behind a residue of profoundly disappointed expectations. Left behind also will be an American people looking more and more for radical change and a thoroughgoing reformation of our increasingly moribund political and financial institutions.

It does not have to be this way.

Here and now, the President can decide the direction of the world economy for a generation. Will it be more of the same—stop-go credit cycles into the future? Or will it be true monetary reform and an enduring legacy of rapid non-inflationary growth?

The failures of past economic policies also suggest that the choice should not be between the austerity of monetarism and the stop-go cycles of Keynesianism. Both well-meaning monetarists and Keynesians care little about the integrity of the monetary standard, believing as they do in academic dogmas that assure them that they can wisely manipulate the quantity of paper and credit money needed to bring about prosperity. Often, the abstract formulas of these experts work well on a computer or in a classroom. But neither the simultaneous equations of an econometrician nor the blackboards of a professor are true substitutes for the real world of the market and its standards.

Only a few economists argue that a thoroughgoing monetary reform on the classical model will fulfill the promise of the Reagan election. It is the present indifference of academic economists, politicians and bureaucrats toward monetary reform that has deferred the promise. The complicity of the elites in the destruction of the historic American monetary standard is an economic heresy which ravages the world. In the economy, the wages of sin are alternating seizures of inflation and unemployment.

Meanwhile, because of the Reagan Administration's timid and uncertain policy toward the Fed, and its failure to understand the principal cause of the colossal deficits, namely, recession, economic growth was held back during the early Reagan years.

As a result, the nation faced the major challenge of postwar American financial policy, as the Fed launched a credit reflation under budgetary conditions unique in our history. Rising government credit demands and historically high unemployment and interest rates, combined with the political decision by the Fed to create a worldwide monetary expansion in order to raise commodity prices, rescue the world banking system, and revive the U. S. economy, could, if sustained for several years, cause a complete collapse of U. S. financial institutions.

Once the wonder of the Western world, American long-term capital markets have already ceased to exist as our forefathers knew them. Whether they have a future at all, whether we shall inaugurate a period of sustained non-inflationary growth could have been determined by the Reagan Administration's monetary policy.

The political stakes are great. That is because a true reform of monetary policy can change a cyclical upswing into a ten-year-long investment boom.

V. The Classical Monetary Policy

President Reagan did not need to accept the economic stagnation and slow growth that have caused inordinate budget deficits. Nor did he have to accept the gradual destruction of our money. The remedies were available, as they are now. They are historic remedies. We *can* stabilize the price level. We *can* grow rapidly again. We *can* balance the budget. We can have full employment and 4 percent interest rates. But we will not have them until we have real money.

Only the President can reestablish confidence in the future purchasing power of American money. That is the way to rebuild faith in the future of the American dream itself.

To do so, an administration must establish a convertible currency, end the era of floating exchange rates, and create a new international monetary order based on a common world currency, the gold standard.

The world needs a unified currency because there is only one economy, and that is a unified, integrated world economy. Through the mechanism of arbitrage, the prices of all national economies are linked indissolubly. There is no such thing as an independent monetary policy, the effects of which are contained within the national economy. Therefore, there can be no monetary policy in the true national interest unless it is consistent with the interests of the international monetary system to which it is inextricably bound.

History shows that the optimum monetary institution of international financial order must be an impartial, global coordinating mechanism, outside the control of any soverign state. Such a coordinating mechanism is a multilateral, fixed exchange rate based on unrestricted convertibility of national currencies to gold. Such a true international gold standard operated effectively between 1879–1914 amidst a sophisticated worldwide fractional reserve banking system, at least as integrated then as ours is today. The true gold standard was successful because it was an efficient world currency regime requiring prompt gold settlements to adjust balance-of-payments deficits. It operated in the manner of a global gyroscope to maintain long run price stability and efficient allocation of scarce capital the world over.

Though the gold standard was imperfect, no world monetary system has worked as well (or less imperfectly).

Even huge gold discoveries never resulted in sustained, high inflation. The vast expansion of gold money in Europe during the sixteenth century and the nineteenth century never caused the price level to rise in excess of an average of 3 percent over a long period. Compared to the past 10 years of central bank managed paper money and floating rates, 3 percent inflation is the essence of stability.

Even the part-time absence of large countries like Germany or the United States from the mid-nineteenth century international monetary order did not destabilize the British led convertible currency regime. Nor, for similar reasons, could the Soviet Union and South Africa disrupt a U. S.-led, modernized real international gold standard today. Gold is the optimum monetary standard because it exhibits, better than any commodity, a necessary virtue of money: Total new gold production in any single year is only a very minor fraction of total supply of gold in existence—about 2 percent. Indeed, the average rate of increase of new gold production is equal to the average rate of gain of productivity since the onset of the industrial revolution. That is why gold is stable money.

Moreover, South African production, approximately 21 million ounces, and Soviet production, approximately 8–10 million ounces, is but a drop in the bucket compared to total world stocks, approximately 2.5 billion ounces. Withholding or selling new production of such small quantities cannot disturb the stability of the gold standard, one rule of which causes the authorities to sell or buy at the established rate all gold demanded or offered. In addition, only with gold does the rate of growth of world money stocks naturally conform to the conditions of the monetarist rule—a steady rate of growth of the money supply, consistent with the long term rate of economic growth. And this is because, unique among commodities, gold is not susceptible to scale production techniques which can vastly or quickly increase its supply through new discovery or invention. Over the long run production statistics show that the supply and demand for gold are stable—just as monetary theory shows that the demand for real cash balances is stable over the long run. The alleged volatility of the price of gold is a curious inversion of the truth. It is not gold that is unstable. On the contrary, the stable long run value of gold is recorded today by the extraordinary and unstable fluctuations in the value of paper and credit money—manipulated as they are by the monetary authorities.

A study of the supply conditions of gold production over centuries shows that it takes a relatively constant rate of application of a certain quantity of capital and labor to produce a constant quantity of gold. Gold production is therefore like a metering device, an optimum standard, a yardstick by which to gauge equitably the relative productivity, over time, of *all* capital and labor in an integrated world market economy. The unique characteristics of the conditions of gold production can be established with respect to no other commodity, product, or man-made banking device.

These conditions explain why gold has been world money from time immemorial. They also explain why gold emerged as the natural standard of the free monetary order. In an imperfect world, the gold standard was freely selected in an open market as the commercial yardstick of free people. It served, less imperfectly than any other contrivance, the economic purposes of exchange, standard calculations of price, and as the enduring repository of saving. *When free to choose,* in the absence of legal tender laws, *free people choose gold as money.*

The gold standard, finally, may be seen as the way to end the mindless speculation and fluctuation of inconvertible national currencies. In particular, the real gold standard spells the end of unproductive speculation in gold and eliminates the inflationary premium which now benefits only the South Africans and the Russians.

The gold standard, a convertible dollar, can end the present financial disorder in America and the world. In plain English, it is the missing link in the search for a lasting economic renewal in America. It is a financial policy which I deeply believe can create the conditions of rapid non-inflationary economic growth. And only rapid economic growth can fulfill the American dream *and* pay for the expanding scale of national defense.

Indeed, the history of the West and of our own country bears witness. After the hyperinflation of the American Revolutionary War and the corresponding economic decline (1775–1789), the new constitutional republic was established upon the bedrock of a new monetary order. It was Alexander Hamilton who brought about the mint act of 1792. By this act, the American dollar was fixed by law to a gold and silver basis. Economic historians and scholars of the period all remark the extraordinary ten-year boom that followed. Low long term interest rates, rapid growth in the work force, and a stable price level were the hallmarks of a return to convertibility at the birth of the American nation.

Napoleon ended financial catastrophe in France, after the paper money debacle of the French revolution, by establishing the gold franc. Financial stability and prosperity followed, generating the revenues which filled the Imperial Treasury.

The restoration of the gold standard in England in 1819–1821 ended the 24-year financial nightmare (1795–1819) of alternating wartime inflation and peacetime austerity and deflation. English economic historians all report that one of England's greatest investment booms followed in the wake of the restoration of currency convertibility in 1821.

America in 1879 ended a 17-year period of floating-exchange rates and paper money, begun in 1862 by the outbreak of Civil War. This period of war and reconstruction was also characterized by a doubling of the price level, then a peacetime deflation. The gold standard and currency convertibility were restored in January of 1879. Real growth of national income averaged 8.4 percent annually for the next four years—and almost 6 percent for a decade.

These are but a few examples, drawn from the only reliable laboratory for economic experiments, the real history of nations and people. These historical cases are the stuff of reality, not airy abstractions drawn from computers and blackboards. They show that the effects of a thoroughgoing monetary reform—the end of irredeemable paper money and the end of floating exchange rates—lead to new faith in the future.

Just as important, the restoration of the monetary standard will encourage, once again, new long term business lending. Between 1879 and 1960, under the gold standard and Bretton Woods, 4 percent mortgage and business loans for 30–50 years were commonplace. And the price level was reasonably stable. Average prices were almost exactly the same in 1914 as in 1879. After a period of inflation and austerity caused by managed paper currencies, a convertible dollar creates confidence in the future purchasing power of money and a boom in *long term lending*—leading to an investment boom, rapid economic growth, a huge demand for labor, and a stable price level. These are the same effects that can again be brought about by virtue of a sound financial policy. The same causes, under similar conditions, *will* tend to produce the same effects.

When I forecast 4–5 percent mortgage interest rates under a modernized gold standard today, some of my younger friends are incredulous. But it was less than 20 years ago, in 1968 at age 30, that I obtained my first home mortgage at 5.5 percent. Even then, in the waning days of the Bretton Woods gold-linked exchange rate system, long term interest rates were low and reasonably stable compared to today.

VI. Real Money and the American Dream

The first and necessary factor for sustained non-inflationary economic growth will be a dollar once again as good as gold. Under the real gold standard, the world will be reassured that the price level in the future will be *permanently pinned down*. The gold standard is an actuarial guarantee to working people that the purchasing power of money will be approximately the same in the future as it is on the first day of convertibility. Professor Roy Jastram has shown that the purchasing power of gold was constant for four centuries, 1540–1940. Permanent inflation and high interest rates are ruled out by the gold dollar. Thus are expectations stabilized and the inflation premium in interest rates eradicated.

Our grandparents lent their long term savings to American railroads (for 50–100 years) at 3 percent under the international gold standard. They did so, and as we shall lend to new industries again, because only the gold monetary standard will restore our faith that the savings we lend to business today will yield us and our grandchildren future rewards paid in honest dollars of similar purchasing power.

It is this faith in the integrity of the monetary standard that will rebuild the foundations of long term capital markets. With the advent of real money, the sluice gates will open and savings, now held at short term, will pour into new, long term debt and equity investments. At first, the rush of a great new supply of long term savings into the credit markets will exceed the demand. As a result, long term rates of interest will fall. As real interest rates fall, the demand for low-cost financial capital will rise—to build businesses and homes. As the investment boom in new technology, plant and equipment gets underway, the demand for labor will rise rapidly. Unemployment will fall.

After the monetary reform, real economic growth will rise to 7 percent per year and be sustained for at least four years. A decade of economic growth averaging 5 percent will be underway. As the tax base expands, tax revenues will pour into the Treasury. For each 1 percent fall in the unemployment rate the government deficit will fall $30–40 billion. Long term interest rates on high quality private debt would fall to 6–7 percent within 12 months of the monetary reform. For each 1 percent fall in the rate of interest, the Treasury could save $10 billion in service costs. The government debt could be refinanced at about one-half current interest rates, thus saving the Treasury $60–70 billion annually. At 5 percent unemployment, the Treasury could save an additional $150–200 billion.

The fiscal effect of rapid economic growth, joined to a refunding of the national debt, would refill the public treasury with increased revenues and balance the budget. Tax rates could then be further reduced.

The monetary reform is the sole remaining path to sustained, long term economic growth and a balanced budget. In truth, an authentic demand for a balanced budget means an end to budget austerity. The demand for a balanced budget is now a demand for rapid economic growth. Today, the demand for sustained economic growth is a demand for a long term investment boom. The demand for a long term investment boom is a demand for restoration of the long term credit markets. The economic demand for savers to lend in the long term financial markets can only be a demand for honest insurance of the value of money rewards to those who have the faith to lend far into the future. The demand for faithful insurance of the future value of money is, by every test of equity and history, a demand for the real gold standard.

Once and for all, if America is to give the world a real money, it is necessary and sufficient to reestablish a free monetary order. Under the American Constitution, a free monetary order consists of a currency of real worth, a gold dollar, ruled by a moral principle—the unimpeachable integrity of a true money. The substance and integrity of the dollar, until 1934, rested upon the right of every American to bring precious metal to the mint to have it freely coined into standard money. Free coinage gave rise to the right to *convert* all paper and bank deposit claims, such as Federal Reserve notes and checking accounts, into the monetary standard. Thus was the dollar referred to as a *convertible* currency. But in 1933 the integrity of the dollar was put in question by government intervention.

Franklin D. Roosevelt unilaterally made contractual paper claims to gold dollars irredeemable. The U. S. government repudiated its covenant to convert Federal Reserve notes into standard gold coin held in reserve for those who trusted the guarantees of the Constitution. Moreover, in 1934, lawful gold money held by American citizens was forcibly confiscated by the government without due process.

As the integrity of our *domestic* currency was destroyed in the 1930s, its *international* substance was eviscerated in 1971 when Richard Nixon unilaterally repudiated the contractual right of foreigners, enshrined in the Bretton Woods Agreement of 1944, to claim gold dollars for undesired paper and deposit dollars. The present era of financial disorder, marked by alternating cycles of inflation and unemployment, originated in these monetary repudiations of 1933 and 1971.

Now is the moment to end this age of financial disorder and redeem the promise of economic growth signalled by the election of Ronald Reagan.

To wipe out inflation, to restore the essential condition for rapid economic growth, full employment, and 4 percent interest rates, to undergird the integrity of the dollar, it is necessary to establish a monetary standard upon the principle of free coinage, the sure foundation of a convertible dollar—to be upheld by the organic law of the land. The law of the land, the law of money must be as it was from 1792—the year of Alexander Hamilton's free coinage act—until 1933. During those 150 years, thirteen impoverished little colonies by the sea rose to world power while their commerce and monetary standard, the gold dollar, engirdled the earth. It is true that protectionism, trade wars, and Federal Reserve deflationary policy after 1929 ended that epoch of growth and created the Great Depression. But these same mindless policies also destroyed the international gold standard.

Now is the time for America to launch a new gold standard era of open world trade, peace and prosperity. Only the U.S. has the power to do so. For the U.S. is the natural leader to restore the equilibrium of the free world economy. It is true that the classical monetary policy is no panacea. Neither was Keynesian and monetarist doctrine. But the latter two are man-made gods which have failed while the former, the gold standard, present from the creation of the industrial revolution, has actually worked in the only laboratory on earth that counts—the real world of history.

The international gold standard is the least imperfect of monetary institutions by which the U.S. can establish sound money, a reasonably stable price level, a long term investment boom, and a general tendency toward full employment. It is true that we do not have the power to make our human institutions perfect, as we are all fallen creatures. But we *do* have the limited power to rule out the wild inflation inherent in the policy of Keynes and the austerity implied in the doctrine of the monetarists. We also have the power to rule out sub-optimal international exchange rate regimes, such as the mercantilist float of today, as well as the superior but defective Bretton Woods fixed exchange rate regime of yesteryear.

VII. The Plan for Restoring the Public Credit

Of course, the experts complain about the difficulty of establishing the gold standard.

We have to ask ourselves and our monetarist and Keynesian friends, as well as the socialists and our foreign allies, one practical question: Are the problems of establishing the gold standard and a new international monetary order greater than living with the practical problems of the high real interest rates, inflation and unemployment characteristic of our catastrophic paper and credit money system?

A reasonable person might answer that establishing the gold standard is not easy. But it is, nevertheless, simpler, beset by fewer problems, and entails fewer unpredictable consequences than the continuing disasters of the past ten years of government managed money. Therefore:

1) The President should announce that, effective within two years, the U.S. will establish a convertible dollar. By statute, the monetary standard will be defined as a dollar with a specific weight of gold.

2) During the next two years, the stabilization period, the President would also propose a specific balanced budget amendment to the Constitution, to become effective four years after the convertible dollars is announced.

3) He would propose a statutory reform of the Federal Reserve System which would have the effect of prohibiting the Federal Reserve from manipulating the monetary standard, its value or its quantity. First, open market operations in U.S. government debt securities by the Federal Reserve would be ruled out. Second, the central bank discount rate would be established, by resolution or executive order, as a market interest rate and the sole banking technique by which the Federal Reserve lends money, against secured commercial paper, to the banking system. Third, by resolution or executive order, any bank reserves required by the Federal Reserve would pay a market interest rate consistent with interest rates paid on the highest quality secured commercial paper.

During the stabilization period, as a result of the proposed reform of the monetary standard, market participants would gradually cease to hedge against inflation or to speculate for a deflation. Gold would begin to settle at a more stable, paper dollar price as the convertibility date drew closer.

4) Ninety days before the end of the stabilization period, the President, after due committee deliberations with appropriate legislative and executive officers, would propose the statutory gold weight of the dollar, or the "price of gold." Setting the price, or gold weight, of the dollar would require great care. It would be stipulated in *The Gold Standard Act,* submitted to Congress shortly before convertibility went into effect. The gold weight of the monetary standard, or the dollar price of gold, would be determined first by reference to the market price of gold at that time. Second, the price of gold would be established at a level certain not to cause a reduction in the average dollar level of nominal wages. Because if the price of gold were set too low, a general tendency toward falling prices might develop, thus putting downward pressures on sticky wages and salaries as well as on

the level of employment. This pressure occurred in 1925 in England when the convertibility of the pound was re-established at a price too low (the prewar parity) and therefore unemployment stuck at high levels. Such an outcome can be prevented by fixing the convertibility price of the dollar at a level not substantially less than the average costs of the marginal productions of operating North American gold mines. History also shows that the price of gold should be no less than the average gross weekly wage rates of major domestic manufacturing, mining and industrial producers. Determining this price would be a simple technical procedure using readily available data, competence and experience easily attained by virtue of the President's power to appoint a commission. This commission would determine the gold value of the dollar monetary standard, ultimately to be approved by Congress.

5) Within this final ninety-day period, the President would propose to Congress all the appropriate statutory reforms of the Fed, and the new laws needed to implement his original declaration. The gold standard act of 1985 would accomplish two fundamental financial reforms now missing from the law of the land. First, the definition of the monetary standard, the dollar, would be established by law. Second, the purpose of Federal Reserve policy would also be established by law. Its primary purpose would be to uphold the value of the monetary standard of the U.S.

After the Congress acted, we would be on the true gold standard. All who wanted coined gold dollars could bring their bullion, paper money or checks to the mint for conversion at the established rate. The new monetary order would *not* be the gold-exchange or reserve currency regime of Bretton Woods. It would be a true, free market gold standard.

6) Most important, in his initial announcement, the President should call for an international monetary conference, under the leadership of the United States, to begin a year later with the goal of establishing a new international monetary order. Here, the terms of a new fixed exchange rate regime, a modernized international gold standard agreement, would be established by treaty, just as at Bretton Woods in 1944.

The monetary standard of the free world would again be a common currency free of sovereign manipulation. The new monetary order would create the greatest economic boom since the beginning of the Industrial Revolution.

If America truly desires to give the world the real money it needs to grow, then we can choose the international gold standard. But it can only be brought into being by the leadership of a strong president. Such an exchange rate regime can also rule out the competitive depreciations and protectionist anarchy caused by floating rates today. And, once and for all, it will eliminate the privileges and burdens of the reserve currency status of the government managed paper dollar. Only domestic convertibility and the true international gold standard can establish a common currency for a free, open and integrated world economy.

Even without sound money, we will survive as a country. It is the nature of working people and businessmen to survive, especially in America. But to what end? In order to subsidize a cartel of high rolling big city bankers and undisciplined Third World elites? In an armed camp? Amidst conditions of permanently high unemployment, inflation and high interest rates? Increasing bankruptcies? Wage and price controls? Is this the stuff of the American dream?

We *can* attain the goals of financial order and full employment and thereby restore hope in the future. But only with real leadership and real money.

2

Toward a New Nationalism: The Second Sacking of the West

Patrick J. Buchanan

"On New Year's Day, 406, the Vandals, announced foes of Caesar . . . crossed from the East the frozen Rhine, moved south through Gaul and Spain, leaving their vandal track, and on into Africa. In 410, Alaric, the Visigoth, sacked Rome . . .

"The Barbarians were coming. Orosius could look over the frontiers and salute them as brothers. Were not many of them being drawn, and that for many a year, into the Roman mercenary army? As we today, so the Roman provincial then, was optimistic. Had not the eminent and cultured Sidonius dined with Theodoric II, the Goth, and found him not so intolerable? The barbarians were flattered to converse at dinner with a Roman. There was talk of establishing a school of studies at Bordeaux with salaried professors."

—Historian George Caitlin, 1939

At the winding down of the 20th century, the second sacking of the West is far advanced. Not with fire and sword, but with pen and paper; and this, too, is welcomed in the name of "progress." In the finance and foreign ministries of the West, the New International Economic Order, the dream and demand of the Third World, is being crafted by the capitalist world, with the blessing and under the supervision of an American regime headed by Ronald Wilson Reagan. Indeed, we are already midway through the greatest peaceful plunder in human history.

The Debt Bomb

That President Reagan, a patriot and nationalist, would reject and resent such depiction goes without saying. But, consider where we have come within a decade.

In 1973, the Warsaw Pact nations, harnessed together in the Kremlin counterfeit of the Common Market called Comecon, had $9.3 billion in debts outstanding to Western Europe and the United States. By 1983, Pact debt had risen nine-fold to $80 billion. With Yugoslavia added, Communist Europe owed $100 billion to the governments and financial institutions of the West. The equal of half a dozen Marshall Plans had been consumed; and at the decade's end half the communist regimes were illiquid, insolvent or bankrupt. Poland, Rumania and Yugoslavia were rudely demanding a rescheduling of old loans and new infusions of Western capital, while threatening a general default that would send the great banks of West Europe toppling like a line of dominoes.

In Latin America, three nations—Argentina, Brazil and Mexico—had accumulated $210 billion in debt. Interest alone on the Mexican debt was running at $250 million a week.

"The figures are beyond comprehension," wrote scholar William Quirk in the *New Republic*. "In June of 1982, according to Treasury Secretary Donald Regan, the poor countries owed $265 billion to Western private banks. Latin America alone owed $168 billion to the banks. Including loans from Western governments and international agencies, the poor countries owed $500 billion. Counting in loans to companies in poor countries, the total was $626 billion of which $400 billion was owed to the banks. . . . Half the poor country debt is due in 1983."

This, then, is the essence of the debt crisis:

After a decade of improvident or, more precisely, lunatic lending, Western governments, financial institutions and banks held $700 billion worth of paper representing loans to the Soviet Bloc and the Third World. Three dozen countries on four continents were in "technical" default, i.e., they had failed repeatedly to meet the original terms of their loans. If these "non-performing loans" had to be written down or written off, as normal banking and accounting procedures require, there would ensue a worldwide banking collapse.

Kamenev on Rockfeller

How did we arrive at a juncture where the United States is presented this apparent Hobson's choice: Either accept the indefinite siphoning of your wealth into the looted vaults of the communist and socialist world to enable them to "service" their debts, or call a halt to the income transfers and risk collapse of the international financial system, the crash of the Big Banks and a repeat of 1933?

How did we reach a point where President Reagan and Secretary Regan are pointedly warned that either they allow this indefinite milking of America's savings or accept the fate of becoming Hoover and Mellon to their own generation? Have we, truly, no other option?

The bank crisis of 1983 is rooted in two events, the "detente" summit at Moscow in May of 1972 and the Yom Kippur War in October of 1973.

"A generation of peace" is what President Nixon hoped would follow from detente; "restraint" on Soviet behavior was the more modest return anticipated by Henry Kissinger. Nonetheless, the deal was struck. In exchange for an end to Soviet adventurism, Russia and her vassal states were accorded unrestricted access to the warehouses of the West.

As the Bloc was without hard currency, and could earn only limited foreign exchange selling furs and vodka, oil and gas and coal, there was a need for credit. Western bankers like David Rockefeller moved with alacrity to provide it.

"Just because a country is technically called Communist," said Mr. Rockefeller, "doesn't mean that capitalist institutions such as the Chase bank can't deal with them on a mutually beneficial basis, and, indeed, we do deal with most of the so-called Communist countries of the world on a basis that has worked out well, I think, for both of us."

Like tourists turned loose for an afternoon in a duty free port, Brezhnev's purchasing agents came West and bought and bought and bought. Food, fertilizer, farm machinery, drilling and pipe-laying equipment, whole plant technology and turn-key projects. The Kama River truck factory, largest in the world, is a blend of Ford technology and Fiat design. Run on IBM computers, it would turn out the truck fleets that would carry the Red Army south into Afghanistan.

Half a century before, Kamenev had predicted, "Foreign capital will fulfill the role Marx predicted for it . . . the foreign capitalists who will be obliged to work on the terms we offer them, will dig their own graves."

For ten years, Western governments and banks competed with one another in the generosity of the terms they offered to Moscow; for ten years the Marxist economies were sustained on capitalist credit. The Soviet military buildup, surely the most awesome and perhaps the most decisive in history, may be said to have been financed by Western banks.

By the end of 1982, with new credit drying up, the Russians were said to be considering a general default. Eighty billion dollars—gone!

The Great Re-Cycling Scam

Third World Debt, which eclipses Bloc Debt by a factor of six, is traceable to the run-up in oil prices in the aftermath of the October War.

Even in retrospect, the numbers astonish. From $2.50 a barrel in 1973, the price of light Arabian crude, benchmark for the OPEC cartel, rose to $34 by 1982—prodded along by Western panic and hoarding after the collapse of the Shah.

The magnitude of the wealth transfer is detailed by Quirk: "In 1972, the Arabs received $24 billion from the rest of the world. In 1982, they received $230 billion. Since all oil prices followed OPEC's lead, in the U. S. the cost of oil went from $20.3 to $225 billion in 1981. . . . The Arabs with the banks brokering the deal had made a major withdrawal from the West."

But these legendary windfall profits presented the OPEC Arabs with a problem: where to park the billions where they would remain secure and grow.

The answer presented itself. Where better than those most solid of institutions, the European and American banks?

The immense and mounting deposits from the Persian Gulf presented the Big Banks in turn with their own problem: where to lend the money where it would earn a higher rate of interest than the bankers were paying OPEC for the privilege of holding it.

This answer, too, presented itself: Why not turn around and lend the money to the Third World which could then use the funds to pay their escalating oil bill and expand their import purchases from the West?

Thus began the great re-cycling scam of the seventies. The cartel would collect and package petrodollars pouring in from Europe, Japan and the United States. The packaged monies would be placed on deposit in the great banks of Tokyo, London and New York. The Big Banks—with the Americans in the van—would turn around and lend the funds at a bit above the LIBOR rate (London inter-bank offer rate) to the cash-starved Third World which would then use the money to buy more oil from the cartel and more imports from the West.

With this steady hemorrhaging of its investment capital—life blood of a free economy—Western economies faltered while the cartel flourished and the Third World boomed. Bankers bored with nursing along loans to the dying industries of Smokestack America reveled in night flights to exotic sites like Buenos Aires and Brasilia to be feted by the finance ministers of the countries of the future.

The money was lent without regard to ideology. "Who knows which political system works?" is how Thomas Theobold, heir presumptive at Citibank, casually dismissed a reporter's question from the *Wall Street Journal*. "The only thing we care about is can they pay their bills."

The banker-statesman incarnate, David Rockefeller, flew into Luanda, capital of the principal African colony in the Soviet Empire, and emerged to announce: "We found we can deal with just about any kind of government, provided they are orderly and responsible. . . . The more I've seen of countries which are allegedly Marxist in Africa, the more I have a feeling it is more labels and trappings than reality."

But, surely, there was a huge economic risk in lending hard currency, without collateral, to socialists and communists: Not to worry, said Leland Prussia, Chairman of the Bank of America. "Countries are different from individuals. We can go bankrupt and disappear. Countries can't do that."

So, in the seventies and early eighties, the seed corn of the U. S. economy was scooped up and carried off to be poured onto the sandy soil of the socialist South and the rocky ground of the Soviet Bloc. Back home, interest rates soared, economic growth was stunted, per capita income, for the first time since the Great Depression, began to fall.

Closing Time

A few Cassandras had warned that the game could not go on indefinitely, that the debts had long ago mounted beyond the capacity of the debtor countries to repay the interest—let alone principal.

By 1980, the Federal Reserve had decided to halt the accelerating inflation upon which the Big Banks had been betting. The American dollar began to rise dramatically against other currencies. Countries with hyper-inflation like Argentina—whose foreign debt had vaulted from $2 billion in 1976 to $40 billion in 1982—found it took more and more pesos, a larger and larger share of export earnings, to service its debt. With the Fed tightening money, a recession took hold in the United States. That recession—coupled with the conservation and conversion to alternative fuels caused by the oil price explosion and accelerated by the Carter-Reagan decision to decontrol—produced a dramatic fall in America's demand for oil. Where OPEC had been pumping 32 million barrels a day in 1979, worldwide sales by the end of 1982 had fallen to 18 million. By spring 1983, they were down to 14 million and the price was about to break as Nigeria and other OPEC countries were desperate for the dollars no longer coming in, upon which they had based their development plans. Meanwhile, new oil coming on stream from Mexico, the North Sea and Alaska compounded OPEC's difficulties. By the spring of 1983, there were gas wars in the United States and a price war had broken out between Iran and Nigeria on one side and Saudi Arabia on the other. The ghost of Adam Smith had risen from its grave and run a sword through the OPEC cartel.

The View from Chase Manhattan

While American consumers were cheering falling gasoline prices and reveling in news accounts of squabbling inside the cartel—*THE SHEIK HIT THE FAN!* exulted one *New York Post* headline—the Big Banks were taking a more somber view.

In 1982, the OPEC surplus, which had been $90 billion the previous year and $110 billion in 1980, disappeared. Beyond that, major cartel members such as Nigeria, Indonesia and Venezuela began having difficulty meeting their debt service. As for the non-oil exporting countries of the Third World, the so-called LDCs (less-developed countries), not a week seemed to pass without one of them arriving in Washington or New York to ask the Big Banks to re-schedule their loans and provide some bridge money until the good old days came back.

Friday, August the 13th, 1982, was the Day of Truth for the Big Banks. Mexico, $80 billion in debt outstanding, came within hours of formal default. With inflation rampant and capital fleeing the country, Lopez Portillo imposed exchange controls, devalued the currency, seized Mexico's banks and confiscated the dollar accounts—swapping the hard currency of Mexico and American citizens for devalued pesos.

Only the intervention of the U.S. Treasury and the Federal Reserve—with the hapless banks forced to pony up another $5 billion—prevented a formal default which would have placed in jeopardy Mexican loans representing 50 percent or more of the equity of nine of the ten largest American banks, and the balance sheet assets of new fewer than 1,000 smaller institutions. As one example of American bank exposure, Manufacturers Hanover of New York had outstanding loans to Mexico equivalent to more than three-fourths of stockholders equity.

Mexico brought home the urgent message to the Big Banks: We are in over our heads and either somebody is going to bail us out, and soon, or we are all going under.

"The problem is liquidity, not solvency," insisted William Ogden, the designated point man for Chase Manhattan. "It is temporary. We need to buy time."

The IMF Safety Net

At Toronto in September of 1982, at the conclave of world bankers and finance ministers, the plan to bail out the Big Banks took shape.

First, the Group of Ten, the Western industrial democracies and Japan, would increase their contributions to the so-called General

Agreement to Borrow of the International Monetary Fund from $7 billion to $20 billion, and permit the IMF to use the funds, for the first time, outside the West. Second, a 50 percent increase in the general funding was agreed to, raising IMF capital from $66 billion to $99 billion. Third, the banks would be prevented from reducing their exposure in the debtor countries and, indeed, would be required to increase it. For every dollar the IMF sent, for example, to Yugoslavia or Mexico—to enable them to continue payment on old debts—the banks would be required to lend new money, thereby increasing everyone's stake in keeping the game going indefinitely, enlarging everyone's vested interest in a renewed inflation that alone could save deadbeat and lender alike.

The public argument for providing the IMF with the $47 billion in new capital was for "structural adjustment loans" to nations with "liquidity problems."

But there were two secret codicils on the hidden agenda. The first was to use the taxing and borrowing power of Western governments to extract from their people the tens of billions necessary to save the reputations, jobs and careers of the foolish and terrified Western bankers. The Bohemian Grove of George Shultz was mounted and riding to the rescue of the Trilateral Commission of David Rockefeller.

But the second secret objective was the creation of new and permanent machinery for the *indefinite* transfer of the wealth of Western people into anti-Western regimes that demand that wealth as a matter of moral right. The IMF was to become catalyst and controller of the New International Economic Order.

Still, the conservatives in the Senate could not see it. With these new billions to the IMF would go irresistible leverage over America's banks, a whip hand to force Manny Hanny and Chase Manhattan to continue making new and risky loans to cover up the old bad debts. The greater the banks' exposure, the greater the clout of the IMF. Should the banks one day balk, the IMF could threaten to wash its hands and walk away leaving the banks to face successor regimes who felt no moral or political obligation to the late dictators and demagogues to whom the banks originally lent their money.

Don Regan and Beryl Sprinkel, Mr. Reagan's Treasury subalterns who had gone to Toronto as acolytes of Reaganomics, returned as construction superintendents for the most audacious foreign aid scheme ever dreamed of. And they sold it to a Senate controlled by the Republican Party.

When the IMF receives this new infusion or capital, and the leverage that goes with it, America's Big Banks will become permanent hostages, subject to indefinite blackmail and extortion by international bureaucrats whose thinking is more akin to Willy Brandt than Ronald Reagan.

Why the Music Has to Stop

Even in the most generous judgment, the Great Bank Bailout of 1983 represents an unexampled triumph of hope over experience.

Rumania has piled up $10 billion in foreign debts and is bankrupt. Can any economist contend that Ceaucescu's Stalinist dictatorship will be made a going concern with another $2 billion in Western capital? Or Poland flat on its back after an infusion of $25 billion? Or Yugoslavia, $20 billion in debt and broke?

The only condition the IMF could place upon such regimes that might enable them to see a day when they could meet their debt service is that they abandon their Marxist systems. Absent such radical reform, sending more billions into the Soviet Bloc amounts to mindless subsidization of militaristic regimes that are as much the enemies of their own people as they are of the West.

The economic treason of underwriting America's enemies aside, where is the rationale for pouring capitalist savings of the West into Marxist economies which the textbooks of the West teach us must inevitably fail?

The bailout of 1983 will succeed, we are told, because the IMF will impose "conditions" upon receiving nations that will put their economies in order and enable them to repay their debts.

But will the IMF tell the Mexican government to surrender the 75 percent of the Mexican economy that regime controls? Will it tell De La Madrid that Pemex, the national oil company, must be disgorged to private enterprise to maximize production? Will the IMF tell Julius Nyerere to give up the Maoist experiment that has converted once-lovely Tanzania into a Third World dump? Will it tell the General in Kinshasa to get up to that Swiss bank and retrieve the billions he has stashed away for a rainy day?

Will the IMF tell India to abandon its atomic weapons program, to cease warring against Pakistan, to stop the forcible sterilization of peasants, to free up industry, to cease diverting our loan and aid dollars to the purchase of French Mirages and Soviet MIGs?

The Administration may have narrowly won congressional approval of the $8.4 billion IMF-Bank Bailout, but the President has only postponed the day of reckoning. The laws of economics cannot be indefinitely suspended.

U.S. bank auditors, with reputations and firms on the line, cannot forever leave on the books as assets loans every rule of accounting tells them are worthless. Smaller American banks with limited exposure abroad are already pulling their cash out, demanding payment as the loans come due.

At a gathering to deal with the Polish crisis, a Hamburg banker captured the mood: "I come into these sessions and I find all these hillbillies. These big American banks have made the loans and sold parts of them to the little ones. And these fellows, who don't know the Baltic from the Barents Sea were all crying, 'I want my money back!'" Said one banker: "We were greedy little pigs. And now we're going to slaughter."

Most ominous for the Big Banks, however, is the political awakening in Latin America, where Uncle Gringo has never been that popular, and within the United States where Big Banks have never been that popular.

How long will the proud people of Mexico accept harsh austerity imposed by the IMF when they discover its purpose is to squeeze out enough of their national wealth to meet the *$250 million a week* in interest payments going to the Yanqui Banks? How long will the people of Argentina, remembering the Falklands war, continue sacrificing to pay off $40 billion to the Americans and the Brits? Already, Buenos Aires is unilaterally altering the terms of its own repayment. The banks, having no choice, are grudgingly going along.

But the greater barrier to the looting of this nation's wealth by its ill-wishers and enemies is a rebirth of nationalism in the United States.

There is a rule taught young journalists: Never overestimate the knowledge of your reader; nor underestimate his intelligence. The American people may not be schooled in matters of international finance, but they are not fools.

When American businesses starved for capital are failing at the Depression rate of 500 a week, when a cab driver in San Francisco is being required by the Bank of America to pay 19 percent for an "unsecured personal loan," Americans have begun to inquire what their Congress is doing shoveling our investment capital out to maintain the credit rating of Mr. Ceaucescu and Mr. Kadar.

What happens when they awaken to the knowledge that the "non-aligned" dreck that treats their country like kitty litter at the UN is not only subsidized with our foreign aide, but is being carried on the books of our biggest banks? When the American people discover that the Soviet nuclear arsenal targeted on Europe and North America was underwritten with Western credit? "How will it be with kingdoms and with kings?" asked Edwin Markham.

"The success of a party means little," Woodrow Wilson declared in his first inaugural, "except when the Nation is using that Party for a large and definite purpose."

If it is perceived to be the "large and definite purpose" of the Republican Party, captured and reconstituted by the men who follow Ronald Reagan, to become the instrument of deliverance for amoral money changers whose highest loyalty is to some neutral flag of commerce then the Republican Party will have no future. And probably deserve none.

You Have No Choice

To those making this case, the pragmatists have what appears irrefutable retort. It runs as follows:

"Agreed, the banks made stupid loans in the decade past. But consider the consequences of blocking future bailouts, of forcing countries like Mexico and Argentina into default.

"If they walk away from their debts, the Big Banks will have to write off billions in bad loans. Bank profits will disappear; dividends will be eliminated; bank stock will plummet. Huge slices, perhaps the whole, of bankers' equity will be eliminated. As equity vanishes, and loan loss reserves mount, new lending in the United States as well as overseas will come to a halt; savings will be threatened; a run on the banks by depositors will follow. We are looking at 1933, when 10,000 American banks went under!"

John Chamberlain, the bard of capitalism, argues the case from the national interest: ". . . despite the outraged feelings of the Populist New Right, Ronald Reagan is not in a position to let Mexico go down the drain. It is not Reagan's fault that the bankers, big and little, mined the whole territory at our southern border before he took office. He must be cursing the day that the Chase bank ever let Mexico have a nickel, but he can't say anything out loud. He can only tell his State Department to tip the world bankers off to their 'duty' which is to bail and bail and bail. . . . It's going to be a long and painful business . . . [but] we are stuck with the bail-out business."

Are we indeed between Scylla and Charybdis? Must we acquiesce in construction of a giant pipeline from Middle America through the IMF into the Third World and back to the Big Banks to maintain the fiction that the loans are good—or risk implosion of the banking system and our own financial ruin?

So the bankers and global bureaucrats would have us believe.

Voltaire's description of history comes to mind—". . . a pack of lies agreed upon." We are not bereft of choice. We are not condemned to perpetual pillage of the savings of the American people with the connivance of their own government.

The Road Out

"There *are* simple answers," Ronald Reagan used to say in the campaigns of 1976 and 1980. "It is just that there are no easy ones." That piece of native wisdom is needed.

The right answer is, indeed, a simple one. It consists, first and foremost, of facing up to, and acting upon, the truth.

The money is gone; it is never coming back. We will no more see again the $80 billion in outstanding credit given the Warsaw Pact than we will see again the World War I billions lent the Triple Entente or the World War II billions sent to J. V. Stalin in Lend-lease.

You could send a naval expedition up the Congo River and you would find Kurtz before you find a trace of the billions sent to Joe Mobutu.

It is no easy thing to concede that the Best and the Brightest of the seventies were as big a fools as their predecessors in the sixties, that the Americans were had once again, that for ten years, we poured the seed corn of the American economy into the drainage ditches and slit trenches of the Third World and reaped for our inebriate's generosity a harvest of insolence and ingratitude. But that is the truth. And it is necessary to recognize and accept and act upon the truth if we are not to re-enact the folly, which Mr. Reagan's Government is even now about to do.

The first piece of business is to notify the Soviet Bloc and the Nonaligned that the game is over, that no more good dollars will come chasing their bad debts, that we are prepared, if necessary, to write off the whole investment, that the United States is not so terrified of default as our cowardly bankers have led them to believe. To make the notification credible, Mr. Reagan should seize the first opportunity of Polish refusal to repay agricultural loans from the Commodity Credit Corporation to declare the Jaruzelski regime in default. Even should Mr. Reagan continue paying off Jaruzelski's debt to American banks, Congress must be persuaded to block any future financing request from the IMF.

The evening the U.S. Congress rejects the next bailout, the lights will be burning late at the Bank of America and Chase Manhattan, Citibank and Manny Hanny. But it will not be the end of the world. The lights will go on again, soon. The paneled offices will be reoccupied—only by different men heading up less ambitious institutions than the Gonzo Bankers who preceded them.

Despite the atmosphere of crisis that has been created, the principal losses threatened by a general writing down, or writing off, of bad loans to the Soviet Bloc and the Third World are to bankers' profits, their shareholders' dividends and their own jobs, salaries, bonuses and perks.

As Paul Craig Roberts, formerly of Treasury, has testified, the entire exposure of the nine largest U. S. banks in the Third World is 222 percent of total capital; their exposure to the three largest debtors, Argentina, Brazil and Mexico, is 112 percent of their capital. While writing down the banks' bad debts might wipe out bank equity, the bad loans are only a fraction of the hundreds of billions in solid performing loans in the bank portfolios.

As former Chase Chairman George Champion has recommended, the American banks should be permitted—if not required—to raise their tax-deductible loan loss reserve from the 1982 level of 1 percent of loans outstanding to 5 percent. While the Treasury would sustain a loss in revenue, the reserve would cushion the banks to take the blows that are coming. Second, rather than increasing their exposure—as the Administration and IMF are still mindlessly demanding—the banks should cease all lending to the Soviet Bloc and to any Third World nation deep in arrears on its debt. Third, bank dividends should be pared back or eliminated to leave the banks more capital to deal with the default loans. Fourth, the enormous and no longer necessary overhead of the Big Banks—the salaries, bonuses, country club memberships, travel expenses, foreign loan departments, excess officers and employees—should be eliminated, as in other enterprises going through the winnowing process that lies ahead. What's good for the Chrysler Corporation is good for Chase Manhattan.

In the last analysis, if there is need for a bailout of any U. S. bank, or any particular Third World country like Mexico, it should be done directly by the government of the United States, not through an institution like the IMF, for which we receive nothing of value in return. If certain countries allied to or supportive of the United States are *in extremis,* send the money directly, and receive in return tangible assets like naval bases, CIA stations, assistance in U.S. diplomatic initiatives, ouster of Russian or Cuban diplomats or "technicians" or support at the United Nations.

A New World Order

The men who tell us "you have no choice," who view any default anywhere with fear and trembling, are men with a stake in the old order.

True, a debtors cartel might default collectively and shake America to its foundations, but with a three-trillion-dollar economy, the United States could accept the shock and remain erect.

But, consider the predicament of our enemies if they walked away from their loans.

The Soviet Empire would be reduced to autarky, total self-reliance. No longer would the West's machinery and technology be coming East on the easiest of credit terms. Any new loans the Bloc received would reflect in the exorbitant interest rate the real risk the bank was taking in lending to an unreliable communist regime. Should the West Europeans continue sending capital East, in the knowledge it would never return—i.e., that it was disguised foreign aid, capitalist tribute to purchase "peaceful co-existence"—then it is time we recognized the symptoms of Finlandization and reset our course accordingly.

The Marxist-Leninist states and the London School of Economics models would at last be confronted with the consequences of their inherently unworkable economic and political systems. If disorder in the East Bloc followed, and upheaval in the Third World, if half the membership of that tyrants' club known as the Organization of African Unity ended up decorating lampposts from Accra to Dar es Salaam, it would not be more than many deserved. As Jefferson wrote to Madison, a little rebellion now and then is a good thing, "as necessary in the political world as storms in the physical."

America First

As stated, there is a rising tide of nationalism in the United States, the visible return of a healthy spirit of patriotism, a belief again in America First, if not forsaking all others, at least *before* all others. While Mr. Reagan rode that patriotic tide into office, he has yet to channel that force into the shaping of new institutions and the abandonment of the old. His Administration has one foot in the future, another in the past.

The time is ripe not only to reject the IMF as over-banker to all mankind, but to discard the husks of institutions that reflect an idealism and an internationalism that no longer correspond to the needs of our time or conform to the spirit of the age.

Since 1945, the United States has poured out a quarter of a trillion dollars in foreign aid. Most of it went directly, but more and more goes indirectly through the United Nations and the World Bank and such progeny as the Inter-American Development Bank and the Asian Development Bank. In February of 1983, Mr. Reagan, astonishingly, announced America's induction into the African Development Bank. Why? Why this inexorable flow of wealth out of the United States into uneconomic regimes that neither share our values nor support our interests? Is it nostalgia for what was, what might have been, political inertia, or the vested interest of the globalist parasites who feed off these institutions, that explains that continued drainage of the national wealth?

The International Development Association, the "soft loan" window of the World Bank, which lends at no interest for 40 and 50 years, is demanding a seventh replenishment of funds to service the clamorous demands of the People's Republic of China. When American businesses are dying for lack of capital, the Reagan Administration has agreed, Congress is actively considering a $750 million a year request.

For what purpose? "We're looking at ports, transportation, education, urban problems and agricultural projects in China," responds A. W. (Tommy) Clausen, Robert McNamara's successor as President of the World Bank. When Mr. Reagan is slicing such pork out of the U. S. Budget, at great political cost, why are we buying pork for the Politburo of the Chinese Communist Party? When Americans face some of the highest real interest rates within memory, why is our money being sent interest free to build Den Tsaio-ping a dual lane highway between Shanghai and Canton? The American working class pays the price, the Peking regime gets the benefit, the World Bank receives the credit. For this, we launched the Reagan Revolution?

"Trade" is the reason, insists Donald Regan of Treasury. We must bail out the Third World, we must make good our pledges to IDA because it is necessary for trade. But if we refuse to ship our wealth overseas, will they refuse to sell us their coffee and copper, their oil and tin? What will they do with it? Eat it?

These international institutions are museum pieces, absurd antiquities like coal scuttles and chamber pots.

In ten years, the World Bank has quintupled its annual lending to more than $13 billion with India the great beneficiary. What do we have to show for it?

The myth that serves the vast foreign aid constituency is "another Marshall Plan"—the recurring hope that somewhere in the subcontinent of Asia or tropical Africa we shall one day replicate the miracle of Europe. But the preconditions for a successful Marshall Plan were peace, a democratic political system, a market economy and people who share the work ethic of the West. Free Asia alone excepted, in what region of the Third World can these be found?

Added together, American foreign aid and the West's lost loans have cost a trillion dollars, a thousand billion dollars wasted, the wealth of an empire sunk, a sum vast enough to wipe out the national debt of the United States. Gone.

It is time to stop.

The symbol of the internationalist creed we have mindlessly followed, the Cathedral to the God That Failed, stands on the East River, the UN, that institutional insult to every noble idea enshrined in the Charter of the United Nations.

Mr. Reagan's re-election would be assured if only he could make in the coming Fall a single short speech to the General Assembly: "We Americans have watched silently the steady decomposition of this institution and its progeny into rabid enemies of the values in which we believe. We have listened patiently as you insulted our friends, disparaged our ideals and defecated upon our hospitality. Now, as that Born Again Christian of an earlier time once said in similar exasperation to the Long Parliament: You have sat too long for any good you have done here. In the name of God, go."

Copyright © PJB Enterprises, Inc.

II
Defense and Foreign Policy Issues

3

Strategic Defense: Toward Assured Survival

Lt. Gen. Daniel O. Graham, U. S. Army (Ret.)

> "Righteous indignation is no substitute for a good course of action."
> —Bismark

In the spring of 1983 the national press was filled with a spate of news articles, interviews, and commentaries on the idea that the United States might build an actual defense against nuclear weapons. That discussion produced a number of interesting assertions, but none more remarkable than the statement made by one of the idea's critics—who argued that the lack of such a defense, and the consequent constant threat of annihilation "has helped keep the peace for more than 30 years."

Like many arguments that are truly dangerous, that statement by Senator Alan Cranston (D-Ca.) made a good deal of superficial sense. Certainly, one must admit that since the defeat of Hitler and Japan, there has been no comparable, all-out conflict among the major powers. No formal declaration has emerged from Congress declaring America's determination to defeat another nation with arms. But in any meaningful sense has the world, or this country, been at peace? Iran and Iraq. Vietnam and Cambodia. Britain and Argentina. Cuba and Angola. Russia and Afghanistan. An article in *USA Today* early in 1983 found almost a third of the world involved in such direct, overt fighting. That, of course, was not all. In the Middle East, Palestine Liberation Organization (PLO) and Libyan terrorists were active in Lebanon, Saudi Arabia, Chad, and probably Southern Egypt and Morocco. Guerrillas fought established, democratic governments in

El Salvador, Peru, and Colombia. Terrorists, though dealt a severe blow by successful anti-terrorist programs in Italy and West Germany, continued to threaten the normal conduct of diplomacy even in the West.

Even if none of these high and low level conflicts had been simmering, could one truthfully describe the world condition as one of "peace" in the spring of 1983? The people of Poland, East Germany, and the rest of Eastern Europe knew only the dubious peace of the slave who is seldom beaten, because the rifle at his back is sufficient to earn his submission. At the bottom line, it would be difficult even to say that the United States was at peace, or felt itself so. In several national polls, better than half of all Americans said they saw a good chance of nuclear war in their lifetime. A far wider majority said they expect, and prefer, to die if such a war occurs. A situation in which most Americans see a "good chance" of a war that will destroy them might be called many things. It cannot plausibly be called peace.

Senator Cranston presumably knew about the invasion of Afghanistan by the Soviet Union and the operations of the PLO. He undoubtedly knew about the fears over nuclear weapons harbored by many Americans; those fears formed the basis of Cranston's successful role in the nuclear freeze movement. So it would be difficult to fault him for poor vision. Nevertheless, his description of what he saw, his choice of words to describe the essence of the reality around him, encompasses a great deal. In fact, it is a neat illustration of the division of thinking between liberals and conservatives on what is arguably the central issue of our time: how to keep—or, rather, establish—peace.

Like military conflict itself, the clash over national security takes place on different levels. The first, on which the division is least distinct, is over the facts themselves. This might astonish us in a country in which leading politicians and journalists lock horns every day over the most straightforward questions: Are the Soviets using chemical weapons? Have the Cubans been shipping arms into Nicaragua? That such basic questions often fail to produce a consensus answer among policy elites would seem to be a matter of serious concern. One might even consider it the heart of our national security problem.

And yet, it isn't. There will always be a good deal of sound and fury surrounding any question of foreign policy fact. For some, no amount of evidence—expert testimony, eyewitness reports, photographs or files—will be sufficient to convince. Nevertheless, it is awfully hard to sustain even a well-honed skepticism over time. Hitler eventually convinced the French, British, and Americans that he posed a fundamental threat to their security. Similarly, the Soviets have managed to convince most of the world that there are chemicals in Asia, a Gulag in Siberia, and a wall in Berlin. Despite the static from above, there is a broad agreement among Americans and their allies in Europe that the Soviet Union is up to nasty things.

As the Cranston parable illustrates, liberals and conservatives differ most significantly not in what facts they see but in how they assemble them. The debate over how many missiles the Kremlin has, or whether the KGB helped shoot the Pope, goes on. It is subsumed, however, by the debate over what to do about it. The national security liberal, like Cranston, views the world of 1983 and sees "peace." He inclines to a solution which will freeze that fragile situation before a new armament program, or an outbreak in Central America, produces tragedy. The national security conservative views that same world and sees "war." The compulsion not to lose that conflict animates his every policy prescription. He wants aid, economic and military, for our allies. He wants a strong Voice of America to spread the truth to countries where truth is outlawed. Above all, he wants dramatic action to right the shifting balance of military power. One irony is that we attach the term conservative to the man who argues for greater vigor in policy and who feels greater compassion for those who suffer under communist domination (or, at least, feels a greater urge to aid them). The more passive doctrine, with the less comprehensive view, is, by contrast, called liberal.

Rarely does an election occur in which the national sentiment on security issues can be distilled neatly from debate over taxes, spending, crime, the environment, and so on. Yet in 1980 and 1982, Americans did express themselves quite clearly on national security, indeed, on the core issue of national security: nuclear weapons. The almost universal reading of those elections was that they signified a complete reversal of opinion: 1980 a mandate for Ronald Reagan and rapid rearmament; 1982, a call to more active disarmament in the form of a nuclear freeze. In fact, Americans expressed an almost identical sentiment in electing Ronald Reagan as they did in supporting a nuclear freeze.

For all their differences, both Jimmy Carter in 1980 and Ronald Reagan in 1982 had one thing in common. They were both forced to conduct a foreign policy and to build a military strategy based on the idea that any decision might mean the end of the world. In a Jimmy Carter, such knowledge was bound to create the sobering realization that if America's nuclear strength slipped too much, it could be the end. Hence, by the end of his term Carter supported an MX missile system with twice the warheads, and costing perhaps twice as much, as the MX later supported by Ronald Reagan. In a Ronald Reagan, the prospect of annihilation is bound to produce some gestures of arms control flexibility that even Reagan might never have imagined. Thus, by 1982 Reagan found himself at Eureka College, his alma mater, pledging adherence to the Carter SALT II agreement he had previously attacked as "fatally flawed."

Superficially, one might argue that in 1980 the American vote could be summarized as for "arms buildup." And then in 1982 Americans voted for "arms control." I would argue that in both 1980 and 1982 the vote was "something different." This is not to suggest a perfect symmetry between 1980 and 1982, nor between the conservative and liberal positions. Given only a choice between more weapons and more treaties, Americans have generally favored more weapons—believing, wisely, that weapons deter Soviet weapons, while treaties historically do not. However the liberal and conservative positions have differed, though, they have more or less accepted the doctrine that our only defense against nuclear weapons is an offense: Blow us up, and we will blow you up. You can hardly blame people for feeling ambivalent about choosing between two policies which essentially provide no certain security. The conservative position bases American peace on the Soviet Union's rationality, on its accepting as viable our threat to destroy them if they destroy us first. The liberal position bases peace on the Soviet Union's malleability, on our ability to coax the Kremlin with the right combination of gestures and compacts into giving up its arsenal as we give up ours.

Americans are to be forgiven if they appear schizophrenic in groping between those alternatives. Their real choice has been: "Give us another alternative." Their preference is for a national security apparatus that protects Americans whether the Soviet Union decides to attack or not. Their vote, unconsciously, has not been "build more offense," or "build less offense." Rather, it has been "build a defense."

That is where High Frontier comes in.

High Frontier is a comprehensive, new U.S. national strategy; it addresses not only our security problems, but also economic, political, and moral issues facing the nation. If adopted, High Frontier would accomplish the following:

- Replace the failed and morally suspect doctrine of Mutual Assured Destruction (MAD) with a strategy of Assured Survival.
- Effectively close the "window of vulnerability" by denying the Soviets a nuclear first strike capability—without deploying one more U.S. nuclear weapon.
- Create a reliably effective deterrent to nuclear war by defending the U.S. and the Free World rather than by threatening a suicidal punitive strike at Soviet civilians with nuclear weapons.
- Create an immediate surge in the high-technology sector of the U.S. economy by opening and securing outer space for private enterprise.
- Provide positive and challenging goals for American youth and a restored image of U.S. success and leadership abroad.

—Do all of the above at costs to the taxpayer below all other alternatives available to meet the current Soviet threat.

—And do so with or without Soviet cooperation.

This is a pretty heady set of claims for the effects of the High Frontier strategic concepts. Certainly, this list of advantages raises both the skeptical eyebrow and the proper question: "If these results can be attained, why isn't High Frontier already national policy?"

The answer is simple. High Frontier, like any idea that challenges the prevailing wisdom, threatens a vast superstructure of intellectual and bureaucratic interests. It upsets the doctrines of Mutual Assured Destruction which have been the keystone of both liberal and conservative administrations for decades. Hence, liberals view High Frontier as a dangerous distraction from arms control. Conservatives see a dollar spent on defense as a dollar that might be diverted from offense—even though there might well be more public support for all military projects under a strategy that promised that some of those projects would actually defend the country. Experts in the military, politics, the academy, and the press have a considerable stake in MAD doctrine. And even those inclined to reject that doctrine face the entrenched attitude of the rest.

Equally important, the High Frontier constituency is broad and dispersed. A strategic defense would protect not just carpenters or insurance companies or women or blacks or Exxon Oil—it would protect everyone. For that very reason it does not excite any narrow constituency to lobby on its behalf. Indeed, as I have said, the terms of debate have been such that the High Frontier vote has been largely inchoate, unconscious. Americans were never given the chance to rally behind a strategic defense.

The High Frontier project itself was launched with much the same uncertainty. The scientists and strategists who began meeting in 1981 did not have an answer. They had only a shared apprehension about the state of the world. And a question: How can the U.S. quickly right the imbalance of power? The search for such an end-run around the Soviet threat led immediately to two areas: strategy and technology. For how could the U.S. hope to catch up and surpass the Soviets using the same approach that allowed us to fall behind? And how could rapid progress be made simply by trying to outbuild the Soviet military machine tank-for-tank, missile-for-missile?

The search for a clear U.S. technological advantage, in turn, led inevitably to space. One such advantage in space is our superior transportation system, the Shuttle. The Soviets trail us in such space transport by eight or ten years. Another clear U.S. advantage is in miniaturization, the ability to make things small, light, and efficient. Because of it, every pound we put into space does five or six times as much useful work as a pound put into space by the Soviets. These advantages are not merely additive, they are compounding. Since the limiting factor in exploiting space is the cost-per-pound to orbit, this superior U.S. technology gives us a very fundamental advantage over the Soviets.

The High Frontier team determined that this advantage could best be exploited by providing a layered strategic defense to nullify the Soviet threat of a first strike against the United States and its allies. Somewhat to our surprise, we found that an effective spaceborne defense could be built in five to six years using off-the-shelf technology, and that emerging technology could greatly strengthen the first layer of strategic defense in 10-12 years. We also found that there were relatively inexpensive and quick options available for point-defense systems to protect the U.S. deterrent on the ground, and thus deny the Soviets a first strike capability until the first spaceborne system could be deployed. None of these defensive systems requires any nuclear weapons. They do not even require lasers or other beam weapons, although such weaponry might figure prominently in the second-stage defense layer in the future.

High Frontier was launched as a search for national security solutions. We found, however, that the core space technology required for defense—like efficient space transport—was the same technology required to open up space to U.S. industry. The unique environment of space—zero gravity, vacuum, perfectly sterile conditions, and unlimited heat sink—provides opportunities for the manufacture of products impracticable to make on earth. It became clear to the High Frontier team that U.S. commercial and military users of space would proceed best in tandem, just as in earlier centuries the merchantman and man-of-war produced 100 years of Pax Britannica on the high seas.

High Frontier, then, was a call for a new strategic direction. It was *not* a list of specific, nuts-and-bolts technical recommendations. Nonetheless, High Frontier identified things that must be done—urgent requirements that must be met in order to gain the strategic goals we sought. To illustrate the feasibility of meeting those requirements, we outlined some of the many options for military and civilian programs that had been proposed by aerospace companies or independent engineers—programs which could stand scrutiny for technology, costs, and timing.

When we elected to illustrate even limited specific programs, great opposition formed within the High Frontier team. Some felt that the illustrative systems would be attacked in detail by naysayers anxious to avoid consideration of High Frontier's basic strategic recommendations. Most of us agreed, but felt that without describing

Strategic Defense: Toward Assured Survival

hardware programs that could support the strategic thrust of High Frontier, the entire idea would be ignored to death along with hundreds of other treatises on strategy that are gathering dust on bookshelves.

The worriers proved at least partly correct. Certainly the first vigorous opposition to High Frontier came in the form of an assault on one of our eight illustrative programs, the first layer of spaceborne defense, which we called Global Ballistic Missile Defense I (GBMD I). The other military systems drew relatively little fire, and the four civil programs practically none.

The contentious illustrative program, GBMD I, comprises a fleet of 432 orbiting satellites. Each satellite would carry 40 or 50 small rockets capable of intercepting up to 80 percent of a Soviet long-range missile attack early in trajectory. The fleet would use almost entirely off-the-shelf technology. It could be built in five or six years at an estimated cost of $15 billion.

Early on, critics assailed High Frontier's GBMD as "defying the laws of physics" and posing costs of up to $400 billion. Some raised broad doubt as to the competency and even honesty of our team. This reaction came mostly from within the bureaucracy from obvious guarders of turf and were not difficult to counter.

This assault, moreover, was heavily reinforced by those who object to High Frontier's basic thrust, itself a threat to such ongoing defense program as the MX race track and dense pack schemes.

"Race track," inherited from the Carter Administration, was a plan to place the MX missile on railroad tracks, presenting Soviet generals with a moving target should they ever attempt a first strike. "Dense pack" proposed instead to cluster MX missiles in a tight basket, in the hope that a Soviet attack would produce such debris and clutter that *some* MX missiles would survive. What both dense pack and race track shared, along with several dozen other MX plans, was this: they reflected a hard-won compromise. By necessity, strategic debate in Washington often starts with answers and ends up with questions. Instead of asking, "what system makes the most sense?" and answering "a High Frontier defense," politicians started with the anwer, "we must have MX" and wound up wondering, "how do we build it?" Once the "build MX" imperative is established, Pentagon planners must sit down and hammer out a compromise. Hundreds of plans are drawn up, methods tested, and public, presidential and congressional inquiries answered. At the end of all this, a delicate agreement is reached to produce this-or-that option. High Frontier, or any other alternative, threatens to de-fund that hard-won compromise weapon and open up a new round of hearings and tests and bargaining sessions. Hence, it gets stern treatment among the very people in the Pentagon that a president or congressman relies on for "technical" advice.

Even so, the great debate about America's ability to actually build a defense eventually died down. Within months of the report's release, too many experts from private industry and public think-thanks had affirmed its technical soundness for the doubters to retain any credibility. Boeing Aerospace Company, without even telling High Frontier, assigned a group of top engineers to study the project. They found High Frontier eminently feasible.

By 1983 the hardline opposition had softened to such an extent that Ronald Reagan could make a bold announcement. Late in March, less than one year after the High Frontier report, Reagan announced his support for the core High Frontier concept of strategic defense. No sooner had Reagan made his dramatic speech, though, than an army of press aides and security advisers scrambled to qualify. The opposition, defeated on strategy and feasibility, shifted to time and cost. "Yes, we support the *idea* of a High Frontier defense," the spokesmen said. "But we recognize that it will take decades to build and cost far more than we can afford just now."

At this juncture, decision makers in government should consider some recent history.

In 1956, President Dwight D. Eisenhower was briefed by a Navy team on a rather ambitious concept for strengthening the U.S. nuclear deterrent. These bold fellows thought that we could build a very large nuclear-powered submarine that could launch ballistic missiles from under the water, and that we could devise a way for the submarine to know its location well enough for these missiles to hit their intended targets in the Soviet Union. President Eisenhower saw the enormous strategic advantages of such a system, and, despite technical unknowns, ordered it built. One month less than four years later, the first Polaris submarine put to sea.

In 1959, as the space age was dawning, Eisenhower recognized the enormous advantages that would accrue to the United States if we could use our advanced technology to create a defense against the long-range ballistic missiles the Soviets had developed. He ordered the Pentagon to conduct an urgent, all-out research effort to determine the feasibility of defending the United States against such missiles. Mind you, this was *before* the Soviets *or* the United States had deployed the first inter-continental ballistic missile (ICBM).

The Department of Defense responded vigorously in an effect named Project Defender. By mid-1962, this highly competent group of Defense Department scientists and engineers had concluded that the United States could deploy a non-nuclear spaceborne defense capable of stopping up to 90 percent of a Soviet missile attack. We could accomplish this within six years of a decision to do so, and could do it with technology already available or confidently expected.

Twenty years later, a group of scientists, engineers and strategists collectively known as Project High Frontier came to the same conclusion. Armed with data that had not been available to President Eisenhower's group, and supported by quantum advances in technology, they concluded that, indeed, the United States and its allies in the Free World could be protected from a Soviet nuclear missile strike in five or six years, and at reasonable cost.

This bit of history should evoke some general and disturbing questions. How could President Eisenhower order the building of Polaris submarines, an effort fraught with enormous technical uncertainties, and get an "aye aye, sir" from the Navy and concrete results in four years? How could President Kennedy, a few years later, order a manned landing on the moon—a project also involving serious technical unknowns—and get concrete results in seven years? And why is it that, today, a system such as the Global Ballistic Missile Defense system of High Frontier—based primarily on 20-year old technology—can be rejected on the grounds of technical problems, long lead times and overall costs? Has the United States over the past 20 years become technologically inept? And why has a concept such as High Frontier had to come from a privately financed, non-governmental effort outside the complex of buyers and suppliers of military hardware?

There are answers and partial answers to these questions, too many to cover in detail. However, they are all rooted in adherence to bad strategy.

The bad strategy is Mutual Assured Destruction, although "strategy" is a flattering term to apply to this odd theory. MAD holds that U.S. security and the avoidance of nuclear war is dependent entirely on the maintenance of a balance of terror which is achieved when both the U.S. and the Soviet Union can absorb a nuclear first strike and still be able to wreak such terrible vengeance that neither side will ever use those weapons. One vital corollary of MAD is that both sides must refrain from defending their citizens because to protect them would deny or ameliorate the terribleness of the vengeance and would therefore be destabilizing.

Another vital and little understood corollary of MAD is its fundamental dependence on effective arms control which assumes the agreement by both sides to retain the balance of terror. Without an agreement with the Soviets as to just how many of what types of nuclear weapons each side must have, the pressure to add more and better offensive systems is continuous. MAD with SALT (Strategic Arms Limitation Treaties) or START (Strategic Arms Reduction

Talks) dictates that each side keep adding offensive weapons because each is dependent upon the surviving fraction of its nuclear force after a first strike by its opponent. This fraction diminishes steadily because of technical improvements in offensive weaponry. Totals of weapons must therefore be periodically increased to insure that adequate numbers survive.

Thus MAD comes in a package, along with avoidance of strategic defense and with a large bag of SALT. Remove any one ingredient and theoretically the entire doctrine collapses, which accounts for the paradoxical tacit alliance between adamant arms control enthusiasts and the offense-only school of military thought. It is reminiscent of the once common support of Dry Laws in some parts of the country by both bootleggers and the Women's Christian Temperance Union.

In reality, despite 15 years of American adherence, MAD was doomed from the start. Its only chance for success lay in the hope that the Soviets would adopt the same doctrine. They did not. They labeled it "bourgeois naïveté"—which indeed it is—and proceeded to work for a war-winning nuclear advantage. They did not eschew strategic defenses. They did not couple their SALT positions to MAD, but instead insured that SALT did not thwart their drive for nuclear superiority.

Our adherence to MAD produced a grossly unstable and dangerous strategic situation resembling a classic scene from a Western movie. Two men face each other down on Main Street, each waiting for the other to go for his gun. Each knows that the man who gets in the first shot has by far the better chance for survival. What is worse, the Soviet gunman stands behind a partial barrier of his strategic defenses. The American stands totally unprotected.

This strange doctrine of MAD, denied from time to time by both our political and military leaders, still underpins the shape of our military forces, the nature of new system proposals (e.g., MX-race track and dense pack) and our approach to arms control. And this is why we are unable to make the moves to insure our security that we could make in Eisenhower's day. Even a bold departure from the idea of MAD, such as Ronald Reagan's 1983 "Star Wars" speech, leaves the reality of MAD weapons, MAD planning, MAD treaties and MAD strategy essentially intact. Cut off only one branch, the tree still remains intact.

After all, diligent bureaucrats in the Departments of Defense and State, in the Arms Control and Disarmament Agency, and elsewhere in government worked for 15 years or more to create and perfect programs and policies to support the MAD theory. When High Frontier challenges that theory, applecarts are upset all over Washington.

Strategic Defense: Toward Assured Survival

To accept High Frontier is to accept the unwelcome news that much of the bureaucracy—in and out of military uniform—has been plowing in the wrong field. Small wonder than that the tendency has been to seek ways to squelch rather than ways to support new concepts.

The mere fact that the critic is biased, of course, does not mean that the criticism is invalid. Still, the closer one looks at the specific objections to High Frontier, the more one can see they issue from an opposition not interested in finding the truth, but in generating as many cavils and roadblocks as possible. Some of these arguments—and some answers—are as follows.

"The technology required to implement High Frontier is not off the shelf. In fact, there are serious technical risks in the proposal for a spaceborne defense."

This is a fading category of objection and already a far cry from earlier charges of "defying the laws of physics." Our scientists and engineers have responded effectively to specific criticisms of technology. However, the most telling fact is that the GBMD I system was deemed technically feasible by a DOD team of scientists and technicians *20 years ago!*

"Well, even if it is technically sound, High Frontier's spaceborne systems will cost far more than you say and take a lot longer to achieve."

The cost and time-to-deploy arguments are completely interdependent. The High Frontier team contends that GBMD I can be deployed in five or six years at a cost of about $15 billion. Early on, these figures were challenged with estimates of "about the year 2000 at a cost of $200–$400 billion." I know of no one who supports this view of cost and timing with the possible exception of one man in Reagan's Science Adviser's office. The former Deputy Secretary of Defense, Mr. Carlucci, and Dr. Eberhardt Rechtin, President of Aerospace Corporation, are on record with an estimated deployment of a High-Frontier-type system in 10–12 years at a cost of $50 billion.

The DOD-Aerospace figures are, in one sense, correct. And they are about the same as those of Boeing Aerospace. They are correct *if* one assumes business-as-usual in system acquisition. Given the Pentagon's incredibly inefficient acquisition procedures, now accepted as "normal," it takes the U.S. 13 years' effort to acquire military aircraft—three times as long as it takes industry to produce a new commercial aircraft of equivalent complexity.

Government and industry authorities agree that about 30 percent is added to the end cost of a system for each year the building acquisition process is stretched out beyond the actual time required for development and production. Hence, High Frontier's estimate of about $15 billion in five to six years would certainly be inflated to $50 billion if the time for acquisition is doubled to accommodate bureaucratic inertia and red tape.

We haven't always been saddled with cumbersome and costly acquisition procedures. The most advanced aircraft in the world today, the SR-71, was obtained in 2½ years; the Polaris submarine, with far more technical risks than High Frontier's GBMD, was obtained in 47 months; and we landed on the moon in seven years from a go-ahead. With business as usual, High Frontier's time and cost schedules cannot be met. With management arrangements recommended in our study, which worked in the past, they can.

One way to look at the cost of High Frontier is this: Currently it costs us somewhere between $50 and $250 million per satellite on orbit. High Frontier's satellites—within our $15 billion estimate—cost $36 million each on orbit, or in the DOD estimate about $100 million per satellite. High Frontier would require 500 identical satellites and thus a production-line effort. Current satellites are hand-tooled and custom-built, only a handful of any one type ever constructed. Unit costs are enormous, with each satellite bearing a large chunk of the research and development expenditure. Economies of scale would push the costs down toward that $36 million figure.

Furthermore, most of the cost objections fail to address the savings which High Frontier would permit elsewhere. High Frontier, for example, would protect 100 MX missiles deployed in our old Minuteman silos for $1 billion, the rough cost of the point defense systems High Frontier proposes. Compare that with $20 billion in Dense Pack costs, or $60 billion in MX-Racetrack, for concrete and construction alone. Current MX plans will require another $20 billion to harden U.S. command, control and communications systems to withstand the full weight of an unfiltered Soviet missile attack and to rebase our strategic bombers. Much of that effort would be unnecessary if High Frontier were pursued.

High Frontier, by destroying the rationale for a Soviet first strike against our current retaliatory forces, restores their original value. Our older offensive systems—Minuteman missiles, B-52 bombers and Polaris submarines in port—would retain their value as a deterrent *if* they could not be destroyed in a Soviet first strike. Thus, much of the money already spent by the American taxpayer would once again contribute to our strength.

High Frontier is a global defense concept. It defends not only America, but our allies in Europe and in the Pacific as well. It is therefore perfectly reasonable that our European allies and Japan could be expected to help pay for High Frontier either directly or in offsets to other U.S. defense costs.

Finally, the growth in the high technology sector of the U.S. economy sure to be sparked by High Frontier would more than offset the military costs. The expenditure of about $5 billion per year to pursue the civil and military programs of High Frontier will not only ensure our security, it will result in a net profit. High Frontier is a strategic bargain of immeasurable worth.

> *"The trouble with High Frontier is the vulnerability of space systems. The Soviets will figure out a way to blow a hole in GBMD and then fire their missiles through it."*

From the start, High Frontier experts recognized that survivability was a key issue. Early in the debate, some Air Force critics argued that spaceborne defensive satellites were an attractive idea but "they will shoot them down as fast as you put them up." This reaction had a familiar ring to it. It is almost precisely the doubt that was expressed by Army generals in the early 1900s when some strategic mavericks suggested that aircraft might actually be used in combat. Largely because of concern for vulnerability, the Army concluded that the utility of aircraft was confined to communications and reconnaissance. U.S. planes were duly assigned to the Signal Corps—which is basically the status of spacecraft in today's military establishment.

As a result of concern for spacecraft survivability, Project High Frontier devoted more analysis to this issue than to any other. Project experts brainstormed on almost every conceivable threat—from throwing sand in the path of satellites to speculative exotic Soviet beam weapons (including a few in the classified category). We considered so-called "peacetime" attacks as well as wartime attacks. While we certainly did not conclude that a defense could be invulnerable, we found no readily available or confidently attainable Soviet threat that would render GBMD ineffective. Each threat became manageable through a combination of technical or operational countermeasures.

When viewed piecemeal—an individual defensive satellite against a given postulated threat—the survivability picture looks bleak. When the total defensive system is confronted with the same threat, though, the survivability problem eases dramatically. A GBMD satellite fleet is remarkably survivable because of the number of vehicles, their relative simplicity and their ability to defend one another from direct ascent threats. In this respect, the large number of vehicles required by a kinetic-energy kill system constitutes a distinct survivability advantage over a system consisting of relatively few beam-weapon kill vehicles.

The important consideration to bear in mind is the strategic reasoning behind deploying a spaceborne defense in the first place. Its primary strategic purpose is *to deter a Soviet first strike.* The purpose is not to survive, not to prevent a Soviet retaliatory strike and not to eliminate totally the Soviet missile threat. When this basic fact is borne in mind, it is clear that even *should* the Soviets devise a means to knock a hole in the spaceborne defensive satellite system through which to launch an ICBM attack on the United States, they could not expect a first strike to succeed. They would never believe that, after an assault on our defensive systems, our offensive weapons would await destruction on the ground. Thus, even if one postulates an effective Soviet attack mode against GBMD, it would not destroy the basic strategic reason for deploying it.

It should also be noted that some of the postulated Soviet counters to GBMD involve massive investment and long lead times. For instance, one study has suggested that the Soviets might mass their ICBMs in a small geographical area in order to "bore through" the defense. That is a physical possibility, of course, but it is fraught with adverse strategic considerations for the Soviet planner, would entail enormous costs and would take a decade to even partially accomplish. And—again—the Soviet first-strike threat would be negated for the foreseeable future.

> *"The big problem with High Frontier isn't technology or costs, it's the effects of it on arms control, especially the ABM Treaty."*

We expected a good deal of concern about the effects of High Frontier on the ABM Treaty and devoted considerable space to the issue in our study. As we traveled the country, however, we found it a non-issue with the public and the press. Curiously, we hear most about it from the Pentagon. ABM treaty or no, the public is highly supportive of defense against Soviet ICBMs. A recent poll showed that two out of three Americans believe we already have a defense against ICBMs; 80 percent said they want such a defense and that cost would *not* be a primary factor in their support of such a system.

Finally, it may well be, as some arms control buffs now say, that agreements will become possible only when defensive weapons are re-emphasized. Consider this: If the United States adopted the High Frontier recommendations, our arms-control negotiators could make a proposal to the Soviets along these lines:

> The most destabilizing of weapon systems on both sides are long range ballistic missiles. Only by using these weapons could either side ever hope to carry out a successful first strike against the other's homeland. We have declared that we have no intention of delivering a first strike against the USSR, but perhaps you do not consider that an adequate guarantee on which to base the security of the USSR and the Socialist Bloc. If nothing else, your heavy expenditures on strategic defenses and civil defense so indicate. You have also stated that you have no intention of launching a first strike against the United States, but we can also reasonably doubt

that such a declaration is adequate to insure the security of our country and our allies.

We are going to deploy a purely defensive, spaceborne defense to insure that we cannot be subjected to a nuclear first strike by any nation or combination of nations. It will be a non-nuclear system which cannot possibly be used for attack of any person on earth. We invite you to deploy a similar system to prevent any nuclear first strike against the USSR. We believe that our current treaty arrangements should be amended to make it quite clear that these bilateral steps toward a stable strategic situation are mutually acceptable. We are willing to agree to measures which will ensure that the systems deployed are unmistakably defensive and non-nuclear.

If we can both look forward to the day when neither side must constantly guard against a first strike on our retaliatory forces and our nations as a whole, then surely we can reduce the total numbers of nuclear weapons on both sides.

This kind of arms control offer has some chance of success. It is not based, as U.S. arms control efforts thus far have been, on the hope of creating more equity in the balance of terror, as required by the Mutual Assured Destruction theory, but on creating a situation of Mutual Assured Survival. Total nuclear weapons stockpiles would be effectively reduced by applying technology that makes the accumulation of offensive nuclear weapons less important to both parties.

True, the Soviets may very well reject the entire proposal. But in doing so, they will declare themselves unwilling to accept any solution that denies them a first strike capability against the United States. Thus, we must proceed with High Frontier whether or not they agree to work for Mutual Assured Survival.

"If we choose to reemphasize strategic defenses, how do we know that the Soviets won't quickly deploy a lot of ABMs?"

We don't. I, for one, am convinced that the Soviets have been preparing for a breakout in ABMs ever since the ABM Treaty was signed. If a U.S. move to deploy spaceborne defenses were to cause abrogation of the ABM Treaty, there is a strong possibility that the Soviets would begin an extensive deployment of ground-based ABMs.

However, one must then ask: so what? The Soviets would be adding to strategic defenses they already have; we would be creating a strategic defense where we have none. Our problem is our vulnerability to offensive weapons, not to Soviet defenses.

Certainly the Soviets could, over a number of years—and at the expense of resources which are now being spent on more offensive capability—deploy enough ABMs to further weaken the effectiveness of our deterrent threat. But with a vigorous U.S. effort to deploy the High Frontier defensive systems, the strength of our deterrent will grow even faster, as its elements are made ever more survivable.

The final attack on High Frontier is an attack on the basic strategy. It is essentially the old "defense is destabilizing" argument. It goes like this:

> *"If the United States moves to defend itself against the most powerful element of the Soviet nuclear arsenal, the Soviets will view it as preparation for attack, and will attack us to prevent it."*

Strangely enough, I get this argument most often from people who have in the past condemned me as paranoid when I voiced concern about Soviet advantages in strategic nuclear power allowed in SALT II. They then insisted that the Soviets are in such mortal terror of the destructive power of a few Polaris subs that they would never use their offensive advantages. The *real* problem such people have with High Frontier is that it offers a solution to our strategic dilemmas that is quite independent of Soviet agreement and arms-control treaties with the Soviets which have long been their "sole solution." High Frontier does violence to the apocalyptic vision of utter destruction of the planet which, it is easy to see, underlies the activist core of the disarmament movement.

We must face squarely the full import of accepting this kind of objection. If we conclude that we cannot deploy a defensive system—which cannot kill a single Soviet—on the grounds that it might be too irritating to the Kremlin, we are accepting the proposition that America can *never again be defended*. We would condemn future generations to live constantly in the menacing shadow of a balance of terror, a balance certain to favor those states most willing to use terror to gain their ends.

We should reject objections based on fears of Soviet reaction even if there were a palpable possibility of violent Soviet reaction. The fact is, such a Soviet reaction is too remote to weigh on the decision. The idea that strategic defenses are "destabilizing" is the odd notion of American so-called defense intellectuals. That idea is totally rejected by the Soviets, as indicated in this reply to a newsman by former Soviet Premier Kosygin:

> I believe that defensive systems, which prevent attack, are not the cause of the arms race, but constitute a factor preventing the death of people. Some argue like this: what is cheaper, to have offensive weapons which can destroy towns and whole states or to have defensive weapons which can prevent this destruction? At present the theory is current somewhere that the system which is cheaper should be developed. Such so-called theoreticians argue as to the cost of killing a man—$500,000 or $100,000. Maybe an anti-missile system is more expensive than an offensive system, but it is designed not to kill people but to preserve human lives. I understand that I do not reply to the question I was asked, but you can draw yourselves the appropriate conclusions.

This is but one example of the oft-stated rejection of Mutual Assured Destruction and its eschewal of strategic defenses. Over the past decade or so, the USSR has spent more on strategic defenses than we have. For every ruble they have spent on strategic offense, they have spent one ruble on defense against nuclear attack. The U.S., on the other hand, has spent only one dollar on strategic defense for every ten thousand dollars spent on offense.

High Frontier's proposals for successful defense, enumerated in the foregoing answers, have had some good effects. The issue, once scoffed at, is now taken seriously. Secretary of Defense Weinberger first voiced support for the basic concept in August of 1982, saying, "What is really needed is the development of a new ballistic missile defense system, based in space, that can destroy incoming missiles before they even get into the atmosphere." Months later, President Reagan delivered his dramatic, though limited, endorsement on national television. High Frontier will never become a reality through the recommendations of bureaucrats whose turf it threatens. Only when America's leaders insist on a new strategic direction will the technical, costing and timing arguments fade. These will disappear overnight when our leaders make the decision.

They will not so readily disappear from the rhetoric of the ideological opposition. For a long time, the left studiously refrained from directly attacking High Frontier. They were hopeful, it appears, that the bureaucracy would do its work for them. Then, on February 3, 1983, Congressman Joe Moakley of Massachusetts fired the first shot. Moakley, along with 79 other members of the House, announced sponsorship of a resolution forbidding any and all U. S. weapons in space.

The *Congressional Record* of February 3 contains Mr. Moakley's assault on High Frontier, which he dubbed "high foolishness." He included a diatribe against High Frontier by a Dr. Bowman, who cites ample objections from unnamed Pentagon critics. The Bowman attack, in a way, illustrates the tacit alliance between the anti-defense spokesmen on the Left and some all-offense thinkers in the Department of Defense. Both insist that there is and should be no defense. At about the same time Moakley and company launched their attack, a new "Institute for Security and Cooperation in Outer Space" was founded in Washington, to be presided over by John Pike, one-time adviser to presidential candidate Barry Commoner. Its objective: defeat High Frontier. The Institute's money is to come primarily from the Rockefeller Family Fund.

The Left really had no choice but to oppose High Frontier, which constitutes an effective counter to the nuclear freeze movement around which the Left rallied and revived the old McGovern coalition. High Frontier appeals to the majority of Americans. It must be defeated if the Left is to avoid a large defection of frightened voters swept up into the nuclear freeze movement.

When the Left finally attacked, it handed the High Frontier concepts lock, stock and barrel to the conservatives. Had they been brighter, liberals might have stolen the concepts and turned them into a rationale to do nothing else in defense. They could have touted High Frontier as a panacea which would allow us to neglect our strategic offensive forces, our Navy and our conventional forces. But they didn't.

High Frontier recognizes the dire threat to our security and liberty and meets it. It saves defense money. It promotes private industry. It is independent of agreement with the Soviet Union. And it restores high moral content to our national security and high hope for the future of America and her Free World allies.

High Frontier is a course of action which can gain the support of a broad spectrum of the American public. It must become a prime issue for conservatives in the 1980s.

4

Space: The New Frontier

Congressman Newt Gingrich and James A. M. Muncy

Exploring and developing space is vital to America's future. Its importance is not economic or military nearly as much as it is psychological and cultural. Liberals argue that our planet is limited. Liberals claim that we face an inevitable Malthusian future in which a population explosion leads to a worldwide standard of living comparable to that of Bangladesh. In this setting of universal poverty, liberalism has the psychological edge over conservatism. If misery is unavoidable, liberals will continue to make people feel guilty for having earned (their own) wealth and tell them, "after all, *we* have to redistribute your wealth because others can't create their own in a world of limits."

If we are to build a Conservative Opportunity Society we must first destroy this liberal cultural and psychological myth of limits. Changing the cultural framework will then have political consequences. One of the keys to creating a conservative opportunity society is the fact that we are in the early stages of a great revolution. Alvin Toffler describes the changes as moving from a Second Wave industrial society to a Third Wave information society. He suggests that it is a transformation comparable to the change from agriculture to industry. We are entering a period of time in which technological changes will dramatically expand mankind's ability to create resources.

One of the key differences between a liberal welfare state and a conservative opportunity society is that liberals believe man is limited by resources, while a conservative opportunity society is based on the belief that man creates resources. History is on the side of conservatism. For 300 years, Western history has been a continuing story of man's making life better by making things better. By inventing better medicines we live longer. By developing better agriculture we eat better. By building better machines we improve our productivity and create more wealth.

Everything we do to prove that mankind has access to a universe of resources decreases the value and power of liberalism's most important dogma. In that setting space is a dagger at the heart of the liberal welfare state. Once you accept that opportunities in space are real, that orbiting the planet and building a space station and reaching the moon are not just circus stunts but in fact real achievements that are harbingers of a better future, then it is psychologically impossible to talk about the limits to growth. Then the only limits left are the limits of a free people's ingenuity, daring, and courage.

So we find ourselves almost exactly in the situation Europe was in 1500 when Christopher Columbus had returned from America and said, "There's a great new world out there and it is open to those who dare." If conservatism takes up that message it can become the daring belief, the imaginative belief, the hopeful belief, the opportunity-filled belief. And it can rally a generation of young people to build a better future.

The problem with conservatism in the last 50 years has been that it learned the wrong language from Herbert Hoover's opposition to the New Deal. When Hoover meant to say "we oppose a *liberal welfare state's centralized bureaucracy*" he instead substituted the word "government." Thus, conservatives for a half century have learned to say they're against government.

But in fact that can't be right. The most popular conservative cause of the late 1970s was saving the Panama Canal. But the Panama Canal was built by government engineers who stayed alive in the jungle because government doctors cured yellow fever. The construction was paid for with government monies, run by a government corporation, and protected by a government army and navy. So, indeed, conservatives are not against a strong government. When discussing anti-drug law enforcement conservatives are for effective, strong government. Conservatives are against big, bureaucratic welfare states.

The question for conservatives, then, is what should a strong government do? Liberals know that limited resources—whether real or imagined—necessitate government intrusion in the marketplace to allocate resources. Conservatives should therefore realize that government can and should explode those limits, thus removing the need for bureaucratic government intrusion. If we live in an age of opportunity we will not need socialistic redistribution of wealth.

The great ages of conservatism have included Alexander Hamilton's First Report on Manufacturers, which urged that the government hasten the Industrial Revolution through the use of protective tariffs; Stephen Douglas's dream of a Transcontinental Railroad; and Theodore Roosevelt's courageous building of the Panama Canal. We must look forward to the next generation now. We must once again be willing to work toward great dreams that, once achieved, our grandchildren will fight to defend.

A modern, activist conservatism must very strongly encourage increasing research and development—especially in the space arena. Success in these areas is intrinsic to any conservative vision of a strong, free, expansive America unhindered by the Limits to Growth myth that justifies a liberal welfare state.

We must very strongly favor those government projects that create the framework in which everything else occurs. That doesn't mean supporting a large bureaucracy. After all, there was no Department of Railroads in 1870. It may well be that rather than having NASA build a permanent space station, legislation should be proposed that provides a tax credit to any corporation or private consortium that builds a permanent space station.

The challenge to conservatives is to be aggressive in developing those research projects that, as Lincoln said, the people can't do for themselves. The first Space Shuttle was clearly not within any corporation's reach. The Transcontinental Railroad would never have been constructed without subsidies. The Panama Canal could not have been built if the U.S. Army Corps of Engineers hadn't built it. So government does have a role to play in what must be essentially collaborative efforts. On the other hand, space should be rapidly privatized and as many different groups as possible encouraged to participate on the economic front.

In fact, American private industry is pursuing business opportunities in space. For several years, investors have reaped profits—and consumers benefits—from communication satellites in stationary orbit above the earth that provide services which range from cheaper long-distance phone calls to videoconferencing. Industry's annual revenues are approaching $10 billion.

Now, essentially the same technology is starting to be used to broadcast directly from space several high quality television channels into people's homes—without cable or local broadcast towers. The market for these Direct Broadcast Satellites is estimated to reach $5 billion or more by 1990. Again, the quality of life will improve and the range of consumer choices will expand.

But neither of these opportunities would have been available if the government hadn't first paid to develop the vehicles that launch the large satellites into the high earth orbit required. And the satellites themselves wouldn't have the large productive capacity they do now—and therefore the commercial payoff—if the government hadn't spurred the development of microelectronics. Indeed, our computer industry leads the world today because we needed small and lightweight electronic controls first for ICBMs, then for the unmanned and manned space probes of the 1960s.

So we should support the temporary but aggressive subsidy of space privatization, much in the same way the government subsidized the first Air Mail postal service. It was largely by subsidizing the Air Mail that we created the airlines industry, which then led to a strong aircraft manufacturing industry. That gave the pre-World War II U.S. Army Corps a much wider selection of airplanes to choose from than it would have had if, in the 1920s and 1930s, the government had not been aggressively encouraging the "right behavior"—namely, the advance of aeronautical technology and production capability. It should be the duty of the state to shape market conditions to encourage right behavior, but not to build a bureaucracy to enforce it.

For example, in the 17th century the British crown granted national charters—delegating tremendous economic, political, and even military authority—to trading companies which undertook the risks of colonizing the New World. Historically in America people were encouraged to move into the frontiers by the granting of free land, etc. Now, just as conservatives favor tuition tax credits to encourage people to invest in the best possible education for their children, and just as conservatives support voluntary prayer in school, similarly we encourage people to aggressively seek out and reap the benefits of space.

The genius of activist conservatism in the past was that it encouraged people to, as Irving Kristol has said, "do well by doing good." In fact, we want to make it profitable for free citizens to do the things, take the risks, and develop the frontiers that make America strong.

Even now this policy is being applied to the commercial development of space. For example, NASA has already signed two—and is negotiating more—"joint endeavor agreements" with private companies of consortia to allow the commerical entity to fly payloads containing industrial experiments for free on the Space Shuttle. The company pays all payload development costs, and as soon as the technological capability being tested is proved, the company must pay for all launch costs as well.

NASA's first such agreement is with a partnership of the McDonnell-Douglas corporation and the Ortho Division of Johnson and Johnson. The project is an experiment in using the essentially zero-gravity environment of near-earth space to manufacture esoteric pharmaceuticals much more quickly, cheaply, and in a purer form than is possible on earth.

Industry and NASA are only beginning to identify the seemingly limitless commercial possibilities space offers. Even so, nearly all experts predict continuing acceleration of space industrialization. According to *Business Week,* "companies from Aluminum Co. of America to Western Electric Co., are beginning to view the heavens with an eye to their scientific and commercial possibilities. In fact, a recent NASA-funded survey turned up 84 companies interested in doing some 244 experimental and commercial projects in orbit."

And in the not-too-distant future, we may very well see the space equivalent of the American westward migration: self-supporting colonies of up to 10,000 free people who harvest the resources of space, whether that is the rare minerals contained in many asteroids or building solar power satellites to provide cheap, unlimited electrical energy to earth. After all, it took 109 years from Columbus's discovery of the New World to the founding of Jamestown Colony. That length of time from our moon landing will be the year 2078. Who knows what we will have achieved by then if we dare greatly and have faith in the capacity of free people?

Of course, much scientific research must be done before these dreams can be attained. Just as government-sponsored research helped create the airplane, computer, and nuclear power industries, the government should support and encourage the expansion of our scientific knowledge-base of space.

Again, this does not necessarily mean that NASA or any other government bureaucracy must or should be the sole—or even primary—agent in developing this new research. Special tax credits for industry-sponsored basic research are one option. Another is encouraging private donations to independent research organizations such as the non-profit Space Studies Institute of Princeton, N.J., which has done much of the seminal research in large-scale space industrialization, mostly with private funds.

Just as Thomas Jefferson had the vision to send Lewis and Clark West to explore the Louisiana Territory to the Pacific, so government should continue to fund the basic scientific research that contributes to our knowledge of the universe and increases our wisdom. For example, many of the early unmanned scientific probes launched by NASA led to discoveries that now have commercial application. And the more recent Viking and Voyager missions all advanced the technologies of communications, microelectronics, and robotics.

As of the late 19th century, the United States rode the crest of the industrial wave that had started a hundred years earlier in Europe to become the most economically advanced nation in the world. Now we face a new industrial revolution—in space. Can we afford not to lead again?

There is great danger that the liberal welfare state will cripple America at the beginning of the Third Wave of human development. Recent history has seen America fall behind economically as the liberal welfare state favors food stamps over research and welfare over development. In automobile manufacture and technology we were caught and surpassed by the Japanese. Europe is catching up to us in the field of commercial airlines and airplanes. Similarly, there is an enormous danger that we may be giving up our huge lead in space development to the Japanese and Europeans. We cannot afford to stop or even to delay our exploration of space. Imagine that Queen Isabella of Spain, upon hearing from Columbus that he had found a New World, said, "Fine, we'll mark that up in our books. Let's break up the ships for firewood. We now know this can be done." In reality great nations have turned their backs on the future and paid great costs as a consequence. In fact, less than 20 years before Columbus first reached the New World, the Ming Emperor of China denied the future as an act of state policy. For many years China's deep-water sailing ships had explored the seas as far as the east coast of Africa, bringing back wealth, knowledge, and a strong competitive desire to advance Chinese technology. By 1432, Chinese expeditions were bigger, more sophisticated, and more powerful than any in Western Europe.

The Chinese bureaucracy was afraid that the spirit of exploration was unsettling society. It wanted to return to a calm, stable, controllable way of life. In 1475 the Emperor decreed that all lands beyond China were of no significance and further voyages were banned. The Chinese people were to limit themselves to sanctioned pursuits such as studying Confucius and creating works of art. This so stifled technological advance and the creation of wealth that when the West finally confronted China some 400 years later, the Confucian system was unable to preserve its independence and ultimately it collapsed.

In the early 20th century, those who controlled the air dominated warfare. Now, those who control space will dominate war—and peace. The military survival of the United States—as much as our cultural, economic, and intellectual survival—depends on how quickly we meet the challenge of the space frontier. We have, in the words of Lt. Gen. Daniel Graham, USA (Ret.) and the Director of Project High Frontier, "only a fleeting opportunity to muster the political will and make a bold and rapid entry into space to frustrate Soviet power ambitions."

The Soviets have long seen the importance of this new military arena. Graham aptly describes their view: "The Soviets integrate military space operations into their strategic thinking. They see space in straightforward terms, as an operational or combatant theater, a critical arena for them to dominate." Indeed, the late Soviet rocket pioneer Sergei Korolev boldly and clearly defined his nation's intended leading role in space by saying that "the Soviet Union has become the seacoast of the universe."

According to the Department of Defense's report, *Soviet Military Power*, the Soviet space program leads U.S. efforts in several key areas. The Soviets launch roughly 75 spacecraft a year (four or five times as many as the U.S., although the higher reliability of U.S. satellites partially makes up for this) with an aggregate payload weight some 10 times that of the U.S. Furthermore, as much as 70 percent of all Soviet launches are exclusively for military purposes, and another 15 percent serve some military functions.

Much more significant, however, is the Soviets' lead in sheer manned spaceflight experience. Soviet cosmonauts have spent over 62,000 hours working, learning, and performing experiments in space, as compared to 24,000 hours for U.S. astronauts. From the largely symbolic Apollo-Soyuz mission in 1975 to the first Space Shuttle flight in 1981, the U.S. flew no manned space missions. During the same period, the Soviets launched and manned several Salyut space stations, including Salyut 6, which remained in orbit for nearly five years and was manned almost continously by 30 cosmonauts performing civilian and military tasks. And in 1982, the Soviets launched Salyut 7, which according to many Soviet space experts is the first truly permanent, modular manned space station.

While the Soviets have been actively learning and experimenting with how space can aid their military objectives, our use has been much more passive, although extremely vital. At the simplest level, we use reconnaisance satellites to gather information about the size, strength, and deployment of enemy tactical and strategic forces. The strategic impact of this capability is especially important, because it is really the only way we can verify Soviet compliance with current strategic arms limitation agreements. Space surveillance is the key to preventing a surprise nuclear attack. Furthermore, surveillance from space has impact on much lower levels of warfare.

A good example of the tactical use of observation satellites was the recent war in the Falklands Islands. U. S. satellite data told the British what the weather was going to be and how the Argentine Navy and Air Force were deployed, so they knew in advance, for example, if and when the Argentines would be able to launch an air strike on their ships or ground forces. At the same time, the Soviets launched several specialized reconnaisance satellites so they could monitor the situation in the South Atlantic, and may have given some of that information to the Argentines. If so, the superior quality of U.S. satellite data doubtlessly helped the British win.

The U. S. Armed Forces also increasingly use military communications satellites for Command/Control/Communications functions. While this allows us to deploy our Navy and other forces anywhere on the globe without losing 0^3 contact, it also leaves our war-fighting capability dangerously dependent on very vulnerable satellites.

For several years the Soviets have tested simple but effective anti-satellite (ASAT) weapons. Their inclusion of an ASAT test in a recent full-scale mock alert of Soviet strategic forces shows their willingness to use it. And while it is hoped that the recently-begun U.S. ASAT development program will deter Soviet ASAT usage, we still must recognize that if our vital military satellites are vulnerable, our entire military system is vulnerable.

We can expect to lose our satellites—especially communications and reconnaisance satellites—very quickly once fighting begins. Indeed, loss of several or all of our satellites may be the first warning of an imminent attack. That threat requires us to rethink our entire satellite program to develop backup satellites that we can launch quickly if we start losing orbiting satellites in a crisis.

Along with these military space activities, which help us wage war more effectively, space offers us a chance to preserve peace and avoid nuclear destruction. In addition to the passive role of treaty verification performed by reconnaisance satellites, President Reagan has called for the development of active strategic space technologies that can actually defend the U.S. and its allies from a ballistic missile attack. On March 23, 1983, the President said in a televised address: "I call upon the scientific community in our country, those who gave us nuclear weapons, to turn their great talents now to the cause of mankind and world peace, to give us the means of rendering these nuclear weapons impotent and obsolete."

Ironically, while this proposal is much less "offensive" than, for example, the deployment of a U.S. ASAT system, it has aroused much greater opposition from liberals who believe space can be a pristine, peaceful place "uncontaminated" by weapons of any kind. What they fail to understand, of course, is that we are already engaged in competition with the Soviets in space. Space was militarized when the Soviets demonstrated their ICBM technology by launching Sputnik, and again when we responded with Explorer I, which was built at the Army's Redstone Arsenal. Furthermore, it is irrational and anti-human to suggest that threatening a mechanical satellite is more horrible than killing people on earth. As Winston Churchill said: "War is horrible, slavery is worse." To preserve freedom we must be prepared to defend it in space as well as on earth.

So the military space arena is a challenge, and although our technological lead in space makes us potentially more powerful, the importance of space to our civilian as well as military sector makes us more vulnerable. We must, therefore, make sure that we avail ourselves of all the defensive opportunities that space makes possible. If we succeed in that effort, we can end the continuing balance of terror of Mutual Assured Destruction in favor of peace and assured survival.

In summary, Americans must be offered a future of opportunity and hope, rather than limits and despair. They must be shown a vision of space that arouses people's energies to meet the challenge of producing a better world that insures the survival of freedom and hope for themselves and their grandchildren. We must commit our energies to a conservative opportunity society of freedom and prosperity for all mankind. *That* is a future people will rally to and work for.

BIBLIOGRAPHY

Bova, Ben. *The High Road.* Boston: Houghton Mifflin, 1981.

Business Week staff. "Special Report: The U.S. Returns to Space." *Business Week* (June 20, 1983).

Graham, Daniel. *High Frontier: A New National Strategy.* Washington, D.C.: 1982.

Haggerty, James. "Military in Space." *Aerospace* (Spring 1982).

Hutton, Richard. *The Cosmic Chase.* New York: New American Library, 1981.

O'Neill, Gerard K. *The High Frontier.* New York: William Morrow & Company, 1977.

Stine, G. Harry. *Confrontation in Space.* Englewood Cliffs, N.J.: Prentice Hall, 1981.

Toffler, Alvin. *The Third Wave.* New York: William Morrow & Company, 1980.

Vajk, Peter. *Doomsday Has Been Cancelled.* Culver City, Ca.: Peace Press, 1978.

5

The U.S. and the U.N.: Time for Reappraisal

Burton Yale Pines

After two centuries of disdain for international organizations, the United States in the post-World War II era has become one of history's great joiners. In short time, the U.S. signed on with scores of groups, ranging from the International Monetary Fund (1945) and NATO (1949) to the Inter-American Tropical Tuna Commission (1949), the North Pacific Fur Seal Commission (1957) and the International Agreement Regarding the Maintenance of Certain Lights in the Red Sea (1966). So vast grew this nation's memberships in international groups, that the State Department had to create in 1954 an entire section to deal with international organizations. By early 1983, the Assistant Secretary of State for International Organizations had a staff of 172 to monitor U.S. relations with 98 international groups. In addition to those, the U.S. has ties to at least 50 other international agencies or commissions. The exact number of international bodies to which the U.S. belongs, in fact, no one in government seems to know.

To some, America's readiness to join international bodies seemed like a betrayal of George Washington's Farewell Address warning that "in regard to foreign Nations . . . have with them as little Political connection as possible." To others, U.S. post-war internationalization was welcomed as a tardy but sensible affirmation of the Wilsonian vision. It was, in truth, neither. U.S. participation in international organizations simply was recognition that the civilized world faced extraordinary threats which could be countered only by active U.S. involvement—indeed, by U.S. leadership. In the years following the German and Japanese surrenders, the globe's industrial economies were shattered and in need of repair. Europe's democracies were weary and confronting menacing Soviet troops farther westward than Lenin ever could have imagined. And the world's financial institutions were reeling from the two decades of turmoil caused by depression and war.

It clearly was in American interests to offer to Western Europe the security crutch provided by the North Atlantic Treaty Organization and the machinery to encourage world trade provided by the International Monetary Fund and the General Agreement on Trade and Tariffs. Yet, what was appropriate in the years following World War II now may be an anachronism. With the contemporary world so different from that of 1946 or even 1955, are there still valid reasons for the U.S. to remain deeply involved in international organizations? It is undeniable, for instance, that the Wilsonian dreams once again seem as hollow as they did a half-century ago. George Washington's admonition, meantime, appears increasingly profound. Yet the United States, as it approaches the 21st century, will find guidance on the question of international involvement neither in Wilson nor Washington. The answers rather are in the lessons learned in the past four decades. Among them:

Universal organizations such as the United Nations and those agencies associated with the U.N., like UNESCO, accomplish so little that the value to the U.S. of membership becomes very doubtful.

On the other hand, organizations of like-minded states with fairly specific purposes, such as NATO or, until recently, the International Monetary Fund (IMF) fulfill a number of their most important aims.

The democratic dictum of one-man, one-vote may work within communities or nations, but apparently cannot be applied to organizations containing large numbers of nations which differ dramatically from each other. Within international organizations, the power to influence decisions should closely resemble the responsibility for carrying out the decisions. At the United Nations General Assembly or in UNESCO, for example, a majority comprised of developing nations which contribute almost nothing to the U.N. budget and bear almost no burden for effecting U.S. programs consistently dictate what those programs should be and even what they cost. It is quite a different matter at the I.M.F. There the weight of a nation's vote is determined by the extent of that nation's financial participation.

Technical organizations must limit their activities and rhetoric to technical matters. This means that the World Health Organization should deal with fighting diseases; the International Telecommunications Union should keep global communications orderly; and the International Atomic Energy Agency should monitor the peaceful uses of the atom. When their agendas and rhetoric become politicized, an organization's value wanes. The matter of South Africa's policy of apartheid or the Israeli occupation of the west bank of the Jordan River are serious political matters but are not appropriate for the World Health Organization, International Telecommunications Union, International Atomic Energy Agency or any other technical agency.

It is time for the U.S. to apply these lessons and reevaluate American membership in international organizations. In the case of basically sound bodies—such as NATO, I.M.F., Organization of American States and the World Bank—this reevaluation probably would lead to minor revisions of the organization's structure and the nature of U.S. participation. When it comes to the United Nations and its many affiliated agencies, however, a reevaluation is certain to prompt a fundamental reconsideration of U.S. membership. For more than a decade and a half, the U.N. has increasingly demonstrated that it is not merely costly and harmless. Increasingly, the United Nations is becoming, as Senator Daniel Patrick Moynihan entitled his 1980 description of his tour as U.S. Permanent Representative at the U.N., "a dangerous place." The United Nations, indeed, is becoming a threat to U.S. national interests.

A list of the U.N.'s failures and shortcomings should puncture the resolve of all but the organization's blindest boosters. The U.N. has failed as a peacekeeper and peacemaker and as a protector of human rights. Its record of caring for refugees is suspiciously mixed, ignoring the legions attempting to flee communist-ruled Viet Nam while allowing the Palestine Liberation Organization to turn refugee camps into armed garrisons. Inefficiency, cronyism, high pay, lavish expense accounts and even corruption and illiteracy have become the all-too-common characteristics of the Secretariat and other U.N. bureaucracies. Meantime, U.N. agencies in New York, Geneva and Vienna serve as valuable cover for Soviet, East European, Cuban and other espionage services hostile to the West.

But even this troubling litany omits what now is the gravest danger posed by the United Nations—its role in affecting the way in which nations and their citizens view critical global issues. Like a House of Mirrors at an amusement park, the U.N. distorts reality—exaggerating some things, diminishing others and obscuring most. Unlike a House of Mirrors, however, the U.N.'s distortions, particularly in the General Assembly and its Secretariat, form a predictable pattern. One characteristic of this pattern is the U.N.'s politicization of issues that merely are technical. Certainly the behavior of Israel, Chile and South Africa are not really the most urgent issues confronting the General Assembly, to say nothing of the World Health Organization, UNESCO, the International Labor Organization and a host of other agencies. Yet these ostensibly technical bodies squander an enormous amount of their time and energy dealing repeatedly with a handful of political matters forced onto the agendas by a bloc of nations strongly influenced by the Palestine Liberation Organization and radical leftist states and groups.

Another aspect of the pattern is the U.N.'s globalization of problems. Bringing a local or even regional matter or dispute to the General Assembly forces every nation to take a stand. Issues which could remain local suddenly gain global importance and almost always, therefore, became more difficult to resolve. Nearly 15 years ago, the Netherlands' chief U.N. delegate Carl W. A. Schurmann complained that the U.N. system "forces governments to take a stand (if not by making a speech, then at least by voting) on a great many questions and conflicts that either do not really concern them or on which they would much have preferred to keep their opinions to themselves." This was echoed in 1982 by U.S. Permanent Representative to the United Nations Jeane Jordan Kirkpatrick in an address to the Anti-Defamation League. "Instead of being an effective instrument for conflict resolution," she said, "[the U.N.] serves all too often as an arena in which conflict is polarized, extended and exacerbated, in which differences are made deeper and more difficult to resolve than they would otherwise be."

Politicizing and globalizing issues are two of the dangers created by the U.N.'s distorted pattern of behavior. Dangerous, too, is the legitimacy conferred on the undeserving, while discreditation goes to those entitled to respect as members of the community of nations. Within the U.N. system, for example, the P.L.O. and South West African Peoples Organization (SWAPO) enjoy near official status and are treated not as the terrorists that they are but as members in good standing of the international community. Israel, South Africa, Chile, and the Shah's Iran, meanwhile, are or have been reviled as pariah states.

Most dangerous, however, is the U.N.'s *de facto* (and sometimes *de jure*) crusade against the free enterprise system. In many respects, the U.N. has become the headquarters, command post and strategic planning center of an anti-free enterprise campaign. In almost every U.N. body and almost always in the General Assembly, seldom is an opportunity lost to attack the free enterprise system. These assaults come as direct attacks on the Western industrial democracies which are the main capitalist nations. They come as attacks on individual industries through increasing attempts to impose international codes of economic regulation. They come too as attacks on the most successful of the capitalist enterprises, the corporation which has grown beyond its boundaries of the country in which it was founded and in which it is headquartered—the multinational corporations. And the U.N. crusade attacks the very essence and philosophical base of the free enterprise system. It is an assault which condemns, almost always without supporting evidence, the notion that the dynamic of growth and economic expansion is individual initiative, creativity and the incentive provided by the opportunity of making a profit. This kind of attack even repudiates the notion of economic growth, substituting for it the naïve and economically self-defeating concepts of wealth redistribution and central planning.

In repudiating free enterprise and by ignoring capitalism's record of success, the United Nations and its agencies have raised to the level of gospel the tenets of what is called the New International Economic Order or, as it is widely known, NIEO. The tenacity with which the United Nations fights for NIEO at every forum, from every rostrum and in every possible publication and statement is awesome. The United Nations Education, Scientific and Cultural Organization (UNESCO), for instance, now deals with educational and cultural matters mainly as a means for promoting the NIEO agenda. A U.N. conference ostensibly called to combat discrimination against women, meanwhile, was transformed into a NIEO pep rally. This obsession with NIEO has converted the United Nations from an organization that might merely have been costly and annoying into a body which threatens those nations committed to democracy, liberty and economic development.

Early critics of the United Nations recognized and predicted the organization's shortcomings. While their warnings then might have been debatable, they now seem only too real. As a result, American public support for the U.N. has plummeted sharply from that heady July 28, 1945, when the U.N. Charter went to the Senate floor for ratification and was approved by a lopsided 89 to 2. This reflected the broad popular backing for the U.N. Support remained high through the U.N.'s first decade and a half. A 1959 Gallup Poll revealed that 87 percent of those surveyed felt that the U.N. was doing a good job. By 1971, however, Americans were having second thoughts and Gallup found that only 35 percent gave the U.N. passing grades. This dropped to 30 percent in 1980, while 53 percent thought that the organization was doing a "poor job." And in March 1981, a Roper Poll discovered that only a slim 10 percent of Americans viewed the U.N. as "highly effective" in carrying out its functions.

Though now disillusioned with the U.N., Americans cannot be faulted for not trying to make the international body succeed. Since the U.N.'s birth, the U.S. has been the U.N.'s most enthusiastic and generous booster. Until 1964, for instance, American taxpayers provided nearly 40 percent of the U.N. assessed budget. Even now with its share reduced, as other nations have industrialized and grown wealthier, the U.S. pays about one-quarter of the U.N.'s bills. In 1983, this probably cost the taxpayer more than $1 billion, bringing to about

$12 billion the U.S. contribution to the U.N. since 1945. By contrast, the Soviet Union pays only 13 percent of the U.N. budget (and is $169 million in arrears) and gets much more benefit from the U.N. than does the U.S. Even more striking is the paltry material support from those who control the U.N. The approximately 120 developing nations who command a permanent U.N. majority together contribute less than 9 percent of the organization's costs. Some of those 120 nations, of course, are very poor; yet others are quite rich. In fiscal 1980-81, for instance, Saudi Arabia paid only 0.58 percent of the U.N. budget and Kuwait only 0.20 percent, while relatively poor Britain and Spain paid 4.40 percent and 1.70 percent respectively.

For nearly its first two decades, the United Nations mainly reflected the concerns of the world's industrial democracies. As new nations were formed and admitted to the U.N., in the wake of the dissolution of the world's empires (except that of the Soviet Union), the balance of power within the U.N. inexorably shifted. From 51 members in 1945, the U.N. grew to 82 by 1958, to 115 in 1964 and now stands at 157 member nations. While there is some merit to the argument that a global organization ought to have a universal membership, this has been translated simplistically into a policy within the U.N. (except for the Security Council) of one-nation, one-vote. As a result, policy-making is divorced from policy-responsibility. A majority of today's U.N. members are ill-prepared to address the issues that come before the U.N. for these nations stand only on the threshold of political and economic development. They have no experience in international matters and can boast little knowledge of any history but that of their own transition from colonialism to independence. In almost every case, moreover, the majority of U.N. members have no respect for or faith in democracy. Yet they determine the policies that the U.N. adopts and which the United States and other democracies are obliged to execute and underwrite. To make matters worse, these policies are becoming increasingly opposed to U.S. principles and national interests.

Supporting Terrorists

Through its resolutions and, what is more alarming, its agencies and funds, the United Nations has been supporting terrorist groups. The Palestine Liberation Organization, the African National Congress and the Pan-African Congress have been receiving material backing from the U.N. According to a Heritage Foundation study, between 1975 and 1981 the U.N. spent or budgeted at least $116 million to support these and similar groups. This figure was compiled solely from public records. The real U.N. outlay for terrorism, including items camouflaged and hidden in innocent-appearing budget items, surely exceeds by severalfold this publicly verifiable outlay. Of this sum, the U.S. taxpayer contributes at least 25 percent.

U.N. support for terrorists takes a number of forms. It ranges from gifts of food, housing and health services to providing radio channels through which a terrorist group can broadcast propaganda. The United Nations Education, Scientific and Cultural Organization (UNESCO) has given money earmarked for education to a wide range of terrorist groups. Totaling at least $8 million for 1981-1983, there is no way to account for how the terrorists actually spent that money. To be sure, the public record reveals no U.N. funds used to purchase arms. U.N. accounting and expense monitoring procedures, however, are widely ridiculed as lax, if not deliberately permissive. There is thus valid cause to question how the P.L.O. and similar groups spend UNESCO's "educational" grants. Even by providing food, medicine and training for civilian cadres, the U.N. allows terrorists to earmark more of their own funds for weaponry.

As important as material aid is the political legitimacy that the U.N. confers on terrorist organizations. Official U.N. recognition amounts to a seal of approval which gives the Marxist-oriented P.L.O., SWAPO, A.N.C. and P.A.C. a definite advantage over their non-Marxist rivals at home. They enjoy U.N. money, aid projects, publicity and international lobbying power not available to their competitors. Example: SWAPO has access to the U.N. Department of Public Information Radio Service with broadcasts worldwide. With this, SWAPO airs special programs on Namibia. The Department of Public Information also provides photographic and exhibition services for special SWAPO events—such as displays which become semi-permanent exhibits at U.N. headquarters in New York and offices in Geneva and Vienna. The U.N. imprimatur makes the terrorists appear to be the sole representatives of their respective peoples. In reality, SWAPO, P.L.O., A.N.C. and P.A.C. face formidable challenges at home from non-Marxist and non-terrorist groups.

The United Nations excuses its support for terrorists by claiming that it has a responsibility for helping so-called National Liberation Movements battle colonialist regimes. U.N. aid for these movements, however, is curiously selective. No backing, for instance, is given to pro-Western National Liberation Movements such as UNITA, now fighting what appears to be a successful guerrilla war in Angola against the Soviet and Cuban backed Marxist regime. Nor has the U.N. been willing to recognize the non-Marxist representatives of the Palestinians or the democratic political parties of Namibia. Instead, the U.N. General Assembly grandly declares and treats the P.L.O. and SWAPO as the sole, legitimate representatives of their respective peoples. These two terrorist groups, for example, hold coveted "permanent observer" status at key U.N. agencies and bodies—including the Security Council—when questions concerning their areas of the world are on the agenda. And while the General Assembly effectively has barred the sovereign state of South Africa from its proceedings, denying the South African delegations even the right to answer charges against it, the General Assembly has asked all U.N. organs to include the A.N.C. and P.A.C. in their meetings dealing with southern Africa.

No terrorist group enjoys U.N. munificence more than the Palestine Liberation Organization. It has full observer status at UNESCO, the International Labor Organization, the World Health Organization and the International Civil Aviation Organization. Affiliation with the aviation body actually permits the P.L.O., whose members are among the most accomplished and violent airplane skyjackers, to attend meetings called to discuss international air travel security. In 1977, meanwhile, the P.L.O. was admitted to the U.N. Economic and Social Council's Commission for Western Asia. This was the first full membership ever granted to a non-country. Since then, the P.L.O. has been allowed to chair the Commission's sessions.

Two U.N. committees were created for and are dominated by the P.L.O.: the Inalienable Rights Committee and the Special Unit on Palestinian Rights. These committees allow the P.L.O. to use U.N. funds to publish a wide variety of publications and mount a public relations campaign, including an annual "International Solidarity Day with the Palestinian People." P.L.O. booklets lauding Yassir Arafat as a freedom fighter and defending the P.L.O.'s use of terrorism are featured at U.N. bookstores. P.L.O. exhibitions, meanwhile, adorn corridors of U.N. buildings. Despite protests from Israel, a P.L.O. U.N. exhibit displayed a map of the Middle East which depicted a state identified as "Palestine" by omitted Israel.

Through its officially sanctioned presence, the P.L.O. has gained inordinate influence at the U.N. On many issues, including a good number of personnel matters, the P.L.O. wields a widely-recognized veto. This not only adversely affects American and Israeli interests, but undermines the efforts of moderate, democratic Palestinian leaders to find a peaceful solution to the Palestinian problem. By blindly supporting the P.L.O., the United Nations actually creates obstacles to the achievement of an Arab-Israeli peace.

The Double Standard

The favored treatment of the P.L.O., SWAPO and a handful of other groups typifies the corrosive double standard increasingly characteristic of the United Nations. Outrages committed by socialist and communist nations almost always are overlooked by U.N. agencies, while minor or even alleged misdeeds in pro-Western countries warrant unrelenting U.N. attention and denunciation. Not only does this waste U.N. resources and undermine the credibility of the organization, but also seems to provide U.N. sanction, by its silence, of some of the world's worst contemporary violations of political and human rights.

The double standard pervades most U.N. operations. At UNESCO, for instance, the draft for the 1984-1989 Medium Term Plan dwells at length on a critique of how Western private cultural institutions, because of "short-term amortization, cost factors and profit margins . . . [bring] about a deterioration in the economic and social status of the artists." The Plan is strangely silent about the artistic repression characteristic of Soviet-style and other socialist states. The double standard is most glaring at the General Assembly. There, the majority of 120 or so Third World and Soviet-bloc nations consistently castigates the U.S. for such crimes as trading with South Africa. Nothing is said, however, about the flourishing South African trade carried on by Zimbabwe and other black African states.

The U.N. is particularly schizoid in defining wars of national liberation. It is fine for the P.L.O. to attack Israeli towns and for SWAPO to mount an armed insurrection in South West Africa (known also as Namibia). These are acceptable battles of "liberation." But it is not a "war of liberation" according to the U.N. lexicon when Solidarity struggles for liberty in Poland or when Hungarians and Czechoslovaks tried to wrest freedom from Moscow's tight grip. The coveted "liberation" label even is denied to non-extremist black African groups such as Inkatha, led by Gaftsa Buthelese, head of the Zulu nation. The Zulus are mounting what may be the strongest internal opposition to the South African government. As such, it would seem, Inkatha should qualify as a national liberation movement. But not by the U.N.'s double standard.

The U.N.'s judgment is seriously flawed by its obsession with South Africa. In the 1981 General Assembly, for instance, 45 resolutions were adopted against South Africa, while over 400 speeches attacked the Pretoria regime. At the Secretariat, about 200 bureaucrats work full time against the interests of South Africa, spending some $40 million in this endeavor. At a time when Soviet troops were marching through Afghanistan, Vienamese forces occupying much of Laos and Kampuchea and Iraqi and Iranian soldiers ferociously battling each other, South Africa's internal affairs surely were not the most urgent item on the U.N. agenda.

Israel, too, is a major victim of the double standard. Almost nothing done by the Israelis escapes the U.N.'s vigilant scrutiny, while very little done to Israel by its enemies seems to warrant U.N. attention. More than a decade ago, for example, the U.N. majority voted to condemn Israel for launching air strikes against terrorist camps in Syria and Lebanon. Nothing was said to condemn those who had provoked the strikes—the terrorists who had massacred Israeli athletes at the 1972 Munich Olympics. At a recent General Assembly session, almost all of the 40 resolutions dealing with the Middle East denounced Israel. Yet no mention was made by any resolution of P.L.O. attacks on Israeli civilians, including women and children. The U.S. routinely is excoriated for supporting Israel, while the U.N. majority says nothing about Moscow's training terrorists who attack Israel. The Israeli diamond trade with South Africa is attacked as still another example of the Jewish state's outlaw behavior; the Soviet Union's diamond trade with South Africa is completely ignored.

In 1982 the General Assembly's Credentials Committee condemned Israel as a "non-peaceloving state." If the U.N. pursues the implications of this, Israel eventually could be denied its U.N. seat since the U.N. Charter specifically states that the organization is open solely to "peaceloving" nations. While the U.N. has no trouble branding Israel, because of its military actions, a non-lover of peace, the U.N. apparently regards as examples of peaceloving behavior the Soviet invasion of Afghanistan, Viet Nam's invasion of Cambodia, Iraq's war with Iran and Libya's threats to Chad and the Sudan. No attempt has been made by the General Assembly to label these breakers of peace as "non-peaceloving" states.

The U.S. also is victim of the United Nations double standard. Little seems to inhibit the U.N. majority from attacking the U.S. by name. Washington was brutally denounced, for example, for shooting down two Libyan warplanes which had opened fire on American aircraft. Washington also was attacked for "unfair" treatment of a Palestinian when the U.S. extradited him so that he could stand trial for murder! While the General Assembly works itself into a rage over such American sins, it remains mute in its refusal even to reprimand the Soviet Union by name for invading Afghanistan or for quashing Poland's quest for liberty. Despite mounting evidence of Moscow's use of illegal chemical and biological weapons in Afghanistan, Laos and Cambodia, the General Assembly has had almost nothing to say on the matter. Instead, it prefers lambasting the U.S. for triggering an "arms race" (ignoring the decade-long Soviet military buildup) and condemning Israeli human rights "violations" while saying nothing about the persistent and systematic human rights offenses in North Korea, Ethiopia, the Ayatollah's Iran and scores of other Third World states and the Soviet bloc.

In Latin America, the U.N. routinely condemns Chile, Bolivia, El Salvador and Guatemala for alleged human rights offenses. This amounts to "a particularly egregious example of moral hypocrisy," U.S. Ambassador Jeane Kirkpatrick told a November 24, 1981, session of the Third Committee of the General Assembly. Those four countries are criticized, she complained, while the General Assembly displays "studious unconcern with the much larger violations of human liberty elsewhere in Latin America, by the government of Cuba." Asked Kirkpatrick: "What are we to think of defenders of human rights who ignore the victims of major tyrants and vent all their ferocity on the victims of minor tyrants?" Castro's near-quarter-century of repression has yet to be condemned or even acknowledged by the U.N.

The double standard indeed is most glaring when it comes to the matter of human rights. "No aspect of United Nations affairs," observed Kirkpatrick at the Third Committee meeting, "has been more perverted by politicization in the last decade than have its human rights activities." The U.N. has all but ignored blatant cases of genocide, such as Indonesia's massacre of much of its Chinese population in the late 1960s, Nigeria's persecution of the Ibos in the mid-1960s, Pakistan's action against the Bengalis in 1971, Burundi's attacks on the Hutus in 1972-73, Iran's devastation of the Kurds in the mid-1970s and Nicaragua's campaign against the Miskitoe Indians that continues still. The United Nations was silent on these well-documented atrocities, as it was while three million Cambodians died in Pol Pot's bloody "utopia" and when as many as 250,000 Ugandans died at the hands of Idi Amin. When the U.S. in 1977 proposed a resolution to condemn the Ugandan dictator's actions, the African nations blocked the matter from coming to a vote.

Attempts at less U.N. hypocrisy in applying human rights standards typcally have been overruled. A 1979 Report of the Subcommission on Prevention of Discrimination and Protection of Minorities, for example, originally referred to "the existence of relatively full documentation dealing with the massacres of Armenians [in the Soviet Union], which have been described as the first case of genocide in the twentieth century." The statement was dropped from the Report's final version. Instead of condemning the Soviet Union's human rights record, in fact, the U.N. actually has lauded it—at least indirectly. When it came time to commemorate the twentieth anniversary of the adoption of the Universal Declaration of Human Rights, the U.N. presented a human rights award to, among others, the Soviet Union's Pyotr E. Nedbailo, well-known in his native Ukraine for publishing anti-Semitic tracts.

The Crusade Against Free Enterprise

It is not only the United States and other democracies that are treated unfairly by the United Nations. Cheated more than all others are the poor nations of the Third World that look to the U.N. and its agencies for help in economic development. From the U.N., however, these nations receive biased advice that ignores the sole model for growth with a record of success—the free enterprise market economy. Though the U.N. spends more than $300 million annually on economic research, the data are often altered and the results manipulated to confirm the premises of the New International Economic Order. Thus, instead of giving Third World states the difficult but useful advice that they need for economic growth, the U.N. tells them that they need only take the wealth of the industrial nations. The U.N.'s NIEO orthodoxy endorses the omniscience of government planners rather than the efficiency of the impersonal marketplace; it champions the idea that all have an equal claim to the fruits of man's output rather than that of rewards distributed according to merit; and it rests on the naïve faith that wealth—goods, crops, minerals, technology—simply exists in nature rather than being produced through creativity, risk capital and hard work. NIEO enthusiasts maintain that technology somehow is the "common heritage of mankind"—a resource belonging to no one and to be shared by everyone. Access to technology therefore becomes a right.

The major target of the U.N. crusade against the free enterprise system is the multinational corporations or, as they are sometimes known, transnational corporations. They are denounced for "flying no flag but profit" and for causing the "decay and deskilling" of Third World economies. The pharmaceuticals are attacked, for example, for being "harmful to public health and welfare" and for marketing both the "cause and cure" of illness. The international firms are blamed for causing inflation, unemployment, poverty and political repression in Third World states. So persistently vilified are the large international enterprises that the very terms "multinationals" and "transnationals" have become tainted, burdened with opprobrium. Only rarely does the U.N. look at the record and acknowledge the critically essential contributions that the multinational corporations have made to Third World economic development.

The U.N.'s attacks on the free enterprise system occur with increasing frequency. Among the many instances:

At one time, the World Health Organization was concerned almost entirely with encouraging medical research and planning and executing health programs. In recent years, however, W.H.O. has been pushed by NIEO advocates into the field of regulation and has become politicized on the all-too-familiar lines of the developed North versus undeveloped South or Third World.

Efforts are underway to regulate the international flow of data. The Third World majority at the U.N. is attempting to restrict a company's access to information stored in its own subsidiary or headquarters if they are in different nations. U.N. agencies, moreover, are trying to impose taxes on the movement of data into and out of countries.

The International Telecommunications Union, for decades an agency concerned only with the technical problems of transmitting communications between nations, is becoming increasingly politicized. This is clear not only from a threat at I.T.U. to exclude Israel, but from demands by the Third World majority within the I.T.U. that underdeveloped countries be granted a very large share of the world's radio frequencies, no matter that they do not have and may never have the technological ability to use them. The Third World majority is also insisting that "rents" be paid for the geostationary orbital slots in which communications satellites are parked.

Under the U.N.'s "Agreement Governing the Activities of States on the Moon and Other Celestial Bodies," a U.N.-affiliated "regime" has been established to govern exploration and extraction activities in outer space. This Agreement specifically favors state-owned agencies at the expense of private enterprise.

Through its Center on Transnational Corporations, the U.N. is preparing a "register" of corporate profits. This is seen as an important step toward regulating the activities of international firms.

The General Assembly in 1980 approved the Code of Restrictive Business Practices. When enforced, it would compel multinational corporations to sell their technology and know-how at punitively low prices in Third World markets. Nowhere does the Code acknowledge the contributions made by the multinationals in spurring the development of economically backward states.

U.N. agencies recently have been attempting to change international patent regulations. The aim is to limit the force of patents to allow Third World nations to exploit new technology without paying for it.

At the 1982 World Conference on Cultural Policies in Mexico City, UNESCO Director General Amadou-Mahtar M'Bow of Senegal led an unrelenting charge against the U.S., the West and the free enterprise system. He and the Third World-dominated conference called for a New World Cultural Order and a New World Information Order. Among other things, these new Orders would clamp down on press freedoms and repress expressions of Western culture in the

Third World. This Mexico City conference mirrored the almost fanatical anti-West and anti-capitalist turn taken by UNESCO under M'Bow's direction. UNESCO publications—printed by the millions, distributed to more than 150 nations and paid for mainly by the U.S. and other Western states—have become an important vehicle for Marxist, anti-American and anti-Western articles. In books ostensibly dealing with education, UNESCO promotes the idea that Western industrial states have acquired their wealth unjustly and thus this wealth may be redistributed to poor nations.

Although there is no carefully coordinated or centrally directed grand conspiracy at the U.N. to undermine the free enterprise system, the NIEO serves as a blueprint or manifesto that is endorsed enthusiastically by just about all of the 120 or so underdeveloped states and even accepted (with reservations) by a number of West European industrial nations. This strategy also was accepted by key Carter Administration officials like Andrew Young. Officially called the Charter of Economic Rights and Duties of States, NIEO was adopted in 1974 at the plenary meeting of the United Nations Conference on Trade and Development (UNCTAD)—the U.N. body that most aggressively attacks the market economy. NIEO is a blueprint for assuring that the free enterprise system never takes root in the Third World. It is designed to penalize not only capitalist firms and capitalist states, but also the citizens of capitalist societies. What NIEO seeks, in short, is to force the transfer to undeveloped countries of the wealth, technology and research from those industrial nations that have created this wealth, technology and research. The transfer is to be mandatory and perpetual; there will be only limited, if any, compensation for the enormous assets involved.

NIEO is not going to be enacted or enforced *in toto* on the industrial West. Its underlying philosophy, however, provides the conceptual rationale and guidance for the U.N.'s attack on the free enterprise system. It is a blueprint providing a checklist of specific anti-free enterprise measures which the U.N. and its agencies individually and gradually can enact.

In at least two critical areas, NIEO already is close to enactment. The first is the New World Information Order. It is an attempt to restrict the operations of the Western press and bestow legitimacy on the state-controlled press of the communist countries and most Third World nations. At issue is not only the matter of press freedom. The UNESCO Declaration advocating the New World Information Order is explicitly biased against the private sector. It mandates preference for non-commercial forms of mass communication. The reason for this, states the Declaration, is to "reduce the negative effects [of] the influence of market and commercial considerations." The Declaration fails to acknowledge the positive influence of a privately owned press in ensuring the competition of ideas and alternate sources of information.

The second area in which NIEO has come close to enactment is the Law of the Sea Treaty. The Treaty is a carefully crafted repudiation of the free enterprise system. It establishes a Third World-dominated cartel; it is designed to control the market place; it discriminates against private deep-sea mining ventures; and it declares that those intrinsically valueless metallic nodules on the seabed, which are transformed into useable and valuable resources only through the costly mining technologies developed by private firms, are somehow part of what is called the "common heritage" of all mankind. As such, Third World nations insist that they are entitled to a large share of the financial proceeds from seabed mining. Third World nations also insist that they be given the pioneering technologies and state-of-the-art know-how of deep-sea mining.

There are a multitude of problems connected with the Law of the Sea Treaty beyond its assault on the free enterprise system. But not the least of its dangers is that it is designed to serve as a model treaty for other issues by which the industrial West is to be coaxed and intimidated into surrendering a portion of its national sovereignty. The Law of the Sea Treaty is a pioneering effort by the U.N. to undermine the West's economic system for the sake of that Third World bloc which prefers to strive to get a share of the West's wealth as a kind of welfare transfer payment rather than to create its own wealth.

After nearly a decade of negotiations, during which the Carter Administration made some devastating concessions, the Treaty draft reached a critical stage in early 1982. It was in final form, awaiting approval by all nations, when the Reagan Administration balked at signing the document. Since then, the U.S. has been seeking, with other industrial states, an alternative that would provide a fairer system for encouraging seabed mineral development.

That the U.N. should be greatly concerned about and devote enormous resources to the economic growth of the Third World is understandable and appropriate. What is puzzling is why the U.N. ignores those Third World economic efforts that have been most successful. Why does the majority controlling the U.N. endorse the economically catastrophic model of a Tanzania rather than the economically booming model of a Taiwan or Singapore? Why has the U.N. majority made the free enterprise system its enemy rather than embracing it as the one economic system with a proved record of success?

The answer in large part is ignorance. Daniel Moynihan has written that many leaders of the countries that once were colonies—the majority of U.N. members—were educated in West European universities, such as the London School of economics, where they learned the economics of socialism. As leaders in their own nation's drive against colonial rule, they found the heady rhetoric of socialism politically useful. They rejected much of what their colonial rulers stood for and swallowed Lenin's contention that imperialism was a direct stage in the development of capitalism—an assertion for which there is no evidence. The major imperial power of the past quarter-century, in fact, has been the Soviet Union.

To a great extent, therefore, the Third World knows little about how capitalism works and how capitalism succeeds. And the U.N. does little to enlighten the Third World. The economic studies and analyses produced by U.N. agencies and departments, such as the New York-based Department of Public Information, have a strong anti-free enterprise and pro-socialist bias. To make matters worse, participating semi-officially in U.N. proceedings are scores of anti-free enterprise groups such as the Interfaith Center on Corporate Responsibility, the Institute for Policy Studies, the World Council of Churches and the National Council of Churches. Among the most active of these groups is the International Organization of Consumers Unions (IOCU). Founded in 1960, it now includes more than 100 consumer associations from nearly 50 countries. Led by Malaysia's Anwar Fazal, I.O.C.U. has cloned a new wave of extremist, anti-free enterprise organizations that include Consumer Interpol, International Baby Food Action Network, Health Action International and Pesticide Action Network. What gives I.O.C.U. and similar groups muscle is the legitimacy they achieve through their association with the U.N. as Non-Government Organizations. These N.G.O.s swell the anti-capitalist chorus and further distort the economic data and guidance available through the U.N. for Third World states.

Particularly distorted are the Third World's perceptions and understanding of the multinational corporations. To be sure, the multinationals are not in the business of altruism. But neither are they necessarily the enemies or exploiters of developing countries. The multinationals-Third World relationship is not zero sum; multinationals have made enormous contributions to economic development. They provide developing states with an integrated package of technology, financial and physical resources, managerial experience, training, entrepreneurial ability and market outlets. Since most multinationals enter a market in a developing country for the long haul, they provide sustained back-up and support services. Multinationals provide technology and make it operational. They take risks. And they account for over half the total fixed capital investment in a great many developing states. Rarely, if ever, is this acknowledged by the U.N. With such skewed information provided by the U.N., it is no wonder that Third World states are ignorant of the free enterprise system's true nature.

U.N. opposition to the free enterprise system also stems from the influence of the Soviet Union and such client states as Cuba. The Soviet bloc enjoys an impressive record of successes in shaping U.N. attitudes. During the 1981 General Assembly, for example, the Third World states on average voted with Moscow 84.9 percent of the time, compared to an average 25 percent agreement with Washington.

The most important reason why the U.N. majority wars against the market economy is because the free enterprise system correctly is viewed as a threat to the authoritarian regimes running most Third World societies. Capitalism, after all, has proved to be history's best guarantor of liberty. Observes Irving Kristol: "Never in human history has one seen a society of political liberty that was not based on a free economic system—a system based on private property. Never, never, never. No exceptions."

The free enterprise system permits the emergence of important centers of independent power which rival and successfully check the authority of the state. To regimes whose only legitimacy is their monopoly of the state's coercive power, it is unacceptable that such independent centers of influence as the large corporation, free trade unions and business associations exist. The U.N. opposes the free enterprise system, therefore, because the vast majority of U.N. members would be threatened by the political, economic and social pluralism concomitant with free enterprise.

The U.S. and the U.N.—What Next?

As the United Nations grows increasingly hostile to U.S. interests and principles, it is time for Washington to reappraise the merits of continued American membership in the world body. Not only does the U.N. cost American taxpayers $1 billion annually and the full time efforts of dozens of senior Administration officials and diplomats. The organization rarely fulfills its most basic missions and has embraced an ideology and adopted programs and rhetoric dangerous to the United States and the world's free societies.

The United States cannot continue with business as usual at the U.N. If the U.S. is to remain a member, Washington must begin working for measures designed to blunt the threats posed by the U.N. This means ending or reducing the politicization of the United Nations system, preventing the General Assembly from globalizing local issues, denying terrorists the legitimacy and support they obtain by association with the U.N. and countering the U.N. majority's crusade against the free enterprise system.

Among the reforms required for continued U.S. membership which Washington should consider:

1) The U.N.'s technical agencies once again must deal exclusively with technical matters. Israeli settlements on the West Bank of the Jordan River, alleged human rights violations in Chile (or, for that matter, the Soviet Union) and the establishment of a New International Economic Order do not belong on the agendas of the World Health Organization, the International Telecommunications Union or the International Atomic Energy Agency. These agencies have been created to resolve critical but non-political problems. Their politicization in the past decade has significantly eroded their value and even credibility on technical matters and opens to question whether U.S. participation is warranted.

The same is true of UNESCO, the sprawling bureaucratic empire ostensibly concerned with culture, education and science. Since the U.S. pays more of UNESCO's bill than any other nation, Americans have a right to demand that their costly investment yield some dividends. As such, UNESCO's education programs in poor, developing nations should emphasaize literacy, mathematics and basic technical skills. UNESCO instead squanders its resources on teaching the virtues of the NIEO. This cheats not only the nation funding UNESCO, but more so the nation that looks to UNESCO for help. The U.S. should refuse to contribute to any UNESCO project that is prompted by political rather than technical concerns.

2) The U.N. must stop funding the Palestine Liberation Organization, the South West Africa Peoples Organization, the African National Congress and similar terrorist groups. If the United Nations refuses to establish the auditing procedures adequate to ensure that terrorists receive no U.N. material support, the U.S. should begin monitoring U.N. expenditures, perhaps through the General Accounting Office. If an audit reveals American funds going to terrorists, the U.S. must halt its contribution to that agency, even if this mean unilaterally reducing the American share of the "assessed" U.N. budget. During 1982–1986, for instance, the U.N. Development Program plans to give SWAPO and other terrorist groups $22 million in aid. The U.S. should pay none of this.

3) The General Assembly's stature must be reduced. Dominated by an intolerant majority that routinely produces a barrage of anti-U.S., anti-West and anti-free enterprise rhetoric and resolutions, the General Assembly should not be allowed to pose as a legitimate and impartial global forum. By participating in the General Assembly, the U.S. becomes an accomplice to that body's mischief. Washington prob-

ably should start sending U.S. representatives to only a few General Assembly sessions, boycotting the rest as an expression of American disdain for the organization. At the same time, the U.S. could downgrade its General Assembly delegation; instead of being top-heavy with ambassadors, it should contain only junior State Department officers. So long as the General Assembly refuses to function responsibly, the U.S. should not treat it as if it were responsible. At UNESCO and other U.N. agencies, U.S. representation and attendance could be similarly downgraded and made more selective.

Even with these changes, Washington still may have cause to reconsider American membership in the United Nations. The U.N. may now be well beyond redemption. If this is the conclusion after extensive, sober analysis, then the U.S. should seriously consider withdrawing from the U.N. and asking it to vacate its Manhattan headquarters.

Whether the United Nations in such an event would survive is unimportant. A world body that has achieved so little is not going to be missed very much. In its place, the U.S. should fashion a new international network whose aims are less ambitious and more modest than those that inspired the birth of the U.N. By now the U.S. certainly must have learned that although international cooperation is important, not all (perhaps not even most) nations want to or are willing to cooperate. If a new international body is to be created in the wake of the United Nations, therefore, it should be limited to like-minded states that will cooperate on a limited number of issues. Washington could propose, for example, a new organization comprising the industrial democracies and those states committed to building a democratic society. The organization would enable the democracies to exchange ideas and cooperate on specific matters and would create a platform from which the democracies could challenge the anti-democratic rhetoric of the Soviet Union, its satellites and the totalitarian states of the Third World.

As for those useful international technical organizations, the U.S. should attempt to reestablish the most important of them as independent agencies. The World Health Organization and International Telecommunications Union, for instance, need not be part of a U.N. system or of any other global umbrella organization. A number of them, in fact, existed independent of the United Nations. W.H.O. predates the U.N., for example, while the I.T.U. is more than a century old. Once decoupled from a General Assembly or similar global bodies, these independent agencies are much less likely to be embroiled in political conflicts. This would free them to focus almost exclusively on the technical concerns for which they exist.

The funds that the U.S. saves by withdrawing from the U.N.

could underwrite bilateral aid programs to those Third World nations serious about economic development. Unencumbered by the self-defeating NIEO obsession with wealth redistribution, U.S. development programs could teach the principles of wealth creation that have made South Korea, Taiwan, Singapore, the Ivory Coast, Kenya and a handful of other Third World nations the envy of the developing states.

A world without a United Nations—or without U.S. participation in a U.N.—in sum would be a world less hostile to the U.S. and the free enterprise system. More important, it would be a world which offers more hope to Third World nations of democratic development and economic growth.

6

Third World Policy to Strengthen Freedom

Major John K. Singlaub U.S.A. (Ret.)

Clear thinking about the Third World begins with the realization that no such entity exists. The term "Third World" inappropriately lumps together all countries outside the Soviet bloc that do not qualify as members of a small club of highly affluent, industrially developed and politically stable nations. The United States, Great Britain, France, Italy, Canada, Denmark, Norway, West Germany, the Benelux countries and Japan are the charter members of the club of highly developed nations. Australia, New Zealand, Taiwan, South Korea, Hong Kong and South Africa qualify as junior members in the eyes of most observers. But beyond that constellation of developed, free enterprise based nations on the one hand and the Soviet bloc, Marxist nations on the other, there is a wide variety in the stages of development among the rest of the countries of the world. Moreover, development must be measured socially and politically as well as economically. Likewise, culture, history and geography may unite or divide nations that are similar or dissimilar in their degree of social, economic and/or political development.

    Consider Argentina and Afghanistan. Both are often classified as Third World, yet they have next to nothing in common. Argentina is Roman Catholic, its population highly literate and well-educated, and possesses diversified and highly complex industry. Except for its antiquated telephone system and chronic political and fiscal instability and irresponsibility, Argentina is a developed nation. Economically, the Argentine has tremendous human resources, a well-educated labor pool, substantial managerial talent and skilled technicians. Further, it is self-sufficient in petroleum and is blessed with large expanses of fertile farmland. It is short on financial capital only because of what might be termed a political backwardness that results in governmental instability and irrational economic policies marked by often ruinously high inflation.

Afghanistan is Moslem, overwhelmingly illiterate, possessing hardly any industry and organized on traditional tribal lines. Almost 70 percent of its labor force is devoted to agriculture. It has no television and only one radio receiver for every 6.4 persons. Afghanistan is underdeveloped by any modern standard. Thus, upon cursory examination, the very notion of the "Third World" generally contributes little to sound analysis.

Worse yet, talk of a Third World sometimes seems to posit the existence of conflicting interests and objectives which in some important ways resemble those that define the struggle between the free and communist worlds. There is clearly no such symmetry among these three so-called "worlds" or communities of nations. The First World nations are democratic in politics, more or less capitalist in economics, pluralist Christian in religion and culture, and scientific in outlook. The Communist World is totalitarian in politics, state collectivist in economics, dogmatically and aggressively atheist in culture, and scientifically limited by the unscientific ideology of Marxism-Leninism.

The Third World is not definable in those same appositional terms. India is democratic, Indonesia is not. But neither is Christian. South Korea has a robust free market economy. Its religions are Buddhism, Shamanism, Confucianism and Christianity, and it is traditionally somewhat authoritarian in politics.

All of these countries are in the process of economic development and the material lot of their people is improving. But economic advancement is not necessarily a unifying threat tying together so-called Third World countries, because others among them are economically stagnant. The concept of the Third World only has utility and meaning in relationship to the contest between the United States-led free world and the Soviet-led communist bloc.

Argentina and Afghanistan, Indonesia, Angola and Chad are not the Third World. They are the contested world, places in Latin America, Asia and Africa where the forces of communism and liberal Christian civilization are engaged in fighting the Third World War. Whether these places prosper or develop would have only academic interest for most of us were it not for the communist challenge to our survival. Most of us would be happy to consign the contested world to missionaries and others with special vocations, at least until such time as the well-being of all of our fellow citizens has been secured. Nonetheless, the sober fact is that there is only one world, and while one might like to be able to live and let live, the Soviet empire is pursuing an agenda that aims for world domination.

What should be U.S. policy with respect to the Contested World? That is a question which must first be addressed as a matter of principle or value, and second as a matter of prudence. Prudence is the prince of virtues because it is the judgmental virtue that balances the desirable against a given situation and determines how to achieve the best possible. Or, as Aristotle teaches, ethics seeks to know what is best, and politics seeks to achieve or promote the best that is possible.

As a matter of principle, we Americans favor political self-government by people united socially and geographically. We favor personal freedom and the rule of law. We are most comfortable with regimes that maximize these values, actualizing and extending them to all members of their society. But experience tells us there are other nations and people with other values, and prudence tells us that their affairs are not our affairs. That first principle, self-rule by people who socially and geographically constitute a community, is, I believe, the predominant American political value in international relations. There are two others. First, nations and international actors must fulfill their treaty and contractual agreements. And second, no nation or ideology should impose itself on another nation or community without the consent of at least a majority of the people of that community.

The fact is, there is only one world in which two world views or values systems are contesting, and given the fact that the contest between these two systems is being waged to a large extent in the Contested or Third World, it is necessary to introduce the idea of geopolitics.

"Politics does not make geography, but geography does make politics" is a strategic maxim. It means that geography gives a particular nation and its military forces advantages and disadvantages. Politicians and their generals start where they are regardless of whether they desire to take over others or desire to stay at home and live out their days in good fellowship with their friends and neighbors. Geography can give a nation defensive advantage. That was the case with the United States throughout the 19th century. It also meant that England, once English politicians decided they wanted to be a world power, had no alternative but to build and to maintain a superior, powerful navy. A big army in Great Britain is no great threat to anybody outside Great Britain. Likewise, a great German army did not invade Great Britain in 1941 largely because it lacked sufficient support across the sea even though the distance was short.

The USSR is the driving engine of the only imperialist enterprise in the world today. We may argue the inspiration of those around the world who are in league with them. One can even contend that the Kremlin Communists are at root nothing more than the sons of the Mongol horde. Yet, the truth remains that the Kremlin is fighting a geopolitical war for world domination and the Contested World is where the war is being fought. We have called the war peace since 1954.

The Third World became a reality when World War III began and although one may argue over the precise date the Third World began, I date it from February 1948. In Czechoslovakia that month, a small Soviet-backed minority seized power, repudiated its people's Christian civilizational roots and the liberal and democratic cornerstone of the Czech nation. I mark that date as the beginning of the Third World War because of the methods used: deceit and violence. How else do communists ever take power? Only by deceit and violence have they ever gained power in the Contested World.

Even now, World War III is approaching a climax. The Caribbean, Southern Africa and the Middle East offer other abundant opportunities for Soviet imperialist adventurism. The first two phases of World War III, Cold War and Detente, have been succeeded by the next step in the Soviet scenario: Envelopment. Soviet Russia is seeking by geographical encirclement to strangle the industrialized nations of the Western alliance. In the case of the United States, she seeks to choke off our access to strategic minerals and energy supplies. The geographical encirclement and economic strangulation of the people of the Western Pacific, Western Europe and the Western Hemisphere is in progress. Gaining nuclear superiority, launching a high seas fleet to challenge the maritime nations, and seizing key regions by creating so-called wars of national liberation or popular front governments are all facets of the overall plan the Soviets devised during the first two phases of World War III. Operating under the nuclear balance of terror, the USSR is applying classical pre-atomic concepts of geopolitics: encirclement, isolation and strangulation.

If the United States is to do what is necessary to save the Contested Third World nations from becoming statistical additions to the long list of Captive Nations, three conditions must exist. First, there must be a national consensus that demands that something be done. We must recognize that it is immoral to stand idly by as one nation after another is forced into submission by a Soviet-armed and -directed minority. Second, we need determined leadership willing to accept the political consequences for going ahead and doing what needs to be done. This means that leaders must actually lead and not merely follow the results of polls of misinformed citizens. This leadership includes a large commitment to the education of constituents. Third, we need to command the fiscal means and resources to impose our will in threatened areas if necessary. We must be so strong that we cannot be blackmailed into inactivity by threats of the imposition of conventional and strategical nuclear arms. It also means that we must have available *now* an unconventional or special warfare capability that includes a large non-military, non-violent, psychological warfare component. This is the arena where we are losing completely because we don't even admit we are under attack.

Today, the Armed Forces of the United States are looked upon as a force designed exclusively for fighting a shooting war or as a force to deter or inhibit the outbreak of such a war. While these are valid and essential tasks for the Department of Defense, they overlook the nature of the struggle in which we are currently engaged. The non-fighting, even non-military, potential of the special operations forces of the Army, Navy and Air Force must be integrated into the overall national strategy for dealing with the conflict in the Contested World.

One of the greatest handicaps to the development and execution of an intelligent foreign policy with respect to the Third World is the American concept of a total separation between peace and war. The worldwide struggle between the forces of freedom and communism does not permit a neat distinction of the conflict as either peace or war.

Unfortunately, the view of the State Department is that war must be avoided at all costs. Diplomacy in the State Department's view is the instrument for maintaining the peace. For them to admit that other agencies or national sources of power, including military force, are necessary to improve the bargaining position of diplomats, is to admit the failure of our primary peacekeeping institution, the Foreign Service of the Department of State.

Though study of Clausewitz may not be required at the United States Foreign Service Institute, one can be certain that the graduates of the Soviet Institute of International Relations understand that "war is a continuation of politics by other means." The Soviet graduates also know that conflict is a continuum from non-violent, political, economic and psychological activity into terrorism, guerrilla warfare, limited-conventional, all-out conventional, and limited-nuclear into all-out strategic nuclear war. They also understand that war at the higher levels of violence can be avoided if you can convince your adversaries that they are in a "peacetime" situation, i.e., there is no shooting war. One graduate of the Soviet Institute of International Relations has stated that "all Ministry of Foreign Affairs officers in embassies, consulates, the United Nations, trade missions and other foreign missions, are monitored by and subject to the direct orders of the KGB. All are soldiers whose job is to wage political, ideological and economic warfare against the capitalist countries and their imperialist sponsor, the United States."

One of our most serious problems in the United States is our failure to understand that we are involved in a protracted conflict with an adversary who has demonstrated a willingness to fight us on any battlefield at any time by any means. The question that we must answer is: Will the American people realize that we are engaged in this war in time for us to win it?

The communist conspiracy is dynamic and ongoing. It cannot rest, so there is no such thing as peaceful coexistence or detente. We are, for example, coexisting peacefully with Cuba, but Cuba is not peacefully coexisting with us because it is fomenting and assisting anti-United States plots and actions elsewhere in the hemisphere and in the world.

We must not be trapped into believing that the Soviets possess any special geopolitical advantage. The existence of mountain ranges, rivers, islands, channels and canals influence events, but they do not determine history. Only men make history. Only men can decide how the geography will be used—for the free world or against it. The Soviet strategy of geographical encirclement of the free world and the strangulation of the industrialized nations by choking off their access to oil and ore through sea power is succeeding *because we refuse to recognize that they are doing it.*

In developing our policies toward the Third World countries, we must base our decisions upon the geopolitical significance of a given area to the Western World or to the Socialist World rather than upon some feeling of compassion or humanitarian concern for the people living there. This is not to say that we should not show compassion for starving people in a geopolitically unimportant part of the world. But our aid in the latter cases should be clearly identified as a humanitarian effort and separate from our foreign aid to nations which can contribute to the defense of the free world.

It has always been difficult for Americans to avoid injecting our natural feelings of compassion and sympathy for the underdeveloped nations of the planet when developing a foreign policy toward them. The tradition of extending a helping hand to the less fortunate has been a part of our national thinking for a century or more. Compassion and sympathy are worthwhile virtues for personal human relations, but must not become the principal consideration when developing a policy for dealing with other nations.

It is particularly important to understand that there is neither altruism nor compassion toward any nation on the part of the planners inside the Soviet Union. Our failure to recognize this, and the assumption that the USSR is motivated by Judeo-Christian concepts of human behavior is a major stumbling block to working out effective foreign policy decisions in which the Soviets are involved. Expecting the Soviet Union to act for humanitarian reasons is pure wishful thinking of the most dangerous sort.

What is needed now is the development of a new conservative foreign policy with respect to the Third World. It is important to recognize that in the development of this new foreign policy there are some built-in barriers. This conservative policy will advocate greater emphasis on the personal freedoms of all individuals. It will emphasize expansion of a free market economy, less governmental control rather than more, and abandonment of the concept of the redistribution of income. The American mass media, with their documented bias against these concepts, will actively aid and abet the critics of the changes. The current bureaucracy, whether in Washington or out in the field, is philosophically biased in favor of more governmental involvement and generally supports the liberal or socialist view. It is comfortable with the status quo and will resist any change. A liberal Congress will be hostile to changes that might interfere with its commitment to social welfare and income redistribution.

These barriers to a more workable foreign policy can be solved by a major infusion of dedicated new people into the bureaucracy. Without a major change in the attitudes of the people who must carry out the policy, any new policy will be frustrated and smothered to death before it is implemented. When the policy finally starts to produce results, the liberal media will have to recognize it just as surely as they finally had to admit that President Reagan's economic policies were, in fact, working. The Congressional barrier will have to be overcome by the direct personal intervention of a conservative president using all the powers of his office to produce the legislative changes needed to implement the new policies. This should not be too difficult to do if the president is determined to continually explain the actual situation to the American people.

A good example of how our bureaucracy fails to represent American or free world principles is the case of El Salvador. Despite the fact that the ownership of private property is fundamental to our democratic concepts, the Carter Administration forced a policy of so-called "land reform" on the Salvadorian government. This was nothing more or less than confiscation of land from the legal owner without any real compensation, a policy whose champion, Senator Charles Percy (R. Ill.), Chairman of the Senate Foreign Relations Committee, would never be able to sell to his constituency in Illinois or for that matter in any other state in the nation. There are still plenty of bureaucrats and members of both houses of Congress who think that this is a good idea, who are making implementation of this socialist concept a prerequisite for future assistance to that war-torn nation.

When contemplating financial assistance to one of the lesser developed countries of the Third World, it is relatively easy to reach a consensus that economic aid should have first priority. One of the problems in supplying economic aid, however, is that, generally, greater political benefits to the recipient country are anticipated than are reasonable to expect. One reason is a tendency to use the Marshall Plan of 1947 as a model for the administration of economic aid. Even those intimately involved in the workings of the Marshall Plan didn't know whether it was simply a device for the rebuilding of Europe or whether its purpose was to render Western Europe a bulwark against Eastern Communism. It did accomplish the former, but whether the latter succeeded is more difficult to perceive. The problem with using the Marshall Plan as a model for economic aid to the Third World is that it was applied within industrialized, though war-damaged, nations with high literacy levels and long established systems of participatory government. Unfortunately, none of these conditions seem to apply in the Third World even today.

While the consensus is that economic aid to a Third World country should have a high priority, we must not continue to provide economic aid to a country simply because such aid is less controversial in Congress than military aid. It is easier to obtain approval of nonmilitary aid in today's Congress than for military assistance.

When one of the primary targets of communist insurgents is economic sabotage, continued economic assistance is akin to pouring money down a rathole. If terrorists are able to sabotage and destroy key sectors of the economy such as transportation, warehousing, loading facilities, power supplies and distribution facilities and are able to intimidate workers to stay from their places of employment, what is the use of "economic" aid? The restoration of internal security must have first priority, whether the pacifists and socialists like it or not. It is a fact of life that without internal security and a certain amount of law and order, social, political and economic progress is impossible. Since the first priority of any government is to provide for the common defense against enemies foreign or domestic, this should be our first priority in assistance to the Third World.

According to those who have studied the problem, the primary obstacle to Third World economic development is big government. Reduce the size and activities of government, and the Third World poverty would be transformed into prosperity more quickly than is now believed possible. Big government destroys the economy in a variety of ways. First, it taxes the efficient, competitive and dynamic sectors of the economy by bidding valuable resources away from the private sector. Big government with welfare state aspirations artificially raises the cost of labor to business in labor-abundant economies by imposing minimum wage laws, encouraging trade unions to increase the cost of labor and in general setting a bad example for the private sector by overpaying its own public employees. Big government also damages Third World economies by trying to promote social justice or income redistribution objectives.

What is needed in the less developed countries is "development without aid," an essential condition for economic development. If a less developed country is intent upon rapid growth, it cannot afford to tax the competitive sectors of its economy. Foreign aid encourages big government and big government imposes such taxes. Foreign aid and rapid growth are, therefore, inconsistent.

It is no coincidence that two Third World countries, Taiwan and South Korea, which have the best records of economic performance during the past decades, did well only after large scale economic aid from the United States was *discontinued*. It was then that both switched to outward looking capitalistic policies of free trade and capital importation which brought prosperity to their economies. The international market place proved a much more potent antidote to poverty than the international transfer of income.

When attempting to measure the progress of a Third World country toward achieving economic independence and democratic representative government, we must not establish an absolute goal of perfectionism and then fault the government and its people if they have not yet reached that goal. We should remember the words of Oliver Wendell Holmes: "The great thing in this world is not so much where we are, but in what direction we are moving." Movement toward the goal is far more important than the fact that it has not yet been achieved.

Today, tens of thousands of young people from all over Latin America, Africa and Asia are being sent to communist countries for schooling and Marxist indoctrination. If the U.S. does not attempt to sell our ideals and philosophy to the young people of the Third World, the next generation will belong to the communists. The tragedy of this is that the West has more to offer in terms of greater personal freedoms, more advanced technology, an economic system that works and a clear alternative to the socialist philosophy. But is that message about the West being heard?

As a part of the continuous year-after-year support to our friends in the Contested Third World, we must begin early cultivation of students with the potential for leadership in government, education, industry, communications, business and religion. For these students the U.S. should locate sponsors in this country to provide them with an appropriate education and help them to understand the American way of life. The great majority of these young people—upon return to their own countries—will be friendly influences and more able to neutralize any negative or anti-U.S. themes being peddled by communist disinformation agents. In addition, some of them could be recruited and trained while in the United States to serve as intelligence agents in the Third World. That technique has been used by the Soviet Union for generations with the result that the USSR has apologists and agents of influence all over the world. When unopposed by people knowledgeable about the West and its philosophy, these communist agents are successful in defending the behavior of the Soviets and in selling their promises to the uninformed. We must at least counter this with our own advocates.

Continuing, long term support by the United States to a Third World nation is perhaps more important than emergency assistance during crisis situations. Americans have a tendency to want to get back to normal or to return to a pre-crisis situation as soon as a problem is solved. We tend to walk away from our battlefields. We certainly did this in Europe and China following World War II. This again is a reflection of our failure to recognize the nature of the protracted conflict in which we are engaged. We must learn to stay the course and to look to and plan for the long haul. The U. S. is inclined to avoid confrontation, to hope that things will work out—to hope for the best. This generally has produced delays in our responses to Third World needs.

In many cases, the U. S. State Department has postponed taking action and providing support in a Third World nation for so long that communist forces have had time to build up a campaign of propaganda that misrepresents the situation in that country altogether. While the U.S. balks at officially proclaiming that the insurgents are supported and directed by the Soviet Union or one of its surrogates, the American public is being convinced by the media that the insurrection is indigenous, representing the normal aspirations of a downtrodden, exploited group of peasants and workers who want only to rid themselves of U.S. imperialists and to establish their own, "national" form of government.

In the past, the U.S. has frequently recognized the need for immediate action to counteract these communist-fomented uprisings. However, because the American public had been manipulated into sympathy for the insurgents, our government made the decision to provide covert, CIA-directed assistance. This is a misuse of covert action, which should be an essential element of a total strategy rather than a desperation response designed to evade misguided and misinformed public opinion.

Friendly nations that come under attack by the communists are entitled to ask the United States for military assistance if their security is threatened. There should be no sinister motive applied to the provision of such assistance. The best qualified Americans should be selected and sent without fanfare to provide advice and assistance in their areas of expertise. These advisers or trainers may be civilian, military or retired government employees. If appropriate to the activity, our military personnel should be in uniform. The presence of a uniformed General von Steuben not only provided assistance to General Washington, but the sight of this professional from Europe provided inspiration to the recruits of the Continental Army.

There are several institutionalized barriers and built-in impediments to providing the most useful assistance to our friends and potential allies in the Third World. This is particularly true in the case of military assistance, but also applies in the agricultural and economic areas as well. The military problems involve four separate areas of the military establishment: people, doctrine, equipment and logistical support. Perhaps most important is the problem concerning people. The personnel selected for a military group assignment are all top-flight personnel from their respective services. The measure of effectiveness for an Army officer, for example, is how well he could demonstrate an ability to move, shoot and communicate with his tank and armored infantry battalions in the defense of, say, Fulda Gap in West Germany. The Air Force Colonel selected to head the air section in a Third World country is promoted ahead of his contemporaries because he ran the best Minuteman ICBM Squadron in Wyoming or was the hottest fighter pilot in the F15 Wing in the Pacific. To excel in these assignments, there was no requirement and no time to study Spanish or learn how to fly and maintain World War II C47 aircraft or how to teach illiterate peasants how to move, shoot and communicate without vehicles, modern weapons or radios.

U.S. Armed Forces are organized, trained and equipped to fight high intensity war at the conventional or strategic nuclear levels. Personnel who speak native languages and who specialize in unconventional and counterinsurgency warfare are not promoted at the same rates or levels as their contemporaries. Eventually they are eased out of the military or they resign because they are not considered competitive for the senior positions.

Because the primary mission of the Armed Forces in the United States is preparedness to fight the most dangerous threat to the nation, the Soviet Union, the doctrine and training of the Armed Forces is focused on that goal. It is assumed that any situation less than the worst case, an all out conventional or nuclear attack, should be handled by a lesser capability. This, of course, is a misguided assumption. Recognizing this, the Soviets have over 250,000 Spetsnaz troops specifically organized, trained and equipped for the very special purpose of conducting unconventional, irregular or low intensity warfare. These troops are military advisers in Cuba, Nicaragua, Angola, Vietnam, Syria, Afghanistan and elsewhere. They create and direct the wars of national liberation. They work for the KGB and have their own personal doctrine, equipment and logistical support systems. Because of their extremely specialized nature and their characteristic continuity of organization and people, they have perfected their philosophy and procedures without interference from the military doctrine of the Soviet conventional and strategic forces.

The problem of providing military equipment to the developing countries of the Third World is that their needs may not be met with the equipment we have available. Equipment designed and produced to provide a high level of combat effectiveness in the NATO environment may have little utility in Third World countries. A small nation fighting an insurrection has no need for a company level radio with one thousand channels. The U.S. Army in Germany does. To make a Third World nation pay for 990 more channels than they need is wasteful. A developing nation with an army whose average soldier stands 5' 6" tall and weighs 120 pounds, has great difficulty using the M1 rifle. So it hardly matters that several hundred thousand of them are available. El Salvador cannot afford to purchase, fly and maintain expensive and complex aircraft even though it has an urgent need for increasing aerial surveillance. It needs large numbers of low cost, simple to fly and maintain airframes—aircraft that the U.S. Air Force has never had in its inventory. Again, the point is that we must reorient our thinking to the special needs of our Third World friends and use the world at large as a source for equipment rather than limiting the aid to what is available in the warehouses of the United States Department of Defense.

Just as the equipment needs of the government soldier in the jungles of El Salvador differ from those of the American soldier in Germany, so will the logistical support system need to be different. Certainly, the introduction of nonstandard supply items will introduce problems into the computers of the U.S. Defense Supply Agency. In a developing nation without computer terminals, it does no good to mail a computer printout to the military adviser telling him to "procure locally" the materials needed to repair the ancient aircraft used there. In a developing country the chances are high that the money is not available to make a local purchase. Again, a special logistical support system must be established to service the special needs of our counterinsurgency efforts in the Third World.

We have spoken of a need to develop a comprehensive total strategy to confront the communists who have been waging a one-sided war against the free world, and especially its only possible defender, the United States. The strategy for this unconventional war must have a significant, non-violent, non-military component involving economic, political and psychological operations that are both offensive and defensive. We could, for example, initiate the following policies to force the Soviet Union to withdraw from the Western Hemisphere and to cease its offensive operations in other parts of the Third World. In the economic field, we should cut off any financial aid, including credits and loan guarantees that directly or indirectly benefit a Soviet bloc country. We should end U.S. participation in any international organization that lends money to the Soviet bloc. We should enforce the prohibition against sale to the Soviet bloc of any item that could be used for military or military-related purposes.

In the area of political warfare, we should give overt material aid and encouragement to any group fighting a communist government, whether in Central America, Africa or Asia. As an added measure of political pressure, we should expel all citizens of the Soviet bloc nations except ambassadors and their immediate staffs. We should require that the United Nations headquarters be located outside the United States by 1986.

In addition to the above, we should make it quite clear that it is the political policy of the United States to support those Third World nations that embrace the concepts of genuine democracy including the holding of free elections, the establishment of a system of impartial justice and support for programs to alleviate poverty, ignorance, illiteracy and disease.

To support and emphasize these economic and political programs, a psychological operations component is essential. This should include a major, worldwide truth campaign using all elements of modern communications to distribute truthful information concerning the errors, fallacies and failures of Marxist-Leninist doctrine. We must listen to and publish the experiences of refugees from communism, and tell the story of the dictatorship, brutality and mass murder that has occurred in every country the communists have captured. We must publicize the true and unswerving objectives of the communists. Communist successes in the Third World have been based upon promises for the future that have never been fulfilled and hopes that have never been realized. There are literally millions of people in the world today who are victims of these false promises who are now ready to expose the brutal reality to any who will listen. We must be ever ready to listen, and to make these truths available everywhere.

7

Foreign Policy and the Conservative Blueprint

Charles A. Moser

It is paradoxical but traditional in American politics for presidential candidates to concentrate on domestic questions during an election campaign. Domestic problems are of greatest concern to the voters and to the candidates themselves, who generally lack expertise in foreign policy. This situation is paradoxical first because, once in office, the president has much more power to set foreign policy than he does domestic policy, where Congress makes the final decisions; and second because a president in office, despite his own disinclinations, is compelled to give great attention to foreign policy simply because of the realities of power in the world. The United States is the only nation with the resources to deal with the global challenge of advancing communist totalitarianism. History has placed this responsibility upon us, and we do not have the option of shirking it.

Moreover, if we continue in the future as we have in the past, under the guidance of a foreign policy establishment that moves in and out of the State Department with the ebb and flow of different administrations, it is quite possible that we may fail to meet that responsibility. If we do fail after we have been provided so many chances to succeed, we shall pay a dreadful price: The holocausts in Cambodia and in Afghanistan, of which the American public and the American media take such scant heed, provide examples of that price. Conservatives must assess the present state of world affairs soberly and accurately if the changes necessary to deal with the mortal danger confronting us are to be made. Despite the ground that has been lost, the United States and the Free World still possess many strengths which, if properly deployed, can lead us to victory and bring about a genuine and lasting peace in the world.

Let us be clear on one point at the beginning: The primary threat in the world today is that of communist tyranny, and it is there that our attention must be focused. The gap between North and South, between the poorer and wealthier nations of the world, between the Third World and the West, the discriminatory policies of South Africa and the authoritarian regime in Chile, even the volatile situation in the Middle East (which in my view is nearing a favorable resolution)—all these problems so dear to liberal hearts are distinctly secondary except to the degree that they are intertwined with the primary conflict between the Free World and the communist movement.

The Soviet Union—the engine behind the world communist movement since the Bolshevik seizure of power there in 1917—has over many decades pursued a constant and coherent strategy; a strategy, moreover, which many Western statesmen have refused even to recognize. The USSR thinks in terms of overall geo-strategic military and political power, and has now attained nuclear superiority over us, which is at present employed primarily for political purposes. The Soviets' advantage in conventional weapons and numbers of troops is also convincing, although the relative performance of American arms in the hands of the Israelis and Soviet arms in the hands of the Syrians during the invasion of Lebanon must have given Soviet planners pause. But Soviet nuclear warheads and conventional arms, though vital to their foreign policy, are by no means its only constituent elements. The communist purpose is gradually to take one country after another across the globe, usually employing the device which Willi Schlamm once called "international civil war"—as in Vietnam, Cambodia and Nicaragua—sometimes using surrogates, such as the Cubans in Angola, or their own troops, as in Eastern Europe directly after the war and in Afghanistan now.

The United States is encouraged to perceive no individual country as "vital to its national interests," especially after our experience in Vietnam, and so no U.S. intervention is triggered, and no country once taken by the communists ever frees itself (which explains the persistent worldwide propaganda campaign against Chile, the nearest thing to a "people's republic" ever to have driven out its masters). Europe is already divided in half; a vast portion of Asia is under communist control; examination of the map of Africa shows that communist power has made appalling inroads there; and now communist revolutionaries are actively working on our very doorstep in Central America after successfully maintaining their Cuban beachhead for nearly a quarter of a century.

There is an interesting historical parallel to this strategy in the fall of Constantinople to the Turks in 1453: Over many decades the Turks had patiently conquered one piece after another of the Byzantine Empire's hinterland, so that when they finally began the siege of its capital, the result was a foregone conclusion: Constantinople had become a small island in a hostile sea. The Soviet Union seeks to gradually deprive us of our hinterland until the final confrontation, at which point the balance of power between the Soviet Union and the United States will have shifted so decisively against us that resistance will be suicidal. Indeed, it is conceivable that we could be subjected to the same sort of "civil war" to which other countries have succumbed. The Soviets are prepared to fight a nuclear conflict if they must, but they prefer to attain power without such drastic measures, and thus far they have been quite successful. Hitler erred in invading several countries in quick succession openly, and with his own armies. The Soviets are much shrewder than that.

Such an alarming picture of our situation in 1984 should not imply defeatist conclusions. On the contrary, only if we have a clear understanding of the seriousness of our situation, only if we realize that we cannot continue with "business as usual," only then can we mobilize our resources effectively. But we must also recognize that we should direct much of our energy, not to the Free World, but to people under communist rule, for it is among those who know what communism truly is and who hunger for freedom that we have our staunchest allies. Often anti-Americanism is strongest in Free World countries, where the population is confused by the sophistries of the media and intellectuals; and pro-Americanism is almost embarrassingly powerful, say, in countries which have long been under the communist yoke. "When the well is dry we know the worth of water," goes the proverb, and we must effectively harness the energies of those who know what it is to be without water.

The first pre-condition for an effective foreign policy for the future is to formulate a long-range strategy, and to recognize the inter-dependency of events in different parts of the globe. Our long-range strategy should be to enable the people of *all* countries of the world to select their form of government through free elections. Communists maintain that political power stems from the barrel of a gun; we believe that political power arises from the consent of the governed. Moreover, we should apply this principle not only to our allies, but to our enemies as well: for example, as of this writing, we press the government of El Salvador constantly to schedule elections and negotiations, but make only feeble representations along these lines to Nicaragua; the matter of negotiations and elections in Afghanistan was raised briefly once by British Foreign Minister Lord Carrington but promptly forgotten when the Soviets reacted negatively. And of course we never dream of raising such questions with the Soviet Union itself, or the People's Republic of China. In short, then, a new foreign policy should everywhere and always seek to expand the areas of political freedom in the world, and to reduce and ultimately eliminate the areas controlled by communist regimes. Such a foreign policy would differ markedly from that of recent administrations, which has generally been only reactive, although not without some positive aspects.

Furthermore, as the Soviets do, we must understand the interrelatedness of the struggle between liberty and tyranny throughout the world, instead of regarding "civil wars" in Vietnam or Cambodia or El Salvador as special cases of conflict with indigenous bases, having no connection with events beyond their borders. To be sure, special conditions do exist in each particular country, but they play a distinctly ancillary role to the overall world struggle. As long as the United States views each "national" conflict as a discrete situation, it will be placed constantly on the defensive, and thus remain on the losing side. The Reagan Administration, in supporting offensive action against the Nicaraguan communist regime partly for the purpose of relieving pressure on El Salvador, understands that the root of the Central American turmoil is to be found not in El Salvador, but in Nicaragua, something the Nicaraguans themselves scarcely bother to deny.

In view of all this, it follows that United States foreign policy must abandon its fundamentally defensive posture in favor of an offensive stance throughout the world. That formulation, however, requires some qualification at the start. For some time now our policy on the use of strategic nuclear weapons has been muddle-headedly "offensive": The doctrine of Mutual Assured Destruction held that the best way to avoid nuclear war was to threaten "offensively" the population of the Soviet Union, and to lay our own population open to possible Soviet attack. In recent years, with the rise of the nuclear disarmament movement and a genuine if somewhat hysterical fear of nuclear holocaust on the part of many people in the West, the absurdity of the MAD doctrine has made it increasingly less tenable politically. President Reagan has made an important step away from this doctrine in ordering intensified research on anti-ballistic missile defense, which is becoming technically more and more feasible. A responsible government should seek to protect its own population, not deliberately subject it to the threat of nuclear incineration. The Soviet leadership has always taken a much more rational view of nuclear war than have American intellectuals: that it is possible to fight a nuclear war from which a "winner" would emerge, especially if that winner has strong defenses against nuclear attack and an effective program to protect its civilian population. At the nuclear level, then, it is high time for the United States to move from an offensive posture to a defensive one, to adopt a doctrine which says that we seek to destroy rockets and weapons, not people (in fact, the strength of the seemingly illogical

European opposition to the so-called "neutron bomb" is, in reality, that it is intended to kill people rather than to destroy weapons). Such a policy makes enormous political sense; and beyond that offers genuine hope of an eventual true reduction in offensive nuclear arms.

Actually, the probability of a nuclear conflict is very small, and American foreign policy must cease to be paralyzed, as it has been in the past, by the specter of a possible nuclear holocaust at a time when genuine holocausts are occurring in such places as Afghanistan without the use of nuclear weapons.

But if the United States does move to a defensive stance at the strategic nuclear level, it should simultaneously adopt an offensive posture at all other levels on which the conflict is being waged—in the area of conventional warfare, and certainly in politics, economics and ideology. Furthermore, we must also see the whole picture here: Just as we must cease to regard individual countries as separate problems, so we must recognize that the struggle between freedom and tyranny is currently being fought at the levels of conventional warfare, economics, and political ideology all at once, that all these connecting levels cannot be viewed in isolation from one another.

If we are to pursue such an offensive strategy, we must first of all understand the nature of the enemy, which is the communist movement and its adherents throughout the world—not world poverty or rightist dictators. The communists are our declared enemies. They are consciously working for our destruction, and will settle for nothing less unless they are themselves destroyed. The hostility between the communist world and the Free World is not based on misunderstanding that can be cleared up through improved communication: The communists know very well what our principles are, and explicitly reject them. Thus, it is pointless even to discuss "negotiations" or "compromise" between communist forces and the forces of freedom in, say, El Salvador.

Once we have clearly identified our enemies, then the objective of a rational and offensively-oriented foreign policy should be to undermine our enemies and support our friends, consistently and in every possible way. That is, no doubt, a formulation which scarcely any American would disagree with; yet, in fact, its implementation will require a radical shift in viewpoint in the American foreign policy establishment, which has for years busily discarded our friends in the hope of appeasing enemies. The best example of this is our treatment of our stanch ally, the Republic of China on Taiwan, and our recognition of the tyrannical Peking regime, our unrelenting enemy, in a program set in motion by one of President Nixon's most disastrous foreign policy initiatives. This, and other instances in which we callously deserted national leaders who had cast their lot with us, demonstrates how distorted our foreign policy has been in the past. It is scarcely likely that the professional diplomats who have conducted our failed foreign policy for so many years will agree to conduct the kind of radically new foreign policy now required, and a major failure of the Reagan Administration has been its heavy reliance on the career foreign service bureaucracy for the management of its foreign policy.

What tactics, then, would a new, conservative foreign policy adopt in the pursuit of its long-range, offensive-oriented strategy of extending freedom to all the nations of the world, including the Soviet Union itself?

For purposes of analysis, it may be well to start with the subjective but crucial area of philosophy, or ideology, in the political arena. Here, as elsewhere, the allocation of financial resources is critical: even philosophers and abstract theoreticians must live, and the production and dissemination of ideas cost money. Historically, Western governments have been reluctant to spend very much to influence the way people think: Even Winston Churchill, Britain's most effective propagandist during World War II, did not understand the importance of allocating substantial funds to propaganda during the war. Communist leaders, on the other hand, have a much greater appreciation of the importance of influencing the minds of their own populations and those of their enemies, and allocate impressive sums of money to this end. Influencing public opinion costs a great deal, and the results are difficult to measure. But since our ideal of government based on the consent of the governed presupposes an electorate with informed views, we should in theory be willing to spend even more than the communists on influencing public viewpoints.

Arguments on the philosophical level must include a solid defense of American principles; support must be given those at home who truly believe in the tenets of freedom—they should have the resources to develop and disseminate their views—and to those who attack and weaken the philosophical bases of Marxism. We must emphasize the strengths of our own system and our enemies' weaknesses in an intellectually rigorous way. We must, in short, ourselves be confident of what we have wrought, and know why we believe as we do. We must not find ourselves in the situation of Dwight Eisenhower in his famous meeting with General Zhukov: Though Eisenhower knew instinctively that a government of free men is superior to a communist regime, he could not sustain his end of a debate on the topic on an intellectual level. In sum, we must stimulate both defenses of our own system and criticism of the communist system as part of an effective foreign policy.

Once the proper work has been done on the ideological level at home, there remains the problem of disseminating ideas to intellectuals and to ordinary people around the world. This again will require increased resources, primarily from the government, but also from private sources. Publications should be made available in quantity to all those who wish them; in particular, libraries of such organizations as the United States Information Agency should be expanded and strengthened. As they now exist, USIA libraries too often mirror the tendency of American culture to denigrate itself. To a degree, foreign intellectuals are impressed if American self-criticism is available in USIA libraries, but what should be emphasized is literature that explicates and defends the philosophy of freedom. At the same time, the government should widely distribute critiques of the communist system, written not only by Americans but especially by emigrés from the Soviet bloc, such as Alexander Solzhenitsyn, who know the system from the inside. In the great influx of intellectuals from Soviet-bloc countries, we have a magnificent pool of talent which only needs support, and which we can exploit in the Free World, in the Third World, and even in USIA installations in communist countries, where even simple window displays of books and pamphlets can have dramatic impact.

Increased resources should also be allocated to radio broadcasts as an instrument of propaganda. Despite jamming, the various language services of the Voice of America should concentrate on providing objective information on world events, especially to communist countries where ordinary citizens are eager for simple information, and on serious commentary on American culture and politics. Another form of radio transmission—very essential because it is directed to our enemies in the world—is Radio Liberty (Soviet Union) and Radio Free Europe (Eastern Europe). The language services of these radios are designed not to duplicate the work of the language services of the Voice of America (although they must do that to some extent in providing international news), but to function as a "home service" for individual countries, to provide information and commentary on the country itself not obtainable elsewhere. But the strict control of information in communist societies causes severe difficulties.

For example, recently I conducted an evaluation of the Bulgarian Service of RFE, which shows that the information base of its broadcasts on Bulgarian topics consists of official radio broadcasts and periodicals from communist Bulgaria, so that RFE in effect re-broadcasts official information back to Bulgaria, often with a negative interpretation. Moreover, present guidelines for RFE-RL assume that the East European listener is exceptionally interested in developments within the communist movement both inside and outside the communist bloc. A new foreign policy would assume, on the contrary, that the East European listener does not particularly care about such developments, and would require that RFE and RL make every effort to develop sources of information independent of the Eastern European regimes. This would mean greater reliance on emigré resources, on the written and spoken word of those who have left their countries for political reasons, which RFE-RL tends to discount. After all, such emigrés are by and large our allies in the struggle against communist totalitarianism.

Exchanges with free world countries as well as with communist countries have a place in influencing public opinion, but again much depends on how such exchanges are handled. In the past many responsible officials have been deeply convinced that we should invite to the United States those hostile to us, in the hope of influencing their thinking, and to ignore individuals sympathetic to our cause since they would always be with us anyway. Under a new foreign policy, such exchanges would include our friends and exclude those who oppose us; and in exchanges with communist countries we would invite specific individuals who we believe are either pro-American or critical of their own societies. The Reagan Administration did in fact move to reform our exchange policies along these lines, but was met, not surprisingly, with complaints from liberal congressional activists, which has stalled such reform.

The battle also needs to be carried to the enemy in the area of international politics broadly defined, including in particular the politics of diplomacy. If we regain confidence in our own values, for example, that confidence should be evident in the behavior of our diplomatic representatives, most especially at the United Nations. One of the brightest spots in the Reagan Administration is the appointment of Jeane Kirkpatrick as Ambassador to the United Nations. Following in the tradition of Daniel Moynihan, she has defended the United States, with self-assurance and fortitude, against the political assaults of our enemies; and she has provided strong counter-attacks to insults to the U.S. By her spirit and her self-confidence, Ambassador Kirkpatrick has engendered a new respect for the United States at the United Nations. In the foreseeable future the United States—if it remains in the UN at all—is unlikely to carry the day on many issues, but it can certainly fortify its diplomatic positions there, particularly if we use the leverage which our financial support of the organization should give us.

Much else can be done on the diplomatic and political fronts in order to support our friends and weaken our enemies. The president, secretary of state, and other high officials should stand up for American policy in a straightforward and unembarrassed manner; they must not waffle under tough questioning (Prime Minister Margaret Thatcher is superb at this sort of thing, and Britons admire her for possessing the courage of her convictions). The president and other high officials must of necessity deal with both friends and enemies, but the manner in which they do this can be very important. When, for example, the president meets with a representative of a communist power, he should make it clear by his demeanor that he finds the meeting distasteful (presidents in the past have sometimes behaved disgracefully in such situations: we may recall Nixon in mainland China, or Carter embracing Brezhnev). In like manner he should be responsive and affable when he meets with representatives of friendly nations. It should be very difficult, if not impossible, for political leaders of communist-oriented groups not in power to meet with the president, and relatively easy for the political leaders of pro-Western movements to obtain such meetings (in recent years the actual situation has been almost the reverse).

In state-to-state relations, the United States should employ diplomatic recognition as a weapon. Recognition of communist governments should be tentative, based on the possibility that, within countries, legitimate movements may arise with more plausible claims to represent the people than the government. For example, when the Jaruzelski dictatorship crushed the Solidarity movement in Poland, the United States should have immediately withdrawn diplomatic recognition from the Polish government; and in Afghanistan we should not countenance even the tenuous diplomatic recognition which we now accord the Karmal regime. A formal break in diplomatic relations is not the calamity many diplomatic professionals think it is: American interests in a particular country can usually be safeguarded without formal recognition, e.g., our relations with Iran after we terminated formal recognition. At the other end of the spectrum, we should re-recognize the government of the Republic of China regardless of the wishes of the People's Republic, and notwithstanding its response to that action.

The Carter Administration unleashed a potent weapon in the political arena in its campaign for human rights, which originally had a substantial impact upon the Soviet Union and other communist countries. The received diplomatic wisdom seems to hold that human rights violations are best corrected in hostile countries through quiet diplomacy and in friendly countries through diplomatic offensives, whereas the correct approach is the opposite: Only the extraction of a public political price can hope to bring communist regimes to grudging compliance with the Helsinki Accords and other international agreements. President Carter for a time understood the importance of strong political gestures, such as the Olympic boycott of 1980 following the Soviet invasion of Afghanistan. Such actions may not be sufficient to stop invasions, but they have their overall benefits, and are far superior to inaction.

On the diplomatic level the United States should adhere to a policy of strict reciprocity in its dealings with communist nations: In no case should a communist embassy in the United States be permitted more personnel than we send to that country. Travel restrictions imposed upon American diplomatic personnel should be met with corresponding restrictions upon communist diplomatic personnel; the circulation of official published materials within the country, as well as the selection of individuals to participate in exchanges between countries should also be reciprocal. Where exchanges are involved, we should not be concerned if some of them are suspended or terminated—they can only function properly if we are prepared to forego them altogether. Likewise, we should not enter negotiations with our communist adversaries believing that it is absolutely necessary to obtain agreement, for treaty negotiations are merely another form of conflict between the Free World and the communist world. It is possible to regulate relatively unimportant matters through treaties, but they never bind a nation for long when its profound national interests are at stake. Moreover, once we have signed a treaty with a communist power, especially in view of the communists' history of treaty violations, we should be quite willing to abrogate it if necessary (in the recent past we have been much readier to abrogate treaties with friendly powers than with enemies).

The global conflict must also be fought on the economic level. Many conservatives, though they may consider themselves anti-communists, object to using economic weapons against our enemies because they believe in free trade and the development of commercial markets. For some curious reason businessmen think there are immense untapped markets in communist countries: Such a belief was a major reason for our recognition of the Soviet Union in 1933, and of mainland China four decades later. In fact, these markets have never materialized, and now major banks have assumed appalling overcommitments in making loans to such countries. All of this demonstrates American business and financial leaders' remarkable lack of understanding of communist economic systems and how they work.

In the communist view, politics and economics are so closely intertwined that a conflict on one level inevitably involves conflict on the other. Communist countries eagerly seek Most Favored Nation status from the United States because of the benefits which it confers, and if pressed will make concessions for such status. They are particularly eager to obtain agricultural products from us because, while their economic doctrine gives a low priority to agriculture, still they must feed their people. The grain embargo President Carter imposed on the Soviet Union after the invasion of Afghanistan had a serious impact on the Soviet economy, and the Reagan Administration made a fundamental error in lifting it. The government itself should have purchased the grain from American farmers who originally expected to sell to the Soviet Union and donated it free of charge to the needy in countries friendly to us. In general, a major objective of our foreign economic policy should be to deny important commodities to communist nations.

Whenever economic sanctions of any sort are imposed upon communist countries, the cry arises that they accomplish nothing (though somehow they are supposed to be more effective when applied against friendly countries, such as Rhodesia, Chile or South Africa). New policy would seek to deprive communist countries of all possible economic advantages through various means, one of which might be the economic device now being used by the Left against South Africa: disinvestment, or persuading large pension and investment funds to divest themselves of stock in any firms doing business with South Africa.

In a free economy it is impossible to direct all foreign trade in such a way as to weaken our enemies and assist our friends, but it is possible to ensure that no credits and loans at below-market interest rates are provided to communist countries. Any commercial arrangements should be strictly on a cash basis. Particularly today, when we know that nations can default on their indebtedness in a massive way, it would be the height of folly to provide communist countries with effective subsidies to our disadvantage.

The United States should as a matter of policy use its financial and economic power—both directly and through international financial institutions—to encourage the development of free market economies in other countries, instead of lending money through governments for socialist or state capitalist projects.

Almost always at some point on the globe, the Free World and the communist world are engaged in armed conflict, whether in relatively low-level irregular warfare, or in combat between established armies. The United States has not formally declared war on any country for more than 40 years, but we have been involved in military clashes constantly since that time, a situation which is certain to continue. A forward-looking foreign policy must be equipped to deal with irregular insurgencies, whether aimed against free governments or communist regimes. Ultimately, the communists believe, the question of who holds power must be settled by force. They are ready to back their adherents with money, arms and equipment, and the United States can do no less in the cause of freedom. In Vietnam and Cambodia we reneged on our commitment to those who trusted in us to help them defend themselves against communist aggression when that commitment became too arduous.

Today, in El Salvador we face a situation similar to that in Vietnam. Our task is to make it clear that we intend not only to defend freedom in El Salvador, but also to eliminate the Sandinista government in Nicaragua by whatever means necessary. The pattern of aggression as characterized in El Salvador is by now familiar: the appearance of well-armed "indigenous" communist irregulars; elections in which the communists refuse to participate; calls for negotiations between the government and the insurgents; a coalition government in which the communists obtain key posts; and finally the ejection of all non-communists from the government. When we are involved in a defensive maneuver, as in El Salvador, the U.S. must resist a political solution so long as there are undefeated armies in the field; we should insist upon a military solution. Furthermore, it is the duty of the United States to resolutely support those who are fighting to preserve their freedom. The signals on these points from Washington should be strong and consistent, not weak and mixed.

In several countries where the communists officially hold power, there are widespread anti-communist armed movements that continue to operate without any substantial American aid. Such movements exist in Laos and Vietnam, in Angola and Mozambique, in Afghanistan and in Nicaragua, although the anti-communist resistance there is more dependent on American aid. In some cases—e.g., Angola and Afghanistan—the freedom fighters control large portions of the country, while the communists hold the capital, the major cities, and the official government apparatus. This existence of true freedom movements provides the United States with an unprecedented opportunity to take the offensive against communist regimes throughout the world.

We should provide these freedom fighters with the food and weapons they need to continue their struggle, and do so without apologies: The United States must declare its readiness to assist freedom fighters everywhere, just as the Soviet Union has openly announced its willingness to help so-called "national liberation movements" everywhere. As a movement of freedom fighters achieves some success, the United States should withdraw diplomatic recognition from the communist regime of that country and encourage the freedom fighters to form a provisional government which may be recognized. The political leaders of the freedom fighters should be welcome in Washington, and the military and political leaders of the freedom fighters in various countries should be encouraged to exchange mutually instructive information on conducting an armed struggle in communist-held territory. On the diplomatic level, Washington should campaign for free elections, for negotiations between the communist government and the freedom fighters and for coalition governments between them. With an offensive-oriented American policy working on their behalf, very probably freedom fighters in a number of countries could oust their communist regimes.

In some sense, nowhere are the communists so uncertain of their authority as in the countries they govern, which is why the major thrust of a forward-looking foreign policy must be directed toward our natural allies: the peoples of communist lands whose desire for freedom has never been quenched, and who, despite decades of disillusionment in some instances, still look to us for help. If we give them genuine hope, they will do much of the work of destroying the Soviet empire from within.

The struggle, then, must go forward on many different levels at the same time, although ultimate success will depend upon all elements working in concert. The Soviet Union will not collapse because of a grain embargo, or a diplomatic offensive, or even if it is effectively defeated in Afghanistan, for instance. But victories on each of these fronts—achieved with unwavering persistence in small increments, over a long period of time—will have a cumulative effect in widening the parameters of freedom in the world and weakening the power of our enemies until they are finally eliminated as players on the stage of world history. But correcting the course of American foreign policy, which has been so misguided for so long, will not be an easy task. We have the physical resources at hand. We need to find the will and understanding, which are within ourselves. If they are supplied, the cause of freedom in the world will certainly triumph.

III
Social Issues

8

Right and Wrong and America's Survival: An Ethical System for the Future

Connaught Marshner

The 1970s and 1980s saw the shattering of previously reliable medical ethics into utter confusion. By the early 1980s the American Medical Association was at the same time on record opposing both capital punishment and federal regulations aimed at restricting infanticide. The AMA, along with other prestigious medical associations, was involved in court cases that sought to preserve unlimited access to abortion. What was going on here? The voice of the medical profession, seeking to "protect" the right to kill an unborn child while opposing society's right to protect itself by punishing a convicted criminal? Protesting measures to interfere with passive infant-killing?

Below the level of organizational posturing, confusion was no less rampant. Scarcely a week went by without newspapers carrying stories of families wanting to cease life-support measures for an injured or ill member, and of families demanding more medical treatment for such a person; stories about doctors refusing to cease extraordinary life support systems, and about doctors urging the cessation of extraordinary means. Many such cases end up in the court system.

In the meantime, debates raged over the propriety of *in vitro* fertilization techniques (extracting an ovum from a woman's body, and fertilizing it with extracted sperm, and allowing it to develop over a period of time in a test tube). Newspapers were filled with headlines describing cases like that of the Boston twins: A deformed twin was killed, the unimpaired one allowed to live by means of surgery performed in the third month of pregnancy. The development of new prenatal diagnostic techniques such as alpha-fetaprotein tests to identify neural tube defects in the unborn, and amniocentesis to permit genetic screening for a multitude of diseases, brought with it fierce debates over the reliability of the tests and the propriety of employing the only means of recourse, namely, abortion, if the results proved unfavorable.

A small but well-publicized pressure group demanding legal suicide gained prominence. Utilization of parts of fetal remains for commercial purposes provoked controversy and confusion. The performance of experimentation on unborn-but-scheduled-to-be-aborted babies provoked charges of inhumanity not seen since the gas chambers.

What *was* going on? Or, rather, what had happened to the standards by which medical practice is guided? What was going on was very simple: Medical knowledge was extending itself from the theoretical into the applied, and nobody knew whether it was right or wrong. *California Medicine,* the Western Journal of Medicine, stated in a landmark editorial in September 1970 what had happened to the standards by which medical practice is guided:

> The traditional Western ethic has always placed great emphasis on the intrinsic worth and equal value of every human life regardless of its stage or condition. . . . This traditional ethic is still clearly dominant, but there is much to suggest that it is being eroded at its core and may eventually even be abandoned. . . .
>
> It will become necessary and acceptable to place relative rather than absolute values on such things as human lives, the use of scarce resources and the various elements which are to make up the quality of life or of living which is to be sought. This is quite distinctly at variance with the Judeao-Christian ethic and carries serious philosophical, social, economic and political implications for Western society and perhaps for world society. . . .
>
> The process of eroding the old ethic and substituting the new has already begun. It may be seen most clearly in changing attitudes toward human abortion. . . . Since the old ethic has not yet been fully displaced it has been necessary to separate the idea of abortion from the idea of killing, which continues to be socially abhorrent. The result has been a curious avoidance of the scientific fact, which everyone really knows, that human life begins at conception and is continuous whether intra- or extra-uterine until death. The very considerable semantic gymnastics which are required to rationalize abortion as anything but the taking a human life would be ludicrous if they were not often put forth under socially impeccable auspices. It is suggested that this schizophrenic sort of subterfuge is necessary because while a new ethic is being accepted the old one has not yet been rejected. . . .
>
> It seems safe to predict . . . that the new ethic of relative rather than of absolute and equal values will ultimately prevail. . . . The part which medicine will play as all this develops is not yet entirely clear. That it will be deeply involved is certain. . . .

It is not too early for our profession to examine this new ethic, recognize it for what it is and will mean for human society, and prepare to apply it in a rational development for the fulfillment and betterment of mankind in what is almost certain to be a biologically oriented world society.

The medical profession, if this editorial is an indication of the situation, had abandoned the centuries-old fundamental principles established by Hippocrates, and in their stead had embraced a relativistic ethic geared to maximizing the quality of life in an evolving world society.

Talk of the "population bomb" and other since-disproved massive propaganda flitzes by future-terrorists reached a peak in 1970. Typical of its era, the *California Medicine* editorial justified the shift in ethics on the grounds of the "ever growing ecological disparity" between people and resources and the new emphasis on the "quality of life, something which becomes possible for the first time in human history because of scientific and technologic development."

The predictions of the future-terror advocates not only have not been borne out, they have been ludicrously disproved. In 1970, for instance, *Life* magazine reported the probability that by 1980 urban dwellers would have to wear gas masks to breathe, and by 1985 the amount of sunlight reaching the earth would be cut in half. Paul Ehrlich's *Population Bomb,* published in 1968, predicted that by 1983—after "almost a billion human beings starved to death in the last decade"—a crop blight would force the United States president to go to war with the Sino-Soviet axis and nuclear destruction would follow.

Meanwhile, another demographic reality has been bearing down upon the United States. It is as relentless, but not as well-publicized. Our society is aging, and will continue to age. In 1981, people 65 years of age and older accounted for 11.4 percent of the population. In 2000, that figure will be 13.1 percent, and by 2050, 21.7 percent. The Census Bureau also predicts a startling increase in longevity. Life expectancy for men is now 71, by 2050 it will be 75; now 78 for women, it will be 83.6 in 2050. Also by 2050, the Bureau predicts, 24 percent of the elderly will be 85 or older—only 9 percent today have achieved that ripe total. The total population will begin declining after 2050, but will increase slightly until then due to immigration (birth rate being at below replacement levels). The death rate will actually exceed the birth rate in 2035, for the first time in our nation's history. This, at least, is the most recently available projection from the Census Bureau, released in November 1982.

What this portends for the Social Security system as we know it is awesome. In 1983, when pressure on the system was unacceptably high, there were 54 people of working age for every 10 Social Security recipients. By the year 2000, this will be 47 to 10; by 2025, 30 to 10; and by 2050, 26 to 10. What will be the economic pressures when, for every person receiving Social Security, there are only two working? Will the system even last until then? Or will the Census Bureau's projections be disproved, as the propaganda blitz for euthanasia begins to be felt, and elderly lives are ended, albeit "humanely" and "with dignity," before their time?

The pressure on the Social Security system was already beginning to be felt in Ronald Reagan's first term, when salvaging Social Security was one of the first major political issues. The few bandaids applied in 1983 promised to solve the problem only so long as bandaids generally can control hemorrhages. In the meantime, millions of dollars per year were being diverted into medical treatment of infertility. The same money could have provided many needed services for the elderly. The irony is that most of the infertility being treated was a result of programs and practices initiated in the 1970s when the terror of reproduction held sway over legislators. The National Center for Health Statistics announced in early 1983 that 45 percent of the nation's couples of child-bearing age have difficulty or inability conceiving children. The NCHS report offered two possible reasons: one was the 300 percent increase of cases of gonorrhea between 1965 and 1976; another the 600 percent increase of the use of the intrauterine contraceptive device, which promotes the risk of pelvic inflammatory disease. These are figures full of irony. For one thing, susceptibility to gonorrhea is increased by being on the Pill[1], which in the late '60s and throughout the '70s was in common use among teenagers anxious to avoid the biological consequences of their liberated lifestyles (a certain amount of this Pill usage can be laid at the doorstep of the federal government's Title X program, of course).

If the 1970s were preoccupied with how to cope with a hypothetical excess fertility, the problem of the 1980s is how to meet the demand to remedy insufficient fertility. Never mind the irony of the 1980s that, in the face of the graying of America, young women were being discouraged by a feminist ideology from seeking motherhood, a measure which might at least have been able to provide future mitigation of the problem.

Demography is a factor in many areas of social and economic policy. An aged population brings certain pressures; a young population brings others. But demography should not influence the medical profession. As long as doctors regard each patient's interest as supreme, it matters not whether that patient's age and condition are typical or atypical of society. When the medical profession adopts the notion that it exists to serve the "quality of life" or the "interests of society," however, then the interests of the individual patient are left unprotected. When the individual patient has no guaranteed rights, he is unprotected. The same is true in areas other than medicine.

It is well to keep Hippocrates in historical perspective. In prior ages, the shaman-figure or witch doctor dispensed both life and death. His ministrations could cure as well as kill—indeed, his people expected him to do both. It was Hippocrates, and the followers of Aesculapius (in Roman mythology, the god of medicine and healing), who made it clear that they were going to practice only life-giving arts, and to dedicate themselves to life under all circumstances; whether it be the life of the Emperor of the life of a slave, they would strive to protect both. This complete separation between killing and curing is the historical significance of Hippocrates. The Hippocratic oath remained a mainstay of medieval ethics for centuries because the preservation of that distinction was critical.

In 1948 the General Assembly of the World Medical Association adopted an updated "Doctors' Declaration" at a conference in Geneva. It reiterated Hippocratic principles:

> The health of my patient will be my first consideration; I will not permit considerations of religion, nationality, race, party politics or social standing to intervene between my duty and my patient.
> I will maintain the utmost respect for human life, from the time of conception, even under threat; . . .

In the wake of the revelations of the abuse of medicine under the Nazi regime, world opinion demanded a restatement of a code of ethics which would protect humanity from the repetition of such excesses. Although in 1947 the British Medical Association suggested that the Declaration be part of graduation ceremonies at medical schools, and that medical ethics should be an essential part of the curriculum, the Declaration is no longer included in the graduating ceremonies at medical schools in England. Clearly, the physicians and psychiatrists of the Gulag have not upheld the principles of the 1948 Geneva Declaration. It is impossible for the Hippocratic principles to be maintained when medicine is subordinate to the state. Only medicine free of coercion can respect individual life. This is why, for optimum care, the patient must be the employer of his doctor. If the doctor's master is government, then medicine is nothing but the instrument of the government. When commanded by government, the medical profession will serve as its hangman.

This is why medical ethics has become a political problem. The medical profession is shepherd of life, but also of liberty, much of which was sacrificed as shown in the 1970 *California Medicine* editorial:

> The criteria upon which these relative values are to be based will depend considerably upon whatever concept of the quality of life or living is

developed. This may be expected to reflect the extent that quality of life is considered to be a function of personal fulfillment; of individual responsibility for the common welfare, the preservation of the environment, the betterment of the species; and of whether or not, or to what extent, these responsibilities are to be exercised on a compulsory or voluntary basis. . . .

Since the problems which the new demographic, ecologic and social realities pose are fundamentally biological and pertain to the survival and well-being of human beings, the participation of physicians and of the medical profession will be essential in planning and decision-making at many levels. No other discipline has the knowledge of human nature, human behavior, health and disease, and of what is involved in physical and mental well-being which will be needed. . . .

In essence, this editorial concedes that principles concerning the future of individuals will simply have to be made as collective decisions henceforth. "Whatever concept of the quality of life is developed" is a far cry from "whatever an individual finds fulfilling or appropriate for himself and his family." The medical profession should be close to the top of the totalitarian heap in making the decisions, the editorial suggests. Where does that leave the ordinary man? the patient? Of very low concern—the words "patient" or "medical care" are not mentioned once in the editorial. The purpose of medicine has become the provision of technical expertise in social planning, not the provision of care to a patient.

If a doctor does not protect the right of his patient, the rights of patients will soon not be recognized by the state. The state will claim its own right (perhaps based on "ecological realities") to define who is and who is not protected, and under what circumstances. If "quality of life" is defined as having one child, then those who have two will be punished. The People's Republic of China has not hesitated to carry that logic into practice, as documented by the reports and photographs of women in late-term pregnancy awaiting abortion and sterilization, that were revealed to the Western World in 1983 by a young scientist who was punished for telling the story. The manipulation of housing and employment to achieve the same goals is a less graphic instance of the state defining who is to be protected, and who is not, according to its own essentially arbitrary criteria.

Fertility control is a dramatic example. Traditionally, fertility has been among an individual's most private concerns. The confidentiality of a doctor-patient relationship was nowhere more carefully protected than in all areas pertaining to reproduction and sexuality. As the sense of wonder was stripped away from those areas of life, however, they not only became matters of everyday conversation, but the medical profession began to relax its standards accordingly. The principle, conceded in practice if not in theory, was that a doctor's medical skill was available to be used however the client wished. Thus, while a doctor may help one woman procure an abortion, he would help another save a pregnancy. His medical skills, in short, became available, regardless of principle. China merely took matters to their next logical step, and transferred to the state the decision-making elsewhere left with individuals. The totalitarian impulse which has come to fruit in China is not without its advocates in the West, however. Simone Weil, the member of the French parliament who achieved legalization of abortion in France, wrote: "The state's absolute power over fertility constitutes the perfect criterion for social organization pushed to its extreme limits, and is also a necessary precondition for the functioning of a utopian society after the complete elimination of chance and free will of individuals."[2]

The political nexus should be clear: Strict medical ethics giving absolute protection and right to the life of the individual, and charging the doctor with a sacred duty to serve and protect life, is diminished only at the cost of transferring to "society" (read: the state) the power to make life and death decisions over the individual. In short, the erosion of Hippocratic ethics is yet another avenue of entry for totalitarianism.

II.

At the base of contemporary confusion is a philosophical problem.

An ethical system has got to work. That means it has got to give people clear answers about right and wrong. An ethical system cannot enforce answers; it cannot make people good—only other people can do that. Some are frightened of a strict ethical system because they think it will lead to intolerance, lack of compassion, a Draconian justice. That does not follow at all. An ethical system does not tell jurors whom to forgive or whom to punish lightly. That is the job of human understanding. Ethical systems deal with principles of justification—not principles of excuse. The excuses are left up to jurors.

In the Western world recent generations have experienced a major breakdown in ethical understanding. More and more people are under the influence of ethical systems that do not yield answers but which encourage people to treat every circumstance in which we face a moral problem as a special case. Treating every circumstance as special will soon eliminate any habit of thinking in clear, objective terms.

There are two main sources of ethical confusion: situationism and consequentialism. Among the intellectual and academic communities, the spread of these systems has been fashionable and deliberate. Acceptance of them has not been universal, however, regardless of the self-assuredness of the *California Medicine* editorial.

One philosopher has said of situation ethics that its adherents no longer think through their moral problems in terms of applicable moral norms or precepts, but tend rather to think in pictures. For instance, the question: What should we do about a deformed child who is bringing great strain and hardship on his family? The situationist first conjures up the picture of the family coming apart: the mother a nervous wreck, the father distraught, other children neglected—all because the new baby, deformed, is costing all they can afford, financially and emotionally, for treatment and life-support. Then the situationist conjures up a second picture: the same family happy and contented, out for a picnic, the deformed child simply not in existence. So, ask yourself: Which picture is better? Surely, you will feel, the second.

Situation ethics, in popular form, consists of one simple rule: You may do whatever is necessary to make the better picture a reality, for that is the "loving thing to do."

The popular situationist begins with a rhetorical advantage because he has grabbed the heartstrings. The traditionalist tries to introduce a moral norm into the picture—in this case, the principle of "no killing of the innocent." The situationist is encouraged to feel that the norm applies only in "normal" cases, not in tragic situations. The situationist exploits the full emotional pull of his original picture. And the "ethical debate" degenerates into a contest to see which picture is more valid or appeals more tellingly to the audience.

Fortunately, the traditional moralist has a more compelling and more principled debate strategy at his command. He can tell the audience that their own interests demand a rejection of picture-thinking and a return to a better way of resolving ethical questions—namely, by applying sound moral norms. First, he will point out that all the word-pictures we draw of our "situation" tend to be focused on self-interest. Each of us likes to picture his situation so as to make *other people* the problem. Which is fine for me, so long as I am the only one drawing the pictures and making the life-and-death decisions. But I am not the only one. Other people are drawing pictures with *me* as part of the problem. Suppose they find me, or you, a terrible inconvenience? Suppose they decide that getting rid of us is the "loving thing to do"? What protection do we have from such "loving" decisions, unless we have some natural *rights* they cannot violate? What is a natural right? It is something which cannot be "rightly" or "justly" taken away from us, no matter how much trouble we are to other people, no matter how "tragic" our existence makes their "situation."

Is it not so? Well, if that is what we mean by a right, than there is a flat and obvious contradiction between situation ethics and our rights. Under the former, our lives, properties and freedoms are conditional upon other people's happiness (or what some authority says is other people's happiness). Under the latter, our lives, properties and freedoms are inalienable. Which would a free nation prefer?

Consequentialism, which has been in existence for a long time, has taken many forms. Machiavelli and Hobbes, for example, seemed to argue in consequentialist terms for proposals that seemed radical in their day. Marx, in justifying revolutionary action, did so in the name of the good which was to come of it. In the English-speaking tradition, Jeremy Bentham and John Stuart Mill both employed consequentialism as a method of ethical reasoning.

Capsulized, consequentialism states that the morally good act is the one which will give the best results. In other words, the goodness or evilness of a given human act is determined by the consequences of that act—rather than what the act is intrinsically. Obviously, then, consequentialism cannot be separated from a system of value judgments about the merits of one result versus another. Germain Grisez, perhaps the foremost natural ethician of the modern age, does not dispute consequentialism because it gives wrong answers, but because it cannot rationally justify *any* moral judgment. "Consequentialism," Grisez says, "is a calculative method. It suggests that the good and bad effects of each alternative be tallied, that the total bad effects be subtracted from the total good effects of such alternative, and that the net results of each computation be compared with the others. The alternative which gets the best—or least bad—score is the one to be accepted." Grisez then points out that this calculation cannot be convincingly done unless the values of the various outcomes can be measured against each other. Often the good and bad effects of one alternative simply cannot be measured against the good and bad effects of another alternative. How, for example, does one weigh the good and bad effects of being a lawyer against the good and bad effects of being a doctor? How does one weigh the value of the life of a defective infant against the costs of treatment or the burdens to the parents, and so on?

When consequentialism is first examined, it seems very sensible. Do what will produce the greatest benefit for all is an appealing admonition. To do otherwise is to seem to prefer another ethical system which may force a person to choose a course of action that brings misery. But that is simplistic. Human experience is not so predictable, nor so formulaic. Human enjoyments and desires differ in kind, not just in degree. "Happiness" means different things to different people. Maybe one can compare the enjoyment of a soft drink to that of a candy bar. But how does one compare the value of a corporate promotion with the value of a happy marriage, say? Satisfying one desire may be mutually exclusive of satisfying another. How can the merit of particular desires be measured? All desires are not commensurable, although consequentialism assumes that all "goods" are proportionate and, therefore, that the "greatest net good" can easily be calculated. It presupposes that, while deliberation is going on, the value standard has been settled, a presumption that almost excludes self-determination. But in actual experience, there *is* self-determination, because people accept one way of being satisfied, or another, in different circumstances, and so their happiness quotient may be very different than even they could have predicted.

In Grisez's words: "Consequentialism is rationally unacceptable because the phrase 'greater good' as it is used in any consequentialist theory necessarily lacks reference. I do not reject consequentialism merely because I think it is dangerous; I reject it because I think it is dangerous *nonsense*—'nonsense' in the sense that inasmuch as expressions essential to the articulation of consequentialism necessarily lack reference, the theory is meaningless."

Situationism and consequentalism are, of course, inconsistent with America's religious heritage. Both Judaism and Christianity are based on revealed precepts; situationism and consequentalism reject revealed Judeo-Christian ethics and modernistic ethics. It is also a source of the currently prevailing confusion, namely, that part of the popular mind is sympathetic with traditional values while part accepts the new morality with its subjective standards.

If order is to be restored to society, and the underpinnings of freedom preserved, America must return to non-consequentalist ethics. What would be the basis for such an ethics? Some say the sole possible basis is revealed religion. This is a mistake. First of all, the Bible and other revealed documents do not answer explicitly all the ethical questions that arise; for instance, genetic screening, nuclear weapons systems, or *in vitro* fertilization about which the scriptures speak only by interpretation.

But from another perspective, society needs a more solid foundation from which to teach its next generation. The fact that "God says it's wrong" does not explain "why it is wrong." And that "why" must be answered, if the loyalty of the succeeding generation is to be preserved for an ethical system. Society pays a tremendous price if all it says to its young is "You mustn't do X because God forbids it." This will work so long as the young are pious. But past that, if adults have no further answer, they have no means of maintaining respect for the system. Worse, this kind of approach produces, ultimately, resentment against God. It is not surprising that people reared on a simplistic "God says it's wrong and that's that" system have turned around and rejected faith altogether. It is only to be expected that when adolescent rebellion sets in, young people will resist being told by God that they cannot do what they want, with no reason given.

Rather, a good system of ethics should show *why* something is harmful. A sound system of ethics needs to explain what the conditions are for human well-being, what are the "goods" intrinsically involved in human well-being. If we can see those, we can build a system of precepts which in effect tell us how to avoid damaging any of the essential "goods."

This work has been done already. Natural law ethics are adequate to the task. The philosophy of natural law has been time honored since the ancient Greeks. Though intellectual fashions change, an objective moral order, knowable by man and within the reach of mankind, can be reasonably seen as the most stable basis of personal, national and international order and happiness.

In recent years, finding and justifying a natural law ethics has acquired fresh strength in academic quarters. Beginning with a famous article by G. E. M. Anscombe in the mid 1950s, an increasing number of academic moralists have abandoned the once-fashionable consequentialist and relativist camps to rediscover the ethical wisdom of the pre-modern natural law tradition. An important breakthrough in bringing this tradition up to date was made by Germain Grisez, whose work has been furthered at Oxford by John Finnis. Two other reconstructions of the natural law tradition have been pioneered at the University of Chicago by Alan Donagan, a convert from Marxism, and Alan Gerwirth.[3]

Natural law is harder to summarize than situationism or consequentalism. According to the philosophy of natural law, human beings are endowed, as the Declaration of Independence says, "by their Creator" with certain natural rights and obligations, inalienable, because they are antecedent, both in logic and in nature, to the formation of civil society. They are not granted by the state, therefore the state cannot take them away. Government, indeed, has the moral responsibility to protect these rights and their exercise. It is the ethical system upon which our nation was founded, and has remained very much a part of our tradition. Natural law ethics experienced a revival after World War II, when there was a universally recognized need for an ethical system which would uphold the dignity of the individual against the incursion of dictatorships. Only a moral order that derives its authority from something higher than our fellow man can offer that protection. The natural law is independent of divine revelation, since its first principles are common to mankind as a whole, accessible to reason. The most articulate scholars who have studied and written about the natural law have, however, been Christian, since the teachings of revelation coincide with natural law. With or without the premise of God, nature does have design and order, with respect to both the physcial and the rational aspects of humanity, waiting only to be perceived.

The gist of natural law ethics is that one must study the nature of man and then proceed to do good and avoid evil in accordance with that nature. What is the nature of man, upon which the whole system is based? How can it be known? Man is a rational animal, Aristotle said, and time has not changed that truth. Man is a living being like other animals, but with the need to learn what is true. Thus, man is oriented to two basic "goods": life, because he is a living being, and knowledge, because he is a rational being. Man tends to those things that enhance life and knowledge. Man can only achieve what enhances life and knowledge through actions. Unlike God, man does not possess the fullness of these goods, but must achieve them through action. In addition, man is ordained by nature to all that renders action coherent and successful. If we are thus ordered by nature, since those requirements of nature are found in each one of us, then we must respect those ordinations in each and every one of us. Our nature is one thing we cannot change.

Man can control his actions, however, and ethical systems are about actions. Under the natural law, all actions are not alike. For instance, a human act is an act that proceeds from the considered, deliberate will of man—acts of infants, by way of contrast, are called "acts of man," for they do not come from the deliberate decisions of will. Here is a basis for a system of justice tempered with mercy—one cannot hold an incompetent or an imbecile responsible for actions that would bring condemnation to the person who proceeded from a deliberate act of the will. Every act has three elements of morality: the object of the action (the action itself, distinct from the circumstances around it); the circumstances of the action (who, what, where, by what means, how, when); the purpose of the action (the reason it was done). An action is deemed morally good if its object, circumstances and purpose are all morally good: An action is morally evil if one of these elements is evil. Some actions are morally neutral.

It is necessary to learn the rules of morality. Natural law ethics is not simple; it is not the sort of ethical system that pleases the dilettante who wants an answer which will allow him to do what he feels like today and a different thing tomorrow. It is a system which will endure, and anything which endures is worth working to acquire. Natural law ethics is not an attempt to derive morals from the leaves and flowers, much less from the birds and bees or from tooth and claw. It is, rather, an attempt to derive ethics from the dynamic requirements of human nature. It is an attempt to discover what goods are so intrinsic to human flowering that we cannot violate them without violating ourselves.

What are the implications of an objective system of morality for public policy? Only an ethical system which establishes absolutes can protect anybody's rights. We need an unchangeable basis for protecting our rights. The rights of individuals are under assault in many areas of life. Whether or not the public hears about it generally depends on the political usefulness of the issue. Every once in a while we hear in the media about some testing done on prison inmates twenty years ago, or about a series of involuntary sterilizations performed on black women in the South. Medical testing without consent, surgery without consent—these are unethical at any time, regardless of who the victim is. But we hear about them (and our public conscience aroused) only when the offenses are publicized by a group that has the resources to make a political issue out of it. But where is the protection for the rights of someone with no political clout? The rightness or wrongness of something should not depend on one's political connections. The gravest weaknesses of situationism and consequentialism are that they reduce right and wrong to political expedience. If the powers that be fear overpopulation, then it becomes morally right to practice involuntary sterilization, and also politically imprudent to protest it. In the People's Republic of China no one can protest what the state has decided are actions in its interest.

But the erosion of rights and of freedom can occur on a less dramatic scale as well. A PhD candidate in education wants to turn in a unique dissertation, so he gets the consent of a friendly teacher to allow him to administer some tests to public school students. In the questionnaire, he asks them about their sex lives, their parents' sex lives, their family money situation, their parents' emotional relationships, and so on. Is this ethical? To the PhD candidate, if it helps him produce an interesting dissertation, it seems ethical. But to the parents, who may find out long after their children's privacy and their own have been violated, consequentialism does not seem very comforting. But because there is no clear basis on which to argue for the protection of the parents' rights, those who would so argue find themselves in a discouraging battle.

The objective facts of demographics and economics are heralding a future in which decision making in medicine is going to become increasingly subjective. Ten people need a kidney machine; only five can be accommodated—how is the doctor to decide which five get treatment? Some form of value-judging of each person's life is the way such dilemmas are currently resolved, in a process called triage. It is so commonplace that many schoolchildren are taught triage by playing classroom games; You're in a lifeboat that can only accommodate 12 people, yet 15 are in the boat. Here are the life stories and qualifications of all 15—you decide which three to throw overboard. Such instruction implies that the individual exists to benefit "society," and "society" has the right to decide when an individual is dispensable. We are raising a generation of children who have been taught a set of ethical premises mutually exclusive of the values of Western civilization, Judeo-Christian morality and American jurisprudence. Accepting a defeatist ethical system will allow for defeatist attitudes elsewhere. If people feel comfortable balancing lives one against another and making life and death decisions, they will accept the fact of scarcity of resources. If the public remains morally outraged at having to decide who gets to use the kidney machine, it is more likely that someone will figure out a way to get more kidney machines so those decisions will not have to be made.

The government must be made responsible in using non-consequentialist ethics in reaching its decisions about public policy. When a governmental ethics advisory board reaches a conclusion on the ethical permissiveness of *in vitro* fertilization or genetic engineering, that conclusion should not be based on consequentialist ethics. Generally, such decisions have been so based, however. The Mutual Assured Destruction (MAD) policy of nuclear defense is based on consequentialist thinking—if they destroy us, we'll destroy them, and since both results will be bad, neither side will start it. Mutual Assured Destruction is an intrinsically immoral nuclear policy—a government cannot rightly do anything that would place the lives of its citizens in direct jeopardy. Citizens' rights ought to be defended by their government—but a consequentialist system of ethics, in which the government decides what is good for itself, is not going to defend these citizens' rights.

Citizens must defend their rights, and they must defend them intellectually, by employing and invoking an objective system of right and wrong. This new traditional ethics is based on philosophical precepts, not on religious precepts, and can be understood and accepted by anyone willing to master the intellectual rigors of it.

Only an ethical system that establishes absolute prohibitions can protect anyone's rights. Our society, our system of government, has always taken for granted that individuals have rights. But as collectivism pervades the thinking of the country, those individual rights are going to be subtly undermined in the unspoken premises of a lot of decisions. The overt attacks can be answered—the subtle shifts may not even be noticed. To say that I have a right is to say that something somebody else might do is always wrong—without exception or obfuscation. That is a hard statement to make, but unless such a hard statement *is* made, ultimately, nobody's rights will mean anything.

The American people are going to have to choose between fashionable situationism or consequentialism and their rights. The easy way out is not the way to a future in which America will remain a free country.

NOTES

[1] Barbara Seaman, *The Doctor's Case Against the Pill* (New York: Doubleday & Company, Inc. 1980), p. 96.

[2] Simone Weil, *Population and Development Review,* Vol 4, no. 2 (June 1978), p. 316.

[3] Alan Donagan, *The Theory of Morality* (Chicago: University of Chicago Press, 1977).

9

Decadence and Reform: Toward A Conservative Educational Agenda For the 21st Century

Allan C. Carlson

The American educational system has reached a critical juncture.* Old theoretical and institutional arrangements are failing. New ones are struggling to come into being. The political task facing the nation well into the 21st century is recasting public policy to meet these changing social and cultural imperatives. Ironically, it is American liberals who are locked into the political defense of a sociologically decadent system. Many conservatives, by way of contrast, recognize the necessity for a basic reconstruction that would set aside deteriorating structural arrangements while recovering those educational principles upon which this nation's form of government and future rest.

Education for a Republic

In considering current dislocation and an agenda for the next century, we must first understand the past. When the United States was founded, the education of youth was an informal, exclusively familial and ecclesiastical affair. Laws and state constitutional provisions during the early national era (1776–1840) continued to show, in the words of legal scholar Samuel Windsor Brown, "the largely religious aim of education, the largely religious nature of the subject matter of

---

*This essay is restricted by design to the discussion of elementary and secondary education. While many of its themes also hold true for higher education, the latter is different enough, historically and theoretically, to merit separate consideration.

instruction; and the considerable part played by the church in the control of schools."[1] So long as the governing majority of Americans continued to be of British descent and within the broad Protestant tradition, this arrangement suited the particular needs of the young nation.

The 1840s, however, marked a basic shift in migration patterns to the United States. First Irish, then German, Scandinavian, Slavic, Jewish and Mediterranean peoples began flowing into the country. Between 1840 and 1930, 50 million non-English speaking immigrants entered its gates. The railroad network built during those decades facilitated their spread across the Midwest and West.

These immigrants, persons almost uniformly unfamiliar with the expectations and processes of a democracy, presented the Republic with a new and serious problem. Aristotle had warned in his *Politics* that, "A given constitution demands an education in conformity with it; for the maintenance of any constitution, like its first establishment, is due . . . to the presence of the spirit or character proper to that constitution." He stressed that a republic required individuals of strong character, exhibiting an internalized moral code and a readiness to accept responsibility and make sacrifices for the public good. The maintenance of democracy, he concluded, ultimately rested on a distinctive spirit, to be inculcated in each citizen through a common, or "public," education.[2]

Mid-nineteenth century American educators came to agree. As constitutional law professor E. D. Mansfield told the College of Teachers in 1835, "it is altogether essential to our national security, strength and peace . . . that the foreigners who settle on our soil should cease to be Europeans and become Americans." He urged that immigrant children be brought into the schools and amalgamated with the existing community in the interests of republican order and Christian morality.[3] Similarly, Horace Mann, the acknowledged "father" of American public education, feared the destructive potential of religious, political and class discord that might develop in a nation of immigrants. Out of such varigated cultural traditions, he urged the teaching of a uniquely American public philosophy that would support the republican ideal, build social harmony and progress, and help the nation fulfill its millenial destiny.

Mann emphasized that the very foundations of democratic government—rational debate and civic unity—were at issue. "In the terms of principles common to all," he wrote in 1848, "is to be found the only common medium of language and of idea, by which [disputing] parties can become intelligible to each other. . . ." Moreover, while the public schools in a culturally pluralistic community had to foreswear sectarian religious instruction, Mann insisted on their continued grounding in the broad Judeo-Christian heritage.

The free school system of Massachusetts, he stressed, ". . . recognizes the religious obligations in their fullest extent; . . . invokes a religious spirit, and can never be fitly administered without such a spirit; . . . inculcates the great commands, upon which hang all the laws and the prophets; . . . [and] welcomes the Bible, and therefore welcomes all the doctrines which the Bible really contains . . ." Teachers in the free schools, he noted, were required to instruct children in "the principles of piety, justice, and a sacred regard to truth, love to their country, humanity and universal benevolence, sobriety, industry, and frugality, chastity, moderation, and temperance, and those other virtues . . . upon which a republican constitution is founded."[4]

As public schooling spread West, these same purposes and principles held sway. According to educational historian Timothy Smith, it was not secularism which triumphed in the schools, but a non-denominational (normally Protestant) Christianity reflecting an evangelical consensus on faith and ethics; one so dominating the national culture "that a majority of Protestants were . . . willing to entrust the state with the task of educating children, confident that education would be 'religious' still."[5] Pastor's wives were frequently pressed into service as the teachers in the new common schools. Early state superintendents of education were commonly ordained clergy. Protestant colleges in the Midwest made teacher training an important element in their curricula. Newton Bateman, Illinois' first state superintendent of schools, actually declared in 1875 that the public schools were "the noblest legacy bequeathed by Christian learning to the nation and to the age."[6]

Furthermore, despite this turn to public schools, the American educational enterprise remained community-based, relying on local leadership and volunteer citizen action to realize common civic, moral and educational purposes. Educational bureaucracies were unknown. As late as 1890, the average state department of education employed only two people (including the superintendent), representing but one official for every 100,000 public school students. The U.S. Office of Education, founded in 1867, had a staff of only six with the principal duty of collecting statistics.

The situation was by no means perfect. The informal Protestant identity of most public schools did drive Roman Catholics to create their own educational system. German-Americans fought hard and sometimes bitterly for the right to educate their children in the German language. Some elements of the mid-century German Lutheran immigration also came to build their own schools for both cultural and theological reasons. Yet even parochial schools, over time, absorbed the prevailing sense of "American Character" and became agents in the adjustment of immigrant children to American culture.[7]

The 20th Century: From Order to Monopoly

The first half of the twentieth century did see some lessening of overt religious symbolism in many schools, a pronounced turn toward professionalism among educators, and the emergence of managerial and scientific experts within the educational structure. Bureaucracies grew rapidly. School districts began to consolidate. Tracking, intelligence testing and vocational education to meet the needs of an industrial economy were among the innovations introduced.

Nonetheless, the new educational theorists continued to place primary emphasis on the role of the public schools in undergirding moral character, reinforcing virtue and building national unity. Urban high schools, in particular, became the carriers of American values and culture. No less an advocate of educational progress and reform than John Dewey stressed that the public schools, "in bringing together those of different nationalities, languages, traditions, and creeds . . . are performing an infinitely significant religious work. They are promoting the social unity out of which in the end genuine religious unity must grow. . . ."[8] Progressive reformer Ellwood P. Cubberly, assessing both the massive waves of immigration and the strains of industrialization, declared that "[t]he task is thrown more and more upon the school of instilling into all a social and political consciousness that will lead to unity amid diversity."[9]

Continuity in the acknowledged aims of American education carried into the 1950s. University of Chicago President Robert Hutchins, a stanch advocate of public schooling, stressed in 1953 that ". . . the purpose of education is to improve men." Echoing Horace Mann, he argued that the members of a democratic society must at least be able to understand one another, which demanded "a common purpose and a common concept of man and society adequate to hold the community together." The task of education, Hutchins concluded, was to discover and order this "hierarchy of values" and "to help understand it, establish it, and live by it."[10] John Childs, in his 1950 treatise on education and morals, also stressed that the schooling task rested on faith "in the possibility of controlling the human enterprise in the interest of cherished ends, or values."[11] Anthropologist Cora DuBois labeled the assimilation of diverse immigrant groups into middle-class American values as "one of the remarkable socio-political achievements of the nation," testifying "to the compelling vigor of its value system."[12] Van Cleve Morris, in his 1957 defense of public education, argued consistent with the 19th-century reformers that "[w]e have socialized education because we realize our national destiny is dependent upon it; . . . without an enlightened people we cannot become an enlightened civilization."[13]

Moreover, while controversies over public education remained numerous and varied, the large majority of Americans continued to express confidence in their schools. Student achievement, evidenced through standardized tests, showed progressive improvement. Enhanced science and math curricula were introduced with relative ease. The schools generally reflected and reinforced the revived patriotic sentiment of the post-World War II era. They even succeeded in conveying a shared religiosity to students drawn from many faiths, without significant rancor or dissent. On the negative side, though, black Americans were often left behind, commonly isolated in segregated, usually second-rate schools. Their demands for equality formed the significant discordant note within an otherwise successful system.

Predictably, the first traumas shattering the old certainties grew out of the race issue. The federal courts, beginning with the *Brown vs. Board of Education* decision in 1954, injected judicial litigation deep into the educational enterprise, a development that accelerated over the next quarter century. By 1980, the Boston city schools alone were governed by 200 separate court orders on matters ranging from minority hiring quotas and school closings to the content of curriculum and the structure of the administrative staff. Unrest among black Americans in the 1960s drove a deep wedge into American life, particularly after Martin Luther King, Jr.'s early and consensus-building emphasis on Christian and democratic values gave way to calls for black power and affirmative action. When hosts of other aggrieved groups—ranging from Hispanics and American Indians to radical feminists and homosexuals—began to press for new legal rights, compensation for past "deprivations," and cultural change, the public schools often served as their chosen battleground.

Other developments rocked the educational establishment. The Supreme Court decisions of 1962 and 1963, outlawing mandatory prayer and devotional Bible reading in tax-supported schools, provided civil libertarians and militant atheists with powerful weapons to drive remaining religious sensibilities and symbols out of the public schools. Demographic changes—the "baby boom" of the 1947–62 era and the "baby bust" of the late 1960s and 1970s—successively caused rapid expansion and painful contraction of facilities and teaching staff. The transformation of the National Education Association from a professional organization into a militant trade union marked the politicization of teaching and the growing estrangement of teachers, administrators and parents. Federal government funding of categorical programs for the education of the poor, the handicapped, the gifted and other special groups tied school systems in regulatory knots and stimulated the spread of educational specialists, consultants and bureaucrats. One researcher recently cited an American elementary school with 91 staff persons, only 33 of whom were teachers with full-time classroom responsibilities, the others being social workers, psychologists, counselors, educational specialists, aides and office staff. Countless special interest groups, ranging from Planned Parenthood seeking to promote its brand of sexual ethics among children to business groups pressing for specialized forms of "vocational education," helped to transform schools into three-ring circuses with many acts but no direction.

Radical Assault and Cultural Breakdown

Yet this growing confusion must be seen as part of a broader cultural disorientation, one emerging independent of the educational enterprise. For several centuries, as example, growing numbers of Western intellectuals had viewed moral judgments resting on Divine commandment, or the Natural Law, as irrelevant to the modern age. Enlightenment philosophers in the 18th and 19th centuries, such as David Hume, Denis Diderot and Immanuel Kant, correspondingly mounted a search for an independent, rational foundation for social morality. John Dewey's call early in this country for a "common faith" resting moral order on democracy and science was a late expression of this quest. Yet by the opening of the twentieth century, it was increasingly evident that "the Enlightenment project" had failed. For those who rejected Divine law, confusion, nihilism and radical moral individualism were left as the alternatives.

By the 1920s, these philosophical diseases had started to spread among American educators. "How can a teacher know what habits should be formed by children?" implored C. C. Cooper in the *Journal of the National Education Association* in 1926. "How can she know the relative importance of these habits?"[14] By the early 1970s, such moral confusion dominated both the media-shaped popular culture and the schools. Philosopher Thomas Nagel caught its broad spirit, suggesting that "nothing or almost nothing . . . which a person does seems to be under his control."[15] In adult society, educators explained, the unrestrained pursuit of fame, power, love and wealth had lost its old status as sin. "Put plainly," theorist Jerome Kagan wrote, "it is extremely difficult for an adult who is poor, powerless, and lonely to feel virtuous because he knows he has resisted the lusts of a corrupt society."[16]

For related reasons, the institutions that had joined the schools in shaping moral character—the family and the churches—evidenced their own breakdowns. Attitudes concerning marriage, sex and children showed dramatic shifts. As late as 1967, for example, 85 percent of Americans judged premarital sex to be morally wrong; by 1979, only 37 percent did. Family statistics in the United States also suggested unprecedented stress. The divorce rate, after declining slightly in the 1950s, tripled between 1960 and 1982, with the number of children affected each year by divorce climbing from 379,000 in 1957 to 1.1 million in 1974. The nation's fertility rate (births per 1,000 women aged 15–44) plummeted from 122.7 in 1957 to only 66.7 in 1975, while the illegitimacy ratio (out-of-wedlock births per 1,000 live births) tripled over the same years. Abortion, considered a felony in every state in 1963, was legalized everywhere by court fiat ten years later. By 1982, over 1.6 million abortions occurred annually. In 1980, single-parent families formed over 20 percent of all families with children under the age of six, up from a mere 8 percent in 1960. Among black Americans, nearly half of all children were growing up without fathers in the early 1980s.

Similarly, those religious denominations within the National Council of Churches orbit—among them Congregationalist, Presbyterian and Methodist—tended to abandon in this period their traditional concern with human sin, individual character and personal salvation, leaning instead toward political action to combat the "sinfulness of social structures." While forming a numerical majority, the remaining religious bodies—including Evangelicals, Pentecostals, conservative Lutherans, orthodox Jews, Mormons and traditional Catholics—remained locked in culturally-imposed or self-imposed enclaves, exerting minimal influence on national opinion and policy. Only during the late 1970s did elements of these groups attempt to break out of their isolation.

In sum, America's cultural consensus, centered on devotion to family, personal morality and the virtues of self-denial, hard work and personal responsibility, began to crumble. What Harvard sociologist Talcott Parsons in 1961 had labeled "a single and relatively well integrated and fully institutionalized system of values in American society"[17] was overwhelmed by the spread of moral and social nihilism. Over the course of the 1960s, virtually every aspect of the American system—from standards of family life and respect for the moral law resting in the Ten Commandments to presumptions in favor of hard work and economic growth—came under radical, sustained and often irrational attack. The educational structure was no exception.

In a time when the public schools are frequently criticized for their amoral, value-neutral stance, it is useful to remember that the Left's assault on America's educational system during the 1960–75 era aimed primarily at the *value-laden* nature of the schools. Widely read, revisionist works such as Michael Katz's *The Irony of Early School Reform*, blasted the tradition of "moral education" as "a kind of intellectual totalitarianism" aimed at reinforcing individual character, social order, the Natural Law and capitalism.[18] As New Left activist Marcus Raskin put it, the values in the public schools could be seen "as the few over the many, white over third world, property and goods over people, man as conqueror of nature, fabricating it (and the people who live with nature) into goods and property which then dominates other people, men over women, continuous growth over regeneration and seeding."[19] Ivan Illich, in his influential book, *Deschooling Society,* charged that "the institutionalization of values" in America's schools leads "inevitably to physical pollution, social polarization, and psychological impotence. . . ." Denying the continued relevance of Western culture, he urged efforts "to find a new balance in the global milieu" through "the deinstitutionalization of values."[20] Likewise, critic Martin Carnoy praised those emerging New Age "free schools" that "demystified" inherited values, cultural norms and social order, thereby helping children to discover "that institutional organization and purpose is [sic] *not derived* from 'natural order' but from peoples' minds." More generally, he urged that a society governed by the Natural Law be replaced by a new social system "in continuous liberation."[21]

This assault on the foundation of the American educational enterprise tended to subside by the late 1970s. Yet it left a permanent legacy: the shattering of the moral and philosophical certainties that had infused curricula; the delegitimation of institutional arrangements; and deep confusion and division over the purposes of education.

This loss of bearing is acknowledged by those educators honest with their constituencies and themselves. Syracuse University Professor Gerald Grant suggests that the American public high school "threatens to become a container for adolescents who receive the ministrations of a greatly enlarged core of specialists in a setting in which presumed equals argue about their rights, and individuals pursue their moral preferences in whatever direction they please."[22] Robert Wood, superintendent of the Boston Public Schools, notes that "the concept of national character—of what it means to be an American—appears to have been effectively shattered by [the Vietnam] war and political turmoil."[23] Editor Stephen Graubard of the American Academy of Arts and Sciences concludes that "We no longer understand how events relate to each other. . . . We seem suddenly deprived of the capacity to imagine or construct vital new institutions; it is not always apparent that we know how to renovate those that already exist."[24]

These are descriptions of a sociologically "decadent" system, one that has lost its sustaining symbols, its courage, its mobilizing energy and its purpose.

In place of confident affirmations of the moral virtues deeply rooted in Western Civilization, America's schools have turned to "strategies" such as "values clarification" which treat all value judgments as relative or equal and tend to generate cynicism toward social morality altogether. Moreover, instead of serving as the means of integrating new immigrants into a distinctly American culture, the schools have embraced bilingual education, "the preservation of minority cultures," and a new ethnicism that are corrupting the true meaning of American pluralism and slowly undermining what remains of America's bonds of national community. Succinctly put, the public schools have betrayed their basic social purposes. Tumbling standardized testing scores, lax academic standards, absurd "life studies" curricula, and growing numbers of illiterate "graduates" indicate that even basic education in reading, writing and arithmetic is slipping beyond the grasp of the educational establishment.

But interestingly, just as the public schools showed signs of advanced decay, private schools—virtually ignored in the 1960s as fading entities—evidenced new vitality. The 1971–74 period, suggests Denis Doyle of the American Enterprise Institute, may be regarded by future historians of education as the crucial watershed when the private schools replaced their public counterparts as the vehicles for progress, expansion and experimentation.[25] While it is true that enrollment in Roman Catholic schools declined 30 percent during the 1970s, the explosion in the number of Christian day schools more than made up for the drop. Since the late 1960s, at least 8,000–10,000 new Christian schools have formed, with an estimated enrollment of over one million. However, despite the myths concocted by their opponents, private schools as a group have done at least as well as public schools in integrating racial groups and social classes. In California, for example, private schools enroll *higher* proportions of black, Asian and Hispanic students than do the public schools. Available evidence also suggests that most private schools accept their students as randomly as do the public schools, belying charges of intellectual elitism. Many of these schools link a traditional patriotism to basic religious education. Toss in their voluntaristic, parent-supported nature and their commitment to "moral community," and the independent schools begin to resemble the institutions envisioned by America's 19th-century, "republican" educational reformers.

Looking Toward the 21st Century

In casting a conservative agenda for the 21st century that responds to this situation, two underlying principles need to be posited. First, a democratic constitution continues to demand a unique character among its citizenry: specifically, autonomous individuals with internalized virtues of responsibility, moral courage and a commitment to the public good. It is true that such individuals are shaped, in large part, by their families and their faith. Yet the power of the schools to support or undermine these values is real. With a clear recognition of the historical rarity and fragility of free societies, America needs to recover that constructive institutional balance between family, faith and school that generates citizens for life in a free republic.

Second, this land still needs strong vehicles for national integration. Embracing a heterogeneous population representing over a hundred distinct ethnic origins, and facing new waves of immigration, the United States can ill-afford a turn to internal ethnic, linguistic and cultural ghettos. Instead of accentuated "pluralism" or social atomization, the rebuilding of a distinct sense of American Civilization stands as the pressing national imperative. At the minimum, this involves affirmation of the primacy of the English language and popular reverence for the ideals embodied in the nation's founding documents: a republican government, social equality, the rule of law, equal opportunity and the individual pursuit of happiness within a framework of virtue. It entails reaffirmation of the traditional or historic middle-class family model as a moral and social entity transcending racial, ethnic, religious and class divisions. And it requires the restoration of a religiously based "public philosophy" in the nation's cultural and political spheres.

With this said, it is critical to note that the recovery of a sense of "American Civilization" cannot be imposed from above. As Alexis de Tocqueville came to understand during his mid-19th-century visit to America, a democratic civilization must arise more or less spontaneously from the people themselves as an expression of shared purposes. The task also requires the positive participation of the whole range of culture-shaping entities: the media, the literary world, religion, the arts, as well as the educational system. This very list of necessary agents suggests the great difficulties involved. Nonetheless, the effort must be made; its success is essential to our common future.

In light of these background principles, a conservative policy agenda in education carrying into the next century would encompass:

1. *Deregulation and defederalization of the educational enterprise.* The U.S. Department of Education, the *de facto* tool of the National Education Association and other entrenched groups, should be eliminated. Some of its less politicized agencies, such as the National Center for Education Statistics, would be usefully retained, although returned to their decentralized homes. Others, such as the Office of Bilingual Education and the National Institute of Education, should go. Simply put, these agencies have failed in their putative scientific tasks, have contributed to the intellectual assault on traditional American norms

and mores, and have violated the basic principles of reform suggested above. Certain categorical "formula grant" programs, such as aid for the handicapped and gifted, should be recast to give maximum flexibility to the recipient states and school systems.

2. *Deconsolidation of the public schools.* The existing public school structure is probably beyond incremental salvation. Even worthy plans such as the widely acclaimed *A Nation At Risk,* suggesting more and longer school days, increased homework, tougher grading, and so on, say nothing to the realities of teachers unions, paralyzing litigation, and the ideological content of textbooks, social science courses and sex education curricula. Thousands of good teachers and creative administrators are captives of legal, political, economic and structural restraints not of their making and not amenable to graduated reform. Only the act of "radical deconsolidation," down even to the building level, can shake the system free of these extraneous factors and reopen public education to freedom, experimentation, creativity and intellectual growth. Individual schools, with neighborhood- or community-based boards, should be left free to structure their own personnel policies, develop their own curricula and reflect the moral and religious standards of their constituencies. Such acts would allow neighborhood schools to restore their ties of community loyalty and to compete freely with private schools for students. As a corollary, state and district educational bureaucracies should be slashed.

3. *Restoration of the "sacred canopy" over the schools.* The Supreme Court's decisions to remove prayer and devotional Bible reading from tax supported schools fundamentally violated an informal, 120-year-old compact between the public schools, parents, churches and the American republic. As theologians such as Michael Novak and Richard Neuhaus have suggested, it is ironic that the courts turned to secularity just as the intellectual hegemony of the "Secular Enlightenment" was faltering. "In a whole host of endeavors," Neuhaus writes, "the cutting edge is [now] moving toward an understanding of a religious character in the nature of the reality of which we are part. . . . [W]e realize that we can only become more mature persons not by outgrowing [religious] mystery but by entering ever deeper into the mystery."[26] One recent survey found that, despite the sweeping changes of the preceding twenty years, 94 percent of Americans still acknowledged that feeling that God loves them and 89 percent still engaged in prayer, figures coming as close to unanimity as polling techniques make possible. It is fundamentally anti-democratic to sacrifice such widely shared affirmations of the Divine to the sensitivities of a tiny minority. The Court's actions two decades ago stand as fundamental moral, cultural and historical errors. They need to be reversed, either through legislative action or Constitutional amend-

ment that would return such decisions to community control. Mechanisms to protect minority religious views within such environments are readily available and should be included in such changes.

4. *A joint program of tuition tax credits and vouchers.* Until the reforms cited above are implemented, "communities of virtue" will remain beyond the reach of the public schools. In contrast, private schools already enjoy "freedom from" externally imposed legal, structural and ideological restraints and "freedom for" the creation of moral codes evoking the "shared commitments" of the community involved. Until the cultural resources have been mobilized to rebuild a pervasive national ethos, it is imperative that public policy foster such small centers of freedom and virtue. A combination of tuition tax credits and vouchers would give all elements of the population, not just the relatively wealthy, access to choice and moral values in their children's education, without demanding inordinate sacrifice. A federal income-tax-credit for a portion of the tuition paid to private schools would aid middle-income families. Title I of the Elementary and Secondary Education Act of 1965, which provides categorical aid for the education of disadvantaged children, could be restructured to parcel out the funds involved (in the early 1980s approximately $3 billion) directly to the parents of such children. Each family would then be free to spend its voucher at the public or private school of its choice. If such a scheme proved successful, state funding mechanisms could eventually be restructured to create a universal voucher system within each state. There is the very real danger that federal or state tax-credit and voucher schemes might serve as the wedge for bureaucratic manipulation or control of independent schools. Strong prohibitions against such abuse of power must be written into law. For reasons of history and cultural unity, tuition tax-credit and voucher plans should exclude schools that discriminate in student selection on the basis of race, with built-in protection for the schools' right of due process and an exception granted to those rare instances where legitimate theological considerations are involved. It is true that the Supreme Court has tended in recent decades to overturn state tax-credit and related plans that indirectly aid church-related schools. Setting aside the sound argument that such decisions reflect a serious misreading of the First Amendment, there is no certainty that the Court would throw out a carefully constructed federal plan. The judiciary has changed its collective mind on this subject before. Given new cultural and social circumstances, it could do so again.

In reviewing this agenda, one critical response would be that defederalization, deconsolidation, and the financial support of sectarian schools hardly seem the means for promoting national unity. Indeed, the proposals outlined above do represent in their aggregate one step backward from a deteriorating situation. The intention, though, is to preserve the very possibility of "communities of virtue," in order to take two steps ahead at a later time toward a reinvigorated national character. Admittedly, there is risk involved. New and deep divisions exist in our society. Moral disorder and social alienation have spread deep. Yet public life ultimately stands at the mercy of private life. Trust must be placed in the people and in those "mediating" structures—families, churches, neighborhoods and voluntary associations—giving meaning to individual lives, as the wellsprings for shared values and renewed democratic community. In a free society, there is no other alternative.

NOTES

[1] Samuel Windsor Brown, *The Secularization of American Education* (1912; reissued: New York: Russell E. Russell, 1967), p. 155.

[2] Aristotle, *Aristotle on Education*, edited by John Burnet (Cambridge: At the University Press, 1913), pp. 105–06.

[3] Quoted in Allen O. Hansen, *Early Educational Leadership in the Ohio Valley* (Bloomington, Ill: Arno Press, 1969), pp. 21–24.

[4] Horace Mann, *The Republic and the School: On the Education of Free Men*, edited by Lawrence A. Crenin (New York: Bureau of Publications, Teachers College of Columbia University, 1975), pp. 94, 106, 111.

[5] Timothy L. Smith, "Protestant Schooling and American Nationality, 1800–1850," *Journal of American History* 53 (1967), p. 687.

[6] Quoted in *Ibid.*, p. 694.

[7] Noted in: Timothy Smith, "Religion, Schools, and the Community of Values in American Culture," unpublished paper (1981), p. 12.

[8] John Dewey, "Religion and Our Schools," *The Hibbert Journal* (July 1908), p. 807.

[9] Ellwood P. Cubberly, *Changing Conceptions of Education* (Boston: Houghton Mifflin, 1909); quoted in David Tyack and Elisabeth Hansot, "Conflict and Consensus in American Public Education," *Daedalus* 110 (Summer 1981), p. 14.

[10] Robert M. Hutchins, *The Conflict in Education in a Democratic Society*, (New York: Harper and Brothers, 1953), pp. 67–72.

[11] John Childs, *Education and Morals* (New York: Appleton-Century Crofts, 1950), pp. 5–6.

[12] Cora DuBois, "The Dominant Value Profile of American Culture," *American Anthropologist* 57 (Dec. 1955), pp. 123–38; republished in Harold J. Carter, editor, *Intellectual Foundations of American Education* (New York: Pitman Publishing Co., 1965), pp. 342–47.

[13] Van Cleve Morris, "The Philosophical Premises Underlying Public Education," *Progressive Education* 34 (1957), pp. 69–74.

[14] Quoted in Jerome Kagan, "The Moral Function of the School," *Daedalus* 110 (Summer 1981), p. 154.

[15] Thomas Nagel, *Mortal Questions* (New York: Cambridge University Press, 1979), p. 25.

[16] Kagan, "The Moral Function of the School," p. 160.

[17] Talcott Parsons and Winston White, "The Link Between Character and Society," in Seymour Martin Lipset and Leo Lowenthal, editors, *Culture and Social Character: The Work of David Riesman Reviewed* (New York: The Free Press of Glencoe, 1961), p. 100.

[18] Michael Katz, *The Irony of Early School Reform* (Boston: Beacon Press, 1968), pp. 128–30, 213–18.

[19] Marcus Raskin, "Notes on Reconstructive Knowledge: Its Nature, Ethics and Teaching It," The Institute for Policy Studies, Nov. 18, 1972; from Martin Carnoy, *Education as Cultural Imperialism* (New York: David McKay Company, 1974), p. 365.

[20] Ivan Illich, *Deschooling Society* (New York: Harper & Row, 1970), pp. 1, 114.

[21] Carnoy, *Education as Cultural Imperialism*, p. 367.

[22] Gerald Grant, "The Character of Education and the Education of Character," *Daedalus* 110 (Summer 1981), p. 145.

[23] Robert Wood, "The Disassembling of American Education," *Daedalus* (Summer 1980), p. 99.

[24] Stephen R. Graubard, "Introduction," *Daedalus* (Summer 1980), pp. v–vi.

[25] Denis Doyle, "A Din of Inequity: Private Schools Reconsidered," *Teacher's College Record* 82 (Summer 1981). See also: James Carper, "The Christian Day School Movement," *The Educational Forum* (Winter 1983), pp. 135–49.

[26] Richard John Neuhaus, "Moral Leadership in Post-Secular America," *Imprimis* 11 (July 1982), p. 3.

10

Family Protection: The Imperative of the Future

Connaught Marshner

In regard to the family, one premise underlies all else: There is no alternative to the traditional family. Therefore, since the well-being of the family is indispensable to our social order, the other institutions of society, especially those influenced or controlled by government, must change or reverse a variety of policies which, in one way or another, deny the family a fair break, scatter its resources, or waste its energy.

Why is there no alternative to the traditional family? All around us, in articles, in sociological and psychological journals, in vocal lobby organizations, in manifestations of popular culture, are descriptions of experimentations with "alternative lifestyles" and their advocates. But these are fads. They will not last because there is no alternative social entity or inter-personal arrangement of the assumption, on a large scale, of the most elementary, rock-bottom job of the traditional family, namely, the care and nurture of children.

The traditional family in American society is the nuclear family—a conjugal pair and their children, characterized by certain values of privacy and domesticity. This has also come to be called the "bourgeois" family, often with a tone of contempt, but sometimes with appreciation.[1] It is a modification of the more extended family pattern of pre-modern Europe and which still exists in many parts of the world. The modification has been in two directions. First, the family household has shrunk from previous ages: Apprentices, servants, hangers-on have disappeared; uncles, aunts, cousins, grandparents now tend to live in other households, other cities. Hence the term "nuclear" family. Second, the family household has become heavily child centered, and concentrated on "private life" and domesticity. In earlier ages, before everybody reported to shop, factory, or office for gainful work, the work-place was not separated from the household.

The bourgeois family emerged in tandem with the modern tendency toward economic diversification and urbanization. The household's tendency toward a private, child-centered direction coincided with its idealization of the "home" as a haven of affection in a "heartless world."[2]

These two modifications should not be minimized or exaggerated: not minimized, because they produce a distinctly modern "ethos" of the family, with a unique value; not exaggerated, because these modifications do not represent a denial or destruction of human history and which is an indispensable feature of human nature. The bourgeois family did not invent a concern with the nurture and formation of children—it is a universal concern—but perhaps it did deepen it. Further, the "nuclearity" of the standard American family is not as strict as has been sometimes supposed. It is undeniable that the prototypical young family, living in the suburbs, mother home all day with the children and no close adult for her to interact with and with whom to share the burdens of day-to-day child tending, has some basis in fact. On the other hand, few young couples are so isolated that there is no family member within hailing distance, should the need arise. There have always been family farms and family businesses, in which the old-world, "extended" pattern has been reproduced and carried on in many respects.

The evidence is overwhelming that the traditional family is the only environment in which children will receive the care they need.

Arbitrary opinion does not determine what children need in order to have a reasonable chance at normal and healthy development. The obvious requirements of food, shelter and motor training can be realized in many environments, but four further conditions are necessary to raise a complete individual. Virtually all research has proved conclusively that for healthy emotional development children need a stable environment; stable relationships with caring loving adults, particularly a single, constant, loving mother-figure in the first four or five years; a fair amount of interaction with all adults; and regularity or predictability in the child's relations with all important adults.[3]

Fashionable "pop psychology" may choose to distort these findings: a spate of articles, for instance, in the heyday of the feminist movement, purported to prove that divorce had no harmful effects on children, and was, in fact, upon occasion beneficial. But after the wave of feminist dominance passed, articles in both professional and popular publications again returned to the more time-honored themes. A *Parade* magazine story in 1983 that contended that "staying together for the children's sake" was really a pretty good idea would not have appeared in 1979—the climate then was such that hard facts contrary to trendy "liberation" would not be heard. In certain types of publications, of course, only the rationalizations for alternative lifestyles would ever be heard.

There is an extensive body of research on children in impersonal institutions, such as hospitals, orphanages, public nurseries or day care centers. Not only does this research make clear that institutions cannot replace the family, it also demonstrates that children given adequate food, shelter, warmth and the best that science can offer—but not given simple, affectionate interaction with a constant caregiver—will fail to thrive. There is no getting around the fact that human infants have a strong, innate tendency and need to form highly individualized bonds with a very small number of adults, a characteristic Bowlby has called "monotrophy." A large and ever-changing staff of caregivers, no matter how well-meaning or how well-trained, simply cannot satisfy this innate human need in a child, despite the claims of social engineers who contend that an institution can remedy the failings of a deficient home environment through "early intervention."

Hospitalized children are beneficiaries of "early intervention"—from the child's point of view, the circumstances are not very different from what they are in a day care center. In such a circumstance, one psychologist observed, the child "will appear cheerful and adapt to his unusual situation and apparently be easy and unafraid of anyone. But his sociability is superficial; he appears no longer to care for anyone."[4] The hospitalization syndrome, as it is called, does not apply exclusively to children in hospitals. Professionally-run foundling homes produce the same effects. A study by Rene Spitz compared the development of children in a foundling home and in a prison with their mothers. Right after birth, the foundling home children were superior by all indications. But after the first two years of life, the children in jail with their mothers proved superior in such areas as walking, speech and toilet training.[5] The implication? A mother, even one not considered very good by other criteria, in a stressful environment is better for a young child than so-called "professional care" without the mother.

This is not to say institutions are terrible; it is to suggest that institutional care should not be preferred to mother care.

The counterculture of the 1960s produced a great spate of "communes" in America, a few of which were still surviving into the 1980s. Motivations for this diverse form of family life were various; the example of the Israeli kibbutz was frequently invoked. The kibbutzim have been extensively studied, but the intensely nationalistic and ideological environment surrounding them makes it difficult if not impossible to draw conclusions which would apply in the United States, where communes have always been on the fringes of respectability. Due to the high level of emotional involvement between adults and children in a kibbutz, kibbutz children seem generally to be emotionally stable and well-developed intellectually. What kind of personality does a kibbutz-raised child have? It is clear that personality and values of a kibbutz-raised child are conformist and collectivist. Children are very dependent on their peer-group, for instance, and they often find life outside the kibbutz intolerable.[6]

The accumulating evidence of child-rearing in American communes is not so positive. Instability in all the relationships significant to the child, and neglect and neurosis, along with all sorts of physical and emotional deprivations, are the dominant findings.[7] Personality is formed in infancy; after the first few years, values are formed to shape the personality. A broken personality may never be overcome. A healthy personality can be molded different ways. The children of the kibbutz have healthy personalities—but are conformist, collectivist adults the kind America needs? No.

To restate the premise: The standard, traditional form of the family is the only one in which children will receive the care they need to grow into stable, competent adults able to continue our society.

Western society, of which America's is a sub-group, has gone through an elaborate process of "modernization," about which much has been written. A large part of this process has been in the direction of replacing vague, family-type bonds of loyalty and duty with well-defined contractual arrangements to cover more and more areas of human existence. The father-figure of the king, for instance, has yielded to elected officials who wield power closely defined by constition or law, and based upon the "consent of the governed." Feudal or paternalistic patterns of labor and management have yielded to the free market of contract and salary. Even marriage has become more "consensual," as romantic attraction has replaced parental arrangement as the basis for entering into marriage.

For the past three centuries this thrust toward free consent and contract has fueled a thirst for "liberation." At the heart of each modern "liberation" movement has been the conviction that the individual must create his own ties, that he or she is under no just obligations other than those arrived at through freely bargaining before consenting. It is not surprising, therefore, that people caught up in the counterculture movements of recent decades should have assumed without question that this consensual model could be extended to every area of life, replacing the last vestiges of the family with a "participating democracy" of bed and board. But here the long-cresting wave of liberationism has broken against an unyielding rock; here at last an aspect of human society was encountered upon which the consensual paradigm could not be fastened. For it is of the very essence of the family that it contains, or is open to containing, non-contracting parties. Our children are tied to us without their consent. They confront us, not with a set of negotiable demands, but with their fixed, unyielding needs. Either we meet those needs responsibly, with stable marriages and homes, or we toss away the future of the human race itself. It is no coincidence that the ultimate liberationism of the Age of Aquarius turned to the ultimate sterility of zero population growth.

Public Policy Implications

Because the family is indispensable to the formation of human persons, it is indispensable to a stable social order. Important components of our social order simply cannot bear the burdens that will arise—indeed, are already arising—if the family fails to function well.

The family is strong when it has a function to perform. When a young adult knew that his father's blessing must come to his marriage or he would lose a valuable inheritance, he was more respectful of his father's views. Here, the family performed the function of transmitting wealth. During a time of devastation, if an individual knew that while alone he would perish, if he combined his efforts with those of his sisters, brothers and other kin they would all survive, he developed an emotional investment in a strong family. Here, the family was performing the function of ensuring survival. In the era before government-subsidized college education, when a youngster wanted desperately to go to college but had no means, if he knew that his older sister would contribute some of her wages, and his mother could get a job scrubbing floors, and his aunts would save their money for him, too, then his family was strong, and the sister, the mother and the aunts were all essential to its strength. These examples are rather simple instances. But at various times in history, conquerors have attempted to extinguish defeated races, e.g., Cromwell's persecution of the Irish. Not only were the Irish deprived of land and property and the means of livelihood, they were herded like sheep to the most impoverished and unproductive lands in the west of Ireland. But the race did not die. Why? Because Cromwell left families intact—he did not systematically separate mothers from children, husbands from wives. And the spirit of the Irish race remained intact, indeed, its character can be said to have become more pronounced. That was a more civilized age than ours in some respects, despite its inhumanity. In more modern times, when the communists were fighting for control of Greece after World War II, they were shrewder: In the villages they sought to dominate, they removed the children, taking them, ostensibly for safety, to camps and shelters far away.[8] They knew that, deprived of their children to protect, the villagers' spirit of defiance would be broken and they would submit to communist domination. (Fortunately for Greece, this policy was far from universally practiced and the nation maintained its independence.) The experience of the black slave in America tells the same story. With the coming of freedom, and no paternalistic masters to provide for its needs (not that all masters had been paternalistic), the black family suddenly had enormous functions to perform. Survival, education, cultural identity, security—all these and more were up to the family to provide. It was with the coming of the welfare state, when the family no longer had its functions, when those burdens were borne by the government, that the black family became weak and dysfunctional.

Sociologist Talcott Parsons convinced a whole generation of social scientists and policy makers that even though the modern family had lost most of its traditional functions, it would survive because it had acquired some new ones. The new function, Parsons maintained, was in the area of "affective self-realization." It used to be that the family was the primary educator—it has lost that function to the modern school. It used to be that the family was the primary caregiver to the sick and the elderly—it has lost that function to doctors, hospitals and nursing homes. It used to be that the family was a preeminent source of authority—but that, too, has been lost to outside experts of all kinds. Still, Parsons maintained, it doesn't matter that the family has become an anachronism: Spouses will look to each other for intensely satisfying forms of personal interaction.[9]

The relevance of Parsons' view is simple: If he is right, then the family is not indispensable to a stable social order. If he is right, family decay will have little impact on the other institutions of society. All will be well, if the family just holds together long enough to give initial care to neonates and toddlers. After that, the school and the other institutions of the welfare state can take over.

Parsons' view, however, can be attacked in several basic areas. The experience of the past 30 years with public schooling, with the welfare state, and with the foibles of a wide range of human-service experts and professionals, amply shows that the family is still a key actor in every one of the areas in which Parsons thought it had lost its function.

Consider the schools. The school does not of itself motivate children to learn. Various sociological theories about school-based motivations were eventually found false, even by the researchers who at first proclaimed them. Nobody now disputes that it is parents who motivate children to learn. Parents set the standards for achievement;

parents supervise homework, parents create a home atmosphere for learning. One consistent finding is the significance of parental involvement in effective schools.

In recent times, the schools have been expected to be agents of social change. From busing to providing hot lunches, the schools have been saddled by government with jobs extraneous to education. Teachers have become social workers as well as, or in some cases, instead of, educators. The curriculum has similarly been cluttered up with subjects formerly taught at home, from driver education to values education, from sex education to alcohol education. This overload has simply eroded the schools' capacity to teach academics. It is ironic that, while the academic base is eroding, more and more attention is focused on the school's teaching of moral values. Educators claim this privilege for themselves, implying that parents with their old-fashioned values cannot do an adequate job of preparing children to be flexible for the modern world. Polls periodically find that parents want schools to teach values, a point seized upon zealously by the values educators, even though the polls fail to distinguish between "traditional" values and the progressive or experimental variety commonly included in values curricula.

Public schools are functionally, and legally, unable to provide essential discipline. Even in "good" suburban neighborhoods, public schools are notorious for their lack of discipline—drugs, alcohol, larceny and assault are all commonplace. If teenagers are difficult for their parents to handle, they are impossible for modern public schools to handle. In all this confusion, the well-behaved students are the ones from homes that expect good behavior. The children with high standards of personal morality are the ones whose parents taught them those high standards—not the ones who had the values clarification programs. The obituary of the family as indispensable to a young person's education was pronounced too soon.

Health care is far from independent of the family. An enormous proportion of health care, from first aid given to children to the nursing of invalids to the consolation of the dying, still goes on in the home. As medical costs have escalated, private citizens have been reaching the limit of their capabilities to pay, both for the medical care and for the insurance to cover it. The federal government has also been reaching the limit of its capacity to extend Medicare and Medicaid benefits. If economic growth is to resume, the welfare state must be trimmed, and to the extent that it is trimmed, the role of the family as a health care provider cannot help but resurface. The validity of this point is not lost upon feminists who consider nursing one's sick or dying kin to be a demeaning role for women; realization of this inevitable trend fuels extreme feminists' defense of the failed policies of the liberal welfare state.

There is more to health care than pills and needles and machines. The growing trend of preventive health care and medical self-help promises to outlast the anti-establishmentarianism of some of its origins. Preventive health care can be accomplished by an individual, but once the individual creates a family unit by marrying and having children, preventive health care is a family function. What one eats is a key ingredient in this kind of thinking—yet how does one develop correct eating habits except by being fed properly as a child? The cultural revolution started by the La Leche League in the 1950s has had vast implications for health care. Not only has the demand for family-centered maternity care come from this and related movements, but the importance of mother and father in the years beyond breastfeeding has been rediscovered. "Breastfeeding as a political issue," the subject of a speech at a La Leche League Convention, discussed the political implications of natural mothering, and did not fail to note the obstacles placed in the path of mothering by modern society. Reforms in health care, thus, do not only draw upon the family as a resource more than had been anticipated; some have, indeed, a family-strengthening effect.

Besides the continuing relevance of the family in those functions Parsons thought it had lost, there is another vitally important function overlooked by him and by most others. This is the formation of character.

Character means more than the code of moral standards to which a person adheres. In its broader sense it includes the traits that enable a person to cope: self-confidence, inner resources, other-orientedness, inventiveness, self-discipline, to name a few. These are the traits that a good, stable family background will yield. They are the traits necessary to sustain a free society, which is a society of nonconformists. That the molding of such character is the historic service of the bourgeois family is the central contention of the outstanding book by Brigitte and Peter Berger, *The War Over the Family*. This is the vital respect in which the traditional family shows its superiority over even the best of its rivals, the Israeli kibbutzim. The American character, or more broadly, the character of Western civilization, must be passed on to subsequent generations if our country as we know it is to survive.

In proportion to the traditional family's failure to do its work successfully, other institutions of society will be swamped with burdens they cannot handle. Social workers will try to build character; government programs will attempt to motivate people to find and hold employment; police forces will try to preserve an order that means nothing to those who violate it because they do not understand it; psychiatrists will try to patch up souls that are bruised and wounded, in order to enable their owners to find something worth living for; prisons will try to instill discipline in people who never learned it as youngsters; the military will try to teach patriotism to recruits who do not know the meaning of loyalty or duty; and it will all be paid for by the federal government, whose Internal Revenue Service extracts greater and greater amounts from citizens not shrewd enough to find loopholes. Is not this the situation of the late 20th century? Is not this the situation which has justly earned the criticism of all points on the political spectrum for being a failure? Is not this, indeed, a system, a society, which will not long survive but will soon fall of its own weight, as the state assumes more and more power simply to keep all the leaks plugged?

This scenario is not inevitable. The failed liberal welfare state can be reversed. The fountainheads of leadership can be unblocked. A free, creative, conservative opportunity can be born and survive. The family is not only irreplaceable in its function of ensuring the emotional health of children, it is also indispensable in its other functions for the good of the nation.

Recommendations

Our free society cannot be separated from the traditional family. America needs strong families to perform their lifelong functions so that the government may be free to perform its functions. Given the unity of purpose, then, between the traditional family and a free nation, public policy ought to ensure that the family has maximum strength, energy, and resources. At the very least, public policy ought to follow the time-honored guideline of medical ethics: First, do no harm.

Political battles have been waged over the question of what government is doing to hurt families, and how policies should change. The first thing to establish, of course, is what constitutes the family. Some partisans in the debate define families from a functional perspective: A family is any group of persons who share living quarters and cooking facilities and have a sense of commitment to the future. When policy change is advocated with this type of "family" in mind, it generally has the effect of discriminating against traditional families, albeit perhaps not intentionally. For instance, for a long time income tax forms were arranged so as not to "penalize" single persons. Along with that, of course, came a penalty to married persons, which went unremedied for years. Proposals to, say, include live-in lovers as "family members" for purposes of insurance will have the effect of pushing up the cost of insurance for real families. The debate over the fairness of making the man who supports his wife and children subsidize the health care of the homosexual couple may be conducted at an intellectual level. But there is a lot of potential for social explosion in that same debate, if the fellow in the factory who has trouble buying new shoes for his children one day realizes that he's been paying for some homosexual's doctor bills. To bestow the honor of the name "family" on a variant lifestyle is to demean both the honor of the title and the honor of the real family. Interesting living arrangements are just that: interesting living arrangements. They are not families. Governmental recognition to that effect is an affront against the traditional family struggling for its own survival and working for that of the nation. The affront is more than symbolic. To continue in arduous work, one must perceive some compensation. Raising a family is arduous work, and those who engage in it ought to feel the appreciation of the nation, and its respect, for their effort. Beyond respect and protection from unjust burdens, the family must be aided in performing its basic function.

Because children do not spring full-grown from the head of Zeus, public policy must support parenthood, and that means public policy must reinforce responsibilities of parents toward their children, as well as, later on, the responsibilities of grown children toward their parents. Because the family is indispensable for producing emotional and cognitive maturity and adjustment of children, public policy must support motherhood—economically, socially, legally. Because the family is a primary provider of social services, public policy must protect the family's functions in that area, and not seek to replace them with institutional services.

Traditionally, there was another role for the family, one that has been much reduced in modern society. This is the transfer of inherited wealth to the next generation. Despite the rantings of socialists that such transmittal is immoral, and despite the taxation patterns of the states and federal government which have too often and too long acted as if it were immoral, this function is a very deep-seated emotion in the human heart. It is conventional to see the cause of this change in inheritance taxes and other legal developments, but there is a deeper perspective.

What has really changed this aspect of the family's work is not legislation but technological change. Change in technology means that there are fewer and fewer stable forms of tangible wealth to pass on to one's children. Real estate, precious metals, antiques—these are the last remaining forms of tangible wealth. Since not many families have them, what this means is that the family's job of handing on wealth has not disappeared but has become less visible, because wealth itself has become less visible. Rapid technological growth has produced a society in which the real wealth is know-how, and the greatest inheritance any child can receive is a good education. When a child goes through school without learning to read, it is not only that young person whose life has been blighted for the future; it is his parents' life as well, since his parents' hope of relying on his aid in old age has been reduced to naught. What is almost worse, one of the deepest impulses of the parent has been frustrated, and the parent's trust in one of the institutions of society is betrayed. It is not surprising that when the education system fails and fails again to educate children to a satisfactory level, that the community not only ceases to support the system, but turns indifferent or hostile toward it.

This has happened with the public school system in far too many places in the country. It is a doubly bitter situation. First the state convinces parents to yield what is naturally their function to its agents, promising that the schools could do a better job than the parents, a claim repeated regularly by professional educators. Then, when the job is clearly not being done successfully, the educators attempt to pin the blame on the parents—"you're not supporting the schools" is frequently offered as an excuse. And, ultimately, the schools deny their responsibility at all—lawsuits by parents of illiterate but diploma-holding high school graduates have regularly gone against the parents, confirming the school's lack of responsibility for its educational product.

Government—local, state, and federal—is responsible for public education in this nation. Each level, and all collectively, have failed in this absolutely crucial area. Whether in terms of excellence, in terms of acquisition of knowledge, in terms of preparation for life as worker—when the government takes over one of the natural functions of the family, and fails at it, government has a grave responsibility to make amends. Failures in education have been so consistent and so severe for the past 20 or more years, that it is incumbent upon government to actively compensate for the weaknesses of its public schools. Families must be given tools to remedy the situation before it is too late for their own children. These tools should include greater parental control of public school promotion and grading policies, curriculum content, and so on. The option of private education must be preserved, as an actual—not just hypothetical—choice. It is ultimately the responsibility of parents to provide for their children's education. Government cannot have it both ways: on the one hand saying, let us do the job, on the other hand saying, if we do a poor job, it's your fault.

The area of values formation, moral education, and the other things which make up the emotional adjustment of children must not be usurped from parents. Toward that end, it is the obligation of government to support parental standards. While a case may be made for why pornography at every newsstand and on every television set is an exercise of freedom, it is more difficult to justify that position when parents specifically do not want their children exposed to such materials. For the pornography to remain legally available is for government to say to parents: Your efforts to form the moral character of your child are not important, are not deserving of support. If a parent has a moral objection to something being taught in the public school, this conflict becomes more personal, with the educators casting themselves as elitists who know better than parents what is good for children. The federal government is already in a similar untenable situation with regard to teenage sexuality. The federal government in effect says to teenagers: "Come get your contraceptives from us, we won't tell your parents." What kind of support is this for parents who are trying to train their children in responsibility, self-control, deferral of gratification—all the virtues necessary for the continuation of our society as we know it? Oh, a case may be made, and routinely is by Planned Parenthood, which receives most of the federal money to carry out this program, that without these services available, more teenagers would become pregnant. But how many children who otherwise might maintain the standards taught them by their parents succumb to the too-easy temptation of deceiving their parents, abetted by the federal government?

Similarly, the government must not support "alternative lifestyles," either with funding or with special protection. To loudly broadcast the message that "gay is good and Washington says so" is to take a position fundamentally hostile to the family's nature and mission, and fundamentally inconsistent with the continuation of a stable order. Now is not the time to explain the fallacies of the homosexual ideology, and why it is incompatible with a stable society. That job has been done masterfully elsewhere.[10] Suffice it to say that a lifestyle that depends upon exploitation, even of children, for sexual gratification, that encourages temporary, even impersonal, contacts in lieu of meaningful relationships (though such are not unknown, they are the great rarity), that militates against permanence and commitment, that thrives in an atmosphere of perversion and violence, that is by nature and definition incompatible with the procreation and continuance of life itself, is not the kind of lifestyle which is going to foster the survival of Western civilization. It has been documented that federal aid directly and indirectly goes to organizations dedicated to the promulgation of the homosexual lifestyle. The homosexual movement constantly agitates for more legal recognition, for special legal protection of its lifestyle as a "minority" entitled to civil rights protection. Numerically, it is a minority indeed. However, that term is a politically laden word, and homosexuals are not a "minority" in the sense that blacks or Jews, or other groups defined by racial or religious characteristics are minorities.

The most important area in which public policy needs to accommodate to the needs of family, however, is in the area of its economic survival.

Public policy must support motherhood. This means that mothers must receive financial protection. Possibly the greatest suffering occurs in the area of non-payment of child support, when divorced or separated fathers neglect their responsibility to provide for the support of their minor children with hardly any penalty attached. No matter how bitter the divorce may have been, the father must not be allowed to punish his children by subsequent non-support. What role the federal government may have to play in correcting the situation remains to be seen. It is unfortunate that federal involvement is necessary at all, but other levels of government seem to have failed, for whatever reasons.

Of course, there would not be so many cases of non-payment of child support if there were not so many divorces. Divorce has become a sacred cow of the human services establishment, which is quick to recommend it as a panacea to most interpersonal problems. It has also become a gold mine for lawyers. The right to divorce is probably more jealously guarded than the right to life itself. For generations, the arbitrators of moral standards, the churches, have taken a softer and softer stand on it, until, today, hardly any moral stigma is attached to it. Meanwhile, pop psychologists have gotten into the act, with books about "creative divorce" and articles assuring divorced parents that divorce, far from being harmful to children, might actually be beneficial. To the women's liberation movement, divorce is an ideological principle—as if its absence is the personification of all repression. How a drastic decline in standard of living, coercion into a workforce unresponsive to the needs of one's children, financial abandonment by the father of one's children, and other sundry consequences can be construed to be liberating may be hard to fathom, but such is the view.

I am not advocating an end to divorce. I am suggesting that divorce be made more difficult to obtain. I am also suggesting that its corollary, marriage, also be made harder to obtain. If it were not so easy to marry it would not be so easy to divorce. This proposal is one which can be attacked from many angles: Libertarians feel it is none of the state's business who does what anyway. I answer, that is not so. If the state is going to ultimately be called upon to maintain the court system to handle the failures, collect child-support payments, provide for day-care arrangements, offer mental health services for the casualties of divorce—then, indeed, the state can be justly permitted to take reasonable measures to ensure a reasonable fitness for that station in life before it is entered into. Traditional value conservatives may object because they feel uncomfortable with the state placing obstacles in the way of what is primarily a religious function. I certainly agree that marriage is a sacred right of life, but not everyone sees it that way, and those who do not are the ones most likely to get divorced. Laws limiting access to marriage would be designed to restrain not the God-fearing Christian, but the person who lacks the sense of the sacred permanence that Christian marriage means. The right to marry is certainly a natural right, one that is inalienable, but that does not mean that the state may not place conditions on it when the right has been manifestly abused. The right to marry freely *has* been abused, and just like any other abused right, in its abuse are the seeds for its control. If marriage were generally undertaken seriously, if marriages were generally permanent, and society were not called upon to bail out the casualties in one way or another, then the government would not need to insert itself into the whole procedure. But when 53 out of 100 marriages end in divorce, clearly the privilege of marrying at will is being abused.

Some will claim that making marriage harder to obtain will only lead to an increase in unsanctioned liaisons. To this, I respond that marriages based on lust do not, as a rule, prove to be permanent unions anyway. Furthermore, the increase in unsanctioned liaisons is not among people who could not get married if they were so inclined. The cultural trends, the self-indulgence without willingness to accept responsibility—these are reasons for the increase in what the census bureau so charmingly calls POSSLQs—Persons of Opposite Sex Sharing Living Quarters. For a time, there were strong economic incentives to remain single, but those have largely been eliminated now.

There remain, however, strong incentives for married couples to remain childless. These must be addressed. In 1950, the dependent exemption on the personal income tax form was $600, an amount that reduced a family's tax base by 24 percent. In 1980, however, the dependent exemption of $1,000 reduced the base only by 8 percent.[11] Is a child born in 1980 worth only one-third of his father, born in 1950? Hardly. Indeed, given the scarcity of babies being born, a case could be made that a baby born today is worth more than a baby born during the boom years. The point is, it costs money to raise a child. Having a child is in and of itself a sacrifice, because of the myriad ways in which it changes life for a couple—from the shift in the circle of friends to the shift in priorities on spending money—life is never as simple, never as much "fun" as when one is childless. Yet children are not only the fulfilling of our nature's deepest personal urges, they are a positive social good.

When a child is born, a family's disposable income drops. That is a considerable sacrifice on top of others already being made: For instance, the typical family in California now pays out over a quarter of its income in total taxes.[12] The battle with inflation is a constant struggle: In 1979 average real wages were lower than in the late 1960s.[13] While that may change from year to year, there remains the disturbing awareness, thanks to a steadily escalating permanent national debt and irregular monetary policies, that it could recur at almost any time. The pressure for the security of two incomes is enormous. Yet, the child, as has been demonstrated, needs the constant, loving presence of an adult, preferably the mother, for the sake of continuity. If the federal government is not going to relieve a family with children of some of its tax burdens, how can families be expected to meet the needs of their children? If the nation's fiscal and monetary policies are not more responsible, how can citizens be expected to form solid families and to maintain them in the face of financial uncertainty? If a father's wage is not adequate to support his wife and children, what is he to do?

All too frequently, the welfare system steps in to provide the wrong kind of incentives for a solution to this situation. A woman alone with children is eligible for numerous different government aid programs. The same woman and children, with a husband, receives scarcely any. While this situation perhaps does not lend itself to the charge that it "destroys families," it is hard to dispute that it acts as a disincentive to form a family in the first place. The high percentage of never-married mothers among low-skilled socioeconomic population groups bears this out. The most damaging evidence of the effect on the family of generous welfare programs is unvarnished statistics from the Bureau of the Census. In 1960, some 70 percent of black children lived with both parents, as did some 92 percent of white children. Then, a few years later came the Great Society, and the geometric increase in government aid programs designed to "help" the underprivileged. By 1978, only 42 percent of black children lived with both parents, while only 85 percent of white children did.[14] Granted, other trends of social decay were occuring simultaneously— but not enough to destroy half of all black families. How has it helped black children to deprive half of them of their fathers? What economic benefit will come from that? What social or emotional improvement will their lives experience?

What is public policy to do? Remedying the situation must become a national priority. Some ideas have already been advanced; others must be welcomed; all must be studied; some must be acted upon. For instance, the child allowance could be increased. Alternatively, a system of family allowances could be introduced, bringing the United States into the company of almost every other industrialized nation. If family allowances replaced the child exemption, the costs to the government need not be increased, though there is the danger that down the road they will be. There is a case to be made for such a policy; Piccione has cogently argued the affirmative.

There is much that can be done to amend the tax codes to relieve burdens on parents. There is also much that can be done to reinforce the responsibility of grown children for their parents. Measures such as the "parental IRA" deserve consideration. This is a tax-free savings plan into which taxpayers could put some portion of their income, not for their own later use, but for the use of their parents when the latter reach a certain age. When Social Security is less and less a security, it is appropriate that the federal government provide some other measures for people to enable them to find elsewhere the reassurance the government formerly encouraged citizens to expect from it. When wealthy children refuse to pay for their parents' needs, forcing their parents into the public recipient rolls, it is no more inappropriate for the children to be required to support their dependent parents than it is for parents to be required to support their dependent children. Trends in this direction will bring shouts of outrage and pain from exponents of the "me first" school of selfishness—but selfishness is no foundation upon which to build a social order.

The tax code includes credits for child care expenses paid to others so that a mother may hold gainful employment. Taxpaying mothers find this a great comfort. But is it just? What about the non-employed mothers, the ones who work 24 hours a day in their homes, raising their own children and foregoing the additional comforts that employment might bring? They have no such tax credit to claim: Are they not, then, subsidizing the mothers who work? And is that just? Might not the tax code seek to add a fairness credit for mothers who spend full-time rearing children surviving on one income to do so?

Many of the human services in our country are provided by volunteers, who give hours of their days to worthy causes—from assisting in hospitals or schools to running church and social service programs to providing such social goods as scouting. Without abundance of volunteers, many of the mediating structures that make life so tolerable would be in even worse condition than they already are. Through tax exemptions, government encourages everything from abortion clinics to homosexual research, and some worthy causes as well. Why not encourage volunteerism? Why not give a personal income tax exemption for volunteerism?

The idea is frequently advanced that this nation needs an explicit family policy. The country needs to go on record supporting family life, the argument goes, and to lay down guidelines for the manner in which it is to be supported. I do not agree. Having an explicit family policy is rather like having an explicit population policy. Putting the government on record on any such private matter as that is only inviting future problems. First of all, there is the obvious political hurdle of formulating language that would be able to pass Congress. Anything that would pass a Congress so polarized on social issues as those of the past decade would be meaningless—the empty rhetoric of politicians on the campaign trail is bad enough; to have such rhetoric as part of official government policy would be more offensive. But it would be worse than that. It would be a document for the future to fight over. We cannot now foresee what pressures might emerge on families 20 or 50 years down the road. It would be impossible to write a document now that would allow for technological developments of the future—and then, when the document failed to speak to the needs of the future, of what use would it be? In the meantime, if something were of political necessity or oversight omitted from the "statement of family policy" it would be construed as a meaningful omission, and regardless of its merits, argued over. If, say, right to life were not included in a statement of family policy, pro-abortionists would attempt to read into that the intent of Congress that the right to life was not meant to be protected—something the nation is not ready to conclude.

But beyond these political and interpretive problems is a bigger one: Is it the business of the federal government to prescribe general guidelines for family life? No. It is sufficient for the government to recognize that stable family life is indispensable to stable national life and to foster and encourage family stability. The national government has no business prescribing what kind of family life people ought to have, or what form their families ought to take, or how they ought to rear their children. Protection against threats is government involvement enough.

Furthermore, there is another principle to be considered: the principle of subsidiarity. Put simply, the principle of subsidiarity states that the level of government closest to any given problem ought to deal with the problem. Thus, since public schools are locally funded and supervised, local government ought to first handle problems with the public schools. Since families live in communities, community government ought to first address the problems families face. Many, if not most, problems faced by families can be ameliorated at the local level: The pornography question, for instance, can often be resolved by a local zoning change or other local regulation. The child support problem, on the other hand, has moved up the ladder of subsidiarity. Local communities have been unable to compel child-support payments because the absconding father will simply relocate; for the same reason state enforcement has been unsuccessful. Some charge that at these levels there has been no serious intention to compel payment. Whatever the reason, since the lower levels have failed to solve the problem, the federal government is being forced into the arena. It would be far better to have solutions and enforcement at local levels, but some remedy is preferable to none. State tax policies could be changed to accommodate family needs. But federal tax policies, obviously, can be addressed only by the federal government.

It is a time-honored American belief that individuals know better than anybody else what is good for them and in a stable society will make the right decisions for themselves. This belief is nowhere more threatened than with regard to families. The explosion of "helping service professions," in tandem with government policies to prescribe conditions in return for provision of services, has been going on for the entire century, and the toll has been gradual but definite. Americans are too willing to cede their own judgment to opinions and decisions made by somebody else. That frame of mind must be reversed; a sense of dependence upon professionals, upon government, upon other experts, will not fit America to face the future. Parents must regain the confidence of their ancestors with regard to raising their children. Parents do know what is best for their children—nosy social workers notwithstanding. The family has no organized, sophisticated lobby in Washington. Nobody, except an occasional Senator, moved by a noble conscience, takes up the cause of the family in Congress. Parenthood in the current age almost implies political consciousness, therefore—nobody is going to defend the family, so the family must undertake its own defense. Perhaps this will change, but if it does, many other things in the political scenery will change as well.

Those things must occur before the passage of much more time if the roots of a stable social order are not going to wither. If the future of America as we have known it is to be secure, the family is the new imperative of the future.

NOTES

[1] Brigitte and Peter Berger, *The War Over the Family* (New York: Anchor Press, 1983), pp. 107–108.

[2] Christopher Lasch, *Haven in a Heartless World* (New York: Basic Books, 1977).

[3] Some of the most valuable references include John Bowlby, *Attachment*

and Loss in three volumes (New York: Basic Books, 1969–1980), Selma Fraiberg, *Every Child's Birthright* (New York: Basic Books, 1977), and Jerome Kagan, "The Psychological Requirements for Human Development" in *Raising Children in Modern America*, ed. Nathan B. Talbot (Boston: Little, Brown & Co., 1976).

[4] Bowlby, *op. cit.*, vol. II, p. 28.

[5] R. A. Spitz, "Hospitalization: An Inquiry into the Genesis of Psychiatric Conditions in Early Childhood" in *Psychoanalytic Study of the Child* (1945) pp. 57–74.

[6] Sources in kibbutz studies include Bruno Bettelheim, *Children of the Dream* (New York: Macmillan Publishing Co., 1969) and Melford E. Spiro, *Kibbutz* (New York: Schocken Books, 1970).

[7] The sorry record can be found in the following: Rosabeth M. Kanter, *Commitment and Community: Communes and Utopias in Sociological Perspective* (Cambridge, Mass.: Harvard University Press, 1972) and John Rothchild and Susan Berns Wolf, *The Children of the Counter Culture* (Garden City, N.Y.: Doubleday & Co., Inc., 1976).

[8] A very moving account of how one family's life was disrupted by this strategy of war is *Eleni* by Nicholas Gage (New York: Random House, 1983).

[9] Talcott Parsons, Robert Bales, et. al., *Family, Socialization and Interaction Process* (Glencoe, Ill.: The Free Press, 1955).

[10] *See* Enrique T. Rueda, *The Homosexual Network* (Old Greenwich, Conn.: Devin-Adair, Publishers, 1982).

[11] Joseph Piccione, "Help for Families on the Front Lines: The Theory and Practice of Family Allowances" (Washington, D.C.: The Free Congress Research and Education Foundation), p. 4.

[12] Jacqueline R. Kasun, "National Economic Policy and the Family." Speech at American Family Forum, June 30, 1980.

[13] *Ibid.*

[14] *Social Indicators III: Selected data on social conditions and trends in the United States*, publication of the Federal Statistical System, Vincent P. Barbera, Director, Bureau of the Census. (December 1980), p. 25, chapter 1/14: "Children Under 18 Years Old in Families, by Presence of Parents and Race of Children: 1960, 1970, and 1978."

11

Making Ends Meet: A Strategy for American Health Care Reform

Ronald F. Docksai

Not long ago, having just completed his medical examination of a woman, a doctor approached his patient to discuss his findings. The doctor said, "Mrs. Harris, I have some good news for you. It is *Mrs.* Harris, isn't it?" The patient replied, "No, it's *Miss* Harris," to which the doctor promptly replied, "Miss Harris, I have some bad news for you."

Call it perspective. Is the proverbial glass half empty or half full? Is the increasing cost of American health care principally the fault of the patient, the medical provider, the insurance company or the government? Are these mounting costs good news for care givers while bad news for consumers, or are they both good news and bad news for everyone? To accept the correct answer to all of these questions as "yes" is to begin comprehending the very difficult public policy dilemmas now confronting anyone trying to solve the Rubik's Cube we call the American health care system.

The Problem

In 1965, total U.S. health care expenditures were approximately $39 billion, representing close to 6 percent of the Gross National Product (GNP). Last year, these figures had increased to roughly $321 billion, and the percentage of GNP for health expenditures was at 10.5 percent.[1] Barring any drastic alteration in U.S. health care reimbursement policy such as that to be outlined later in this chapter, the Department of Health and Human Services estimates that by 1990 total health care expenditures will exceed $750 billion, and this will account for at least 12 to 13 percent of our GNP. While the standard rate of inflation for the total American economy is now somewhere between 3 and 4 percent, and is by anyone's count good news and a significant drop since the double digit inflation days prior to 1980, the current rate of hospital costs' inflation has *risen* from roughly 12 to over 14 percent for fiscal year 1984. From March 1982 to March 1983, the consumer price index increased 3.6 percent for the U.S. economy as a whole, while the CPI for medical care increased by 10.6 percent.

This is why double digit inflation continues to plague the budgets of Medicare and Medicaid, each of which grow in geometric proportion yearly as parts of the budget of the Department of Health and Human Services. Federal and state government budgets must devote more outlays to health care, while health benefits consume ever larger shares of private employee compensation and private insurance premiums increase from 6 to 21 percent a year.

The public image fostered by partisan Democrats and the more fashionable media depicts the status of public health funding under the Reagan Administration as reflecting the dark side of a Dickens novel. We are led to believe that much of the recent increase in private and state/local public health care spending is a function of, and in inverse proportion to, big federal health care spending cuts. This is perfectly wrong. In fact, the federal health and human services budget has been growing at 2 to 4 percent higher levels since Ronald Reagan became President than during the most generous years of the Carter Administration. Non-defense expenditures rose 9 percent in 1982, including 11 percent increases in health and human services and a 12 percent increase in Social Security.[2] Washington these days is spending 240 percent more on human services than did the federal government during the Kennedy Administration, 1960–1963. Consider this a long-winded way of saying that runaway health cost inflation cannot be blamed on federal niggardliness. Health and human services remains the principal "growth industry" item in the federal budget, as it is in private, state and local aggregate spending plans.

This having been said, it is reasonable to then question whether or not this higher growth rate of federal health care spending is such a bad thing. Doesn't the high level of American health expenditures testify to the comparably high level of compassion of the American people, or to the technological superiority of U.S. health care providers and scientists? Is our mounting U.S. health care spending level largely a function of the improved access to medical care for our poor and our elderly?

To these questions, Simon says no. The discernible consensus among economists and health planners holds that the superior quality and accessibility of American health care, still the best of any industrialized country in the world, is that U.S. health care excels in spite of the inefficiencies popularly portrayed as a wild frontier of free market economics, in reality rivals American agriculture as the most regulated and centrally (i.e., federally) directed part of the U.S. economic system. Ironically, it has been during Republican, more than Democratic, administrations that U.S. health care has been increasingly centralized. During the administration of President Gerald Ford, in particular, the federal Health Planning Act was shepherded through Congress and signed into law, mandating a federal regulatory health planning apparatus which remains administratively cumbersome and systematically injurious to competition among health care providers.

"Health planning" not only names a federal program, but also a state of mind. It is the shared belief among American liberals that by limiting the supply of health care, we can limit the demand. We are told to do this by putting price controls or instituting new ceilings on medical services, thus forcing providers to offer these medical services less expensively. What health planning has done is to reduce these services, inadvertently raising their respective price in many medical specialties as these reduced quantities of health providers fall subject to the inevitable and invisible hand of the marketplace. And because adequate health care is not being provided at a lower cost, the more budget-minded members of Congress naturally respond by trying to restrict eligibility while reducing the level of benefits per individual patient. This is how the two previous generations of PT-109 liberals and the Chase Manhattan Bank variety of "conservatives" have failed in their sincere but woolly minded attempts to solve the prevailing conflict between ongoing social needs and the inelastic capacity of the federal government to address them.

What has been (and still is) happening in American health care over the past several decades is an increase in the spending growth and the inefficiencies in our system because of the ever-widening gap between the provision of medical services versus the out-of-pocket payment for them. Marketplace principles *alone* will not solve this problem, given the unique way we as consumers behave in the marketplace of medicine. That is, in most marketplaces, such as those we might haunt to buy a suit, an automobile, an insurance policy or a pizza, we as consumers limit how much we buy to what we feel is necessary, based mostly on how much something will cost. In turn, the haberdasher, the salesman, the insurer or the pizzamaker will resist the temptation to charge us the highest price possible, to the extent that they and we are sensitive to the competition over who successfully solicits our purchasing dollar. But this is not how we normally behave in the medical marketplace. The rational consumer is less than fully discriminating when ill or injured. When choosing a doctor or medical practitioners, it is reputation, familiarity or geographic proximity rather than how much a doctor charges that determines whom we seek for medical assistance. Fairly accurate is the in-house surgeon's joke that the definition of a "fair price" for a medical service is one-half of that which a patient was willing to pay *before* the tumor was removed. Despite all the bad press doctors, nurses and health professionals seem to generate during these iconoclastic times, it is still the physician rather than the patient who makes the decision whether or not we should be hospitalized, what services we will need and how long we should stay. And because the majority of Americans today have some form of hospital insurance, the system of "third party payment" fully anesthetizes us from sensitivity over the price of the care we receive.

In fact, considering how few incentives for cost-consciousness are built into the present health care system, it is surprising that hospital cost inflation has not grown more rapidly. To the extent that we might be at all economical when shopping for health care, the present third party payment system, which *de facto* redistributes the cost of health care to everyone, fosters the belief that it is someone else paying for the bulk of the care we receive. And that is the rub. The villain is not the provider, the insurer, the patient or the government by and of itself. It is all of the above, because the present system insulates both the merchant and the buyer of health care.

The Solution

If there were one quick fix to solve the problems thus far described, national politicians would have stood up for it long ago. As it is, Congress would rather stay seated. The track record of congressional action is unimpressive. It contrasts vividly with the formidable and ever expanding library of data from House and Senate hearings on the subject of controlling health care costs. Under Ronald Reagan's Secretaries of Health and Human Services, first Richard Schweiker and later Margaret Heckler, the administration introduced "health care competition" legislative proposals which Congress relegated to inactive status. Senators Hatch, Dole, Hawkins and Durenberger made legislative yardage for the administration within their respective committees and subcommittees. However, there is so far no more sense of urgency among their Senate and House colleagues than among Americans in general. Yes, many citizens complain about health care cost inflation as reflected in their monthly medical premium statements or, as transparently seen when their camouflage is lifted, in our individual tax rates. These gripes, however, remain at the level of complaining about the weather or long ticket lines at ball games. No one expects the situation to get much better anytime soon, and no one will be held *particularly* accountable as it continues to worsen.

This powerful and prevailing inertia in the general public's consciousness concerning health care cost inflation is the key symptom of the inflationary disease in question. There is an understandable temptation for politicians to select "whipping groups," i.e., special interests singled out for public blame because they are the most politically expendable from the politician's viewpoint. So, Democrats might blame health cost inflation on hospitals and doctors. Republicans might attack big government in general, since federal subsidization over the years did at least partly contribute to the imbalanced health costs' supply and demand. Either way, it is less than half the story. Not providers or the public sector alone, but consumers, labor unions, insurance companies and employers—all of us who are insulated by the third party payment system fuel the fires of this system's inflation.

A systematic political effort to upset this status quo any time soon would require a joint congressional and executive branch policy venture not now politically foreseeable. Whatever we might think of its end product, Congress was able to fashion a bipartisan compromise which eased the Social Security fund's fiscal solvency situation, at least for the short term. If a similar effort is launched to systematically contain health care costs through federal action, it will only be after public awareness is raised to a higher consciousness level. The public can generally accept the "price" of paying for health care reform only after concluding that any other alternative is economically unacceptable. Such a "reform movement" should include these key legislative and administrative objectives:

A) Whether in the form of a tax cap (i.e., ceiling) on the amount of employees' health insurance an employer may write off or in some way manipulate the federal tax code to make the costs of health insurance more visible to employer and employee alike, Congress will have to institutionalize policies forcing all of us to accept more responsibility for the health insurance we purchase. Among federal employees, a voucher program that gives insurance purchasers a choice in selecting the insurance they ultimately buy will serve as the first real demonstration of a more competitive health model. The United States Office of Personnel Management (OPM), charged with the mission of overseeing the U.S. civil service and the Federal Employees' Health Benefits Program (FEHB), is finalizing the draft of such a "health voucher" proposal. It must still run the gantlet of full executive-level approval and the more perilous legislative course to be negotiated in

Congress. The federal government *already* pays 50 to 75 percent of its employees' health insurance premiums. We are talking about 10 million people, a third of whom are retirees.

Under the OPM voucher system as it has been proposed, all federal workers would be given a voucher annually, a voucher being a promissory cash note. The voucher would be calculated to cover a standard health basic benefits plan. Workers who wish service coverage to include additional items such as dental care, respiratory or occupational therapy, etc., would pay the difference in higher premiums out of their own pockets. Thus emerges the built-in incentive for workers to shop around; i.e., *buying health insurance* operates according to the conventional laws of supply and demand, unlike most other areas of health care. Also, insurance companies have an incentive to put together more economical plans since they are now competing for workers' out-of-pocket dollars. History reveals that all of us become more discriminating shoppers when the currency with which we traffic in the marketplace is our own hard-earned wages, rather than third party payments.

Those who oppose the voucher plan do so mainly because they recognize that is it also a Trojan Horse for removing controls from the health care industry. It takes the federal regulatory training wheels off the slow and expensively running cycle we call the current U.S. health care system. Ironically, the principal squeamishness over reform is sounded by those same private insurance health care providers who have grown too comfortable as the administrative vassals of the federal government. The free marketplace is uncertain and dynamic. For every insurance company and enterprising health care provider desiring more competition within the present U.S. health care system, there is also within our overly regulated environment the marginally satisfied, middle-aged company that has grown secure under the fetters of a health care system more Yugoslavian than American. The voucher proposal, like any new idea, is definitely a threat to their comfortable existence.

B) A corollary to the voucher concept is the urgent need to "cap" federal subsidization of employer-based health insurance plans. For example, as Harvard's business administration expert, Dr. Regina Herzlinger, recently observed, "Since the Depression, employer-provided insurance against virtually all health care expenses has become an unwritten national policy. Most programs are generous, requiring no employee contributions for the cost of the insurance and providing extensive benefits, frequently covering up to $500,000 of medical expenses. In many programs, employees pay only 10% to 20% for their health expenses [the co-insurance rate] after their payment for the first $150 of these expenses [the deductible amount]."[3] Dr. Herzlinger surveys the actuarial landscape of health care insurance, making a thoughtful case for "catastrophic only" insurance, i.e., insurance that protects against financially catastrophic medical events, but not for items under, e.g., the $1,000 limit. "To insurance equity, eligibility would be scaled to income. The financial magnitude of the catastrophic event for a person earning $100,000 is probably quite different."[4] Under the Herzlinger plan, consumers would be motivated to shop for insurance health care items as we do for other consumption items.

Desirable or not, it is at least unlikely that the U.S. insurance plan landscape will ever be dominated by "catastrophic only" kinds of plans. However, *limiting* federal tax subsidization of the insurance industry is necessary to spur greater efficiency and reduce overall costs in providing care.

C) The great demographic explosion destined to affect all of us is the growing geometric increase in the number of Americans 65 years and older. By the turn of the century, the proportion of elderly as defined against our total population will have grown 35 to 40 percent.

As superior medical technology and circumstances allow more of us to live longer, the increased life expectancy brings with it increased need for both acute and chronic forms of health care for the elderly. With the Medicare and Medicaid trust funds already seriously in the red, the United States does not now have the resources to construct and maintain the number of nursing homes needed to house and care for the increasing number of senior citizens to be institutionalized. Aside from the dollar costs, there are the social costs. Increasing numbers of elderly citizens don't want to live in nursing homes, no matter how newly constructed or richly maintained. Citizens do not lose their dignity, self-respect or desire for personal independence after their 65th birthdays. To the extent that they are physically able and emotionally capable of doing so, nearly every senior citizen prefers to remain among family and friends. They usually prefer living alone in their own houses or apartments than being semi-privately bunked in impersonal institutions with all their benevolent but nonetheless routinely administered restraints and curfews. For many Americans, the contemplation of being sent to a nursing home is a prelude to death.

Both humane and economical purposes are well-served by rewriting the present Medicare and Medicaid laws to expand their provisions for home health care services for the elderly and disabled. The resulting competition between nursing homes and alternatives to institutionalization would in itself be good for the U.S. health care system in general. Because most studies on the subject conclude that home health care services per unit cost are only one-quarter to one-half as expensive as an equivalent form of nursing care in an institution, the only real cost question is how to limit "utilization costs." That is, how do we limit eligibility under an expanded home health care services program so that it does not revert to an automatic entitlement grant for every elderly citizen or relative desiring to sign up for it.

Actually, these questions have already been effectively answered by Senator Orrin Hatch (R-Utah), who as chairman of the Senate Committee on Labor and Human Resources, has introduced legislation to launch a cost-effective form of home health care.[6] While the Congressional Budget Office (CBO), the General Accounting Office (GAO) and other numbers' watchers differ on the amount, the savings over the long-term promise to offset the increasing burdens on the Medicare trust fund.

More than any other health care proposal currently being discussed anywhere in government, home health care effectively diverts the otherwise certain collision, which we face before the end of the present decade, between the increasing need for human services and the increasing costs and limited resources available to provide them.

As legislatively defined by Hatch, the home health care proposal is a clever means of effectively reprivatizing a large part of the health care system. Private and non-profit home health care agencies, rather than the federal government or some other public sector satellite, would substantially fund and entirely administer home health care.

D) In its health and human services budget the federal government must place proportionately greater emphasis on health promotion and disease prevention.

This fiscal year, the Department of Health and Human Services will spend over $55 billion on health care and medical services, i.e., for "after the fact" health care. Institutional bias and the ever-present difficulty of the public sector to incorporate new ideas are the principal culprits in government's failure to use the new information discovered by health leaders like heart specialist Dr. Michael DeBakey, HHS Assistant Secretary Dr. Edward Brandt, and others. By redirecting HHS and NIH support for epidemiology, biostatistics and behavioral medicine, the public sector's research functions would take advantage of new American technologies in preventing diseases and ailments before they become a public health epidemic. Economists and health planners in and out of government all agree that preventing disease is eminently less expensive and more efficient than caring for ailments after they arise.

In General

The foregoing elements of a solution to our immediate U.S. health care containment problems are only "interim." They do not include the essential and recently implemented regulatory proposals for prospective payment (i.e., "diagnosis related groups," DRGs) or the several other elements of a competitive health care system model already in their embryonic stage of implementation. The common denominator in all of these parts of a systematic solution to health care's rising costs is the recognition that to the extent that federal policies of years past have created this unprecedented cost inflation the arm of the federal government must be involved in its solution.

Such a solution, however, must use the regulatory arm of the federal government to deregulate major portions of America's health care system. Other alternatives, such as a Ted Kennedy-like national health insurance system of sperm-to-worm coverage or the existing, over-regulated and increasingly costly status quo, are unacceptable. Unless we are willing to further compromise the quality of American health care, policymakers and those who influence them must gear our economy and community for a more competitive health care system.

NOTES

[1] Statistics quoted from and explained in testimony of Joseph F. Boyle, M.D., representing the American Medical Association before the U.S. Senate Committee on Labor and Human Resources hearing in health care cost containment, May 19, 1983.

[2] "Human Services Programs," Heritage Foundation, Backgrounder, No. 242, January 26, 1983.

[3] "Limit Employees' Health Plans to Big Bills," the *Wall Street Journal* (June 6, 1983).

[4] *Op. cit.*

[5] Letter by Dr. Donald J. Devine, director, U.S. Office of Personnel Management, outlining OPM's voucher proposal, May 10, 1983. (*See* Congressional Record index.)

[6] Extension of remarks by Senator Orrin G. Hatch for introduction of home health care legislation, June 23, 1983. (*See* Congressional Record index.)

12

Zwap, Zing, Broing, or Computers Are Not Just Toys

John C. Grunden

In the family room of house "A" is a strange and alien sound—zwap, zwap . . . zing . . . broing, broing—above the muted sound of an exasperated mother yelling for quiet and a return to the good old days of cartoons. Across the street in house "B," an eleven-year-old boy takes time to "de-bug" a program for a four-week family backpacking trip into the wilds of upper Oregon. Mom is having trouble interpreting the "essentials" portion of the print-out and disagrees with the basic data. Long before Dad gets home from work, the problem is solved; the family begins their packing amid busy "chit-chat" about having the software left in their home computer control the lights and the heating/air-conditioning system in their absence.

Just what is this machine that has invaded homes across America and created such divergent scenarios? How or why could a machine be on the January 3, 1983, cover of *Time* replacing its annual "Man of the Year" selection? Are we ready for a future that combines the ultimate in technological advancement with all that is in us as thinking, feeling, caring humans? Is this the "future" we are talking about, or is it here now—quickly and quietly manifesting itself in our family lives, our work places, our institutions? How are we to react to a technological revolution if, indeed, we are in one? Will it change the way we live? Will it change our family structure? What impact will it have on how we work and how we govern ourselves as a free people? Inherent in the very nature of information exchange is the concept that man never loses knowledge by sharing it with another. If my vision is correct and man is, in fact, on the cutting edge of an era when information—unlimited information—is literally at our very fingertips, then it is clearly evident that success in every sphere of our lives will depend on how we choose to unleash the boundless opportunities presented *and* on how we choose to act with (not react to) change. To understand where we are today, an enlightened person must first examine where we've been and what has brought us to this point.

The idea of a mechanical apparatus to assist man in the computational process is not new. For many centuries, the abacus has been utilized for calculating and to show resulting numerical values. Slide rulers, adding machines and calculators are all refinements of inventions that originated centuries ago. The electronic, infinitely programmable computer which calculates, shows results and even stores data traces its heritage back almost two hundred years. Christopher Evans's exceptional work, *The Micro Millennium,* is a fascinating and easily read chronological history of the computer. Innovations in the past couple of decades in the entire field of electronics have been phenomenal. In particular, the development and refinement of the transistor and the silicon chip helped speed up the rush to "miniaturize" equipment, making it easy to place in any home or office. Refinements are still occurring at a staggering pace in a field where competition, market share, innovation and high profits are the words of the hour. Indeed, the threshold has already been crossed. We are rushing to computerize our businesses and to purchase the newest microcomputers for our homes. As refinement, availability and competition drive the prices down, the rush continues to accelerate. Has the impact of all this really hit us yet? To what degree can we expect the "age of information" to alter our lives?

In *The Third Wave,* renowned futurist Alvin Toffler examines the information revolution. In detailed historical treatment, he discusses the Agrarian and Industrial Ages, describes the societal changes in each period, and convinces us that we have entered the "third wave." He argues that the age of high tech and information is sufficiently powerful to be dubbed a new era and will have as great an impact on the world as agriculture and industry did. Central to his thesis is that man will not have as much time to prepare for the changes as he had in the first and second "waves." In terms of "third wave society," he examines the family, religion, environmental issues, education, medicine, business, corporate structure, economics, politics and government—every sphere of our lives. And, he gives us his views on how we adjust to these changes and utilize them to our advantage.

Let's go back to family "A" and family "B" for a minute. In the first scene, perhaps the family purchased only a home electronic video game. The child is obviously captivated by the sounds and instant feedback from his own actions. He is ready for active participation. The parent in this scene is not "tuned in" to games, is frustrated and aggravated by the droning on of the noises, feels isolated from the child, and is having difficulty coping with this invasion into his life. My observation of home video games is that parents play them for a short while when they're new but quickly lose interest and go on to other activities. Children seem to delight in playing the games over and over again, long after they have actually figured out the program and become expert at racking up points. Many educators believe that children's enjoyment of repetitive behavior comes from the good feelings of successful accomplishment. They therefore repeat actions over and over again to reinforce their sense of well-being.

Family "B" presents a totally different picture. They obviously used their complete home computer to practical advantage in helping to put together their outing. The key difference is that they approached the task together and worked as a family on the project. Thus, the machine actually brought the family together in an area that appealed to each one of them. This same family may be using their computer to assist the children in the learning process, or helping Mom or Dad do some of their office work at home. Because it is happening so rapidly, there is no way at this time to accurately measure just what is going on in terms of actual application of home computers. That the general public is indeed aware and getting in on the act, is obvious. In June of 1982, Ed Faber, President of Computerland Corporation, said, "There are presently about 750,000 home computers, exclusive of video games. Of these, about 450,000 were sold in the last two years. In 1983, we expect there will be about two million operating in homes. . . ."

And it goes beyond the home application. The original large and rather primitive computers developed during World War II were designed and used for military purposes. The British Colossus "computer" broke the Germans' Enigma Code. The Harvard Mark I was built in cooperation of Harvard, I.B.M. and the United States Navy. Shortly thereafter the Moore School of Engineering in Pennsylvania built the Electronic Numerical Integrator and Calculator (ENIAC), which was utilized in weapons testing at Aberdeen Weapons Proving Grounds.

These machines were initially mostly single purpose equipment, quite large (the Harvard Mark I was eight feet high and fifty-five feet long and had almost a million individual parts), and created tremendous amounts of heat.

Today, a globe-traveling gentleman wears a wristwatch that, in addition to giving him the correct time, has many other functions. Two days prior to his wife's birthday or their anniversary his watch provides him with an appropriate musical reminder by playing "Happy Birthday" or "Happy Anniversary." And the watch has been so programmed for fifty years ahead!

If automobiles had been developed and refined at the same rate, in today's market, one could purchase a Rolls Royce automobile for $49.45, it would seat hundreds of passengers, and get 2,500 miles per gallon.

What does all this mean for us today as a society? Where will it take us?

Fact: Electronic technology and computers are here. This is a reality with which we must deal. In terms of the conservative viewpoint, we cannot and must not simply react to these changes. We must translate their advantages into sound practical methodologies that will improve the quality of life for all.

A combination of sound conservative ideals, free enterprise, national defense needs, quality higher education and the entrepreneurial spirit motivated the development of Harvard Mark I and ENIAC. These same ideals have provided the fertile ground for continuing research and development and the environment that has allowed the fantastic growth of an industry that is ushering us into the hi-tech and information-based society Toffler calls the "third wave."

Conservatives, especially, are at a real crossroads.

Imagine my shock and dismay several months ago when I interviewed a Professor of Information and Computer Science from a major university. His initial statement was: "Although it was the qualities and strengths of you conservative guys that helped all this get started, it's grown so fast that computers are already serving the individuals and serving human needs . . . so . . . it must now be an issue that the liberals are going to use."

While computer applications up until the last few years have been used primarily by the military, in space exploration and in the corporate world, and the technology fostered by conservative perspectives, they are now beginning to have an impact upon the family and individuals. It is imperative that conservative ideals continue to light the way. The information-based society and hi-tech world can accomplish the ultimate goals of less government, decentralization, individual freedom, everything we cherish, *if* properly focused today.

The crucial first step is to put together an all-encompassing game plan integrating all of our ideals and goals into a hi-tech and information-based society.

A starting point is the government operation itself. Conservatives have for years worked for a less centralized and more efficient government. Cannot a more fully, properly data-based and computerized federal government be a tremendous step in that direction? Computers are too efficient to allow a multitude of agencies and a myriad of bureaucrats to be diversely handling the same problem, each writing a separate and often conflicting regulation, engendering tremendous duplication of personnel and paperwork.

Wherever and as quickly as possible the government must be

made to "clean up its own act." Utilizing available technology in the appropriate areas is the first step.

Legislation as it relates to the computer industry is another key area of concern. Current government taxes, regulations and programs, however, fail to promote, and in most cases even prevent or hinder developments in this important business. Congressman Newt Gingrich (R-Ga.) has proposed the "Family Opportunity Act" which offers incentives and tax credits directly to families who purchase home computers and the accompanying software. One can hope that this bill is only the first of many.

Why is it so important?

It would certainly assist an industry important not only in the United States but one of the key industries in the world marketplace. Such legislation would create many jobs, and on two separate fronts. The most obvious are the jobs with the industry itself, but perhaps more important, it could assist and foster a whole new "electronic cottage industry." Home computers allow many to work, partially or totally, from their homes. One of the major home computer manufacturers even uses this concept in its advertisements. While there is clear disagreement among many experts as to the eventual scope of "electronic cottage industry" in this country, all agree that it is growing.

On a corporate level, it is already happening. In certain types of businesses which are paperwork intensive (banks and insurance carriers, e.g.) many of their functions can be performed "off premises" by means of tying employees and their home computers into the corporation's mainframe computer via existing telephone lines. Allowing employees to work in their homes on their small computers is the ultimate in "flexible work schedules." The efficiencies and opportunities are staggering.

Employers and workers both can gain financially from this type of arrangement. An employer can pay less while the employee realizes more net income because of avoiding certain costs inherent in traditional workstyles (travel, clothing, babysitting, etc.). It also allows more individual freedom in selecting where one will live as it is no longer necessary for the employee to reside close to the employer. Decrease in the number of commuters would probably ease some of the burden on our already congested highway and mass transportation systems.

There is also a sizable portion of our society which in the past found it difficult if not impossible to find productive work. The physically handicapped, the elderly, the economically disadvantaged, and the parent at home with small children now have the opportunity to become meaningful and fruitful segments of the work force. If conservatives can lead the charge in helping solve real human needs and, at the same time, decrease people's dependency on others—then it seems to me that this is a genuine opportunity to answer the liberals' charge that conservatives are uncaring.

Regarding our opening scenario, family "B" seems to be a much healthier and more closely knit family. The changes brought on by this new era are going to strengthen the family unit in very positive and constructive ways. In the past, could we have imagined many children knowing or understanding much about the family budget? Now, children are actually helping to write computer software, providing input on family decisions and understanding why and how a budget works.

Our innovative game plan must include putting computers into every school in the country. If youngsters disenchanted with school will pump quarters into video games in a local arcade, could not this zeal for electronic participation be better channeled through their schools? Computer literacy provides a tremendous opportunity to assist all students to rise to new and higher educational levels, as opposed to today's practice of establishing the lowest common denominator as the equalizing factor. Every child in America should have the essential training necessary to live in our information-based, hi-tech society.

Many a good concept has been channeled to select portions of our society because no action was taken to insure accessibility. Consider the case of the "Montessori" method of educating pre-schoolers. Around the turn of the century, Dr. Maria Montessori, an Italian physician and educator, developed a unique system for helping mentally handicapped children to learn. It was an extremely successful method. She therefore reasoned that if the technique worked so well for the handicapped, then it would also benefit normal children. Her techniques quickly spread through Europe. The Netherlands even adopted it as the official system of public school education. In the U.S. however, the Montessori method is mostly limited to private, fairly expensive pre-school centers. The use of computers in schools could go the same way unless action is taken now; otherwise high tax-base areas and private institutions will continue to have the edge over less-advantaged public schools.

And it is not just the elementary and secondary levels of education that need attention. The United States Bureau of Labor Statistics has released a report estimating that by 1990 we will need a minimum of 450,000 people with degrees in Information Science and Computers. At the current rate our institutions are turning out graduates in this field, we will have only 120,000 by then. What will this shortfall cause? Will foreign universities be able to pick up the slack? Should we allow our domestic industry to become strangled from a lack of academically trained personnel? Should U.S. industry lose its prominence in the world market? If not, the problem must be addressed now.

By embracing and promoting the advancing electronic technology, computerization and hi-tech society, conservatives have an excellent focal point for sweeping in changes that fortify our values. A positive approach to the computer revolution is energy efficient, socially uplifting, ecologically sound, assists the decentralization process, is responsive to the individual, expands our knowledge base, and is a relatively inexpensive capital investment.

IV
Institutional Issues

13

Bureaucracy: An Inherent Evil?

Paul M. Weyrich

For at least the last twenty-five years, conservatives have been criticizing bureaucracy. We have been right to do so. In fact, we don't know just how right we've been.

Most of the attacks have been on government bureaucrats and the bloated, inefficient and meddlesome departments they inhabit. By 1980, a majority of the American people had come to share a common dislike for the federal bureaucracy. They were tired of its elitism, its disregard for the right of each American to run his own life. They were sick of its inability to produce anything useful, despite huge doses of tax money. They had come to realize that despite high-flown rhetoric about "helping the poor," or "improving education," or "consumer service," these bureaucrats' real interest was in building their own little empires. The majority of Americans showed what they thought of the federal bureaucracy in 1980 by voting for Ronald Reagan and a Republican Senate. The fact that neither the President nor the Senate has done much to cut the federal bureaucracy down to size is a tragedy, but it is not the fault of those who put them in office who put them there to throw the rascals out.

Conservatives were right about government bureaucrats, but they shouldn't have stopped there. Bureaucracy no longer stops with government. We find it—more and more—in private business and industry. We meet it in small companies as well as large. While efforts were concentrated on going after the government bureaucrats, bureaucracy has crept around our flank and wormed its way into almost every part of our lives. More and more of us get up in the morning and go to work in a bureaucracy. And we hate it.

What is bureaucracy? It is a way of organizing any department or company. In a bureaucracy, the overall goals and purposes—what it is supposed to do in the world beyond its own walls—have broken down into smaller and smaller pieces until each piece is small enough to be done by one person. The piece may be fitting a taillight on a car on a production line, or managing a department in a store, or commanding an infantry battalion (military services can be bureaucracies, too), or commenting on a town's request for a federal grant. These individual pieces are called "jobs."

All these jobs are supposedly linked together in a great chain that ends up producing a product. But each person is kept rigidly within his little box, his job. If he reaches out beyond his job—if, say, the worker on the automobile assembly line suggests that the taillight he is putting on the car is not very well designed—he is told, "That's not your job. Don't concern yourself with that. That's another department, and they will get mad if you start interfering with their job." Not all car companies or other businesses take this approach, of course, but many do.

Faced with this attitude, what does the person who works in a bureaucracy do? He cannot think about what his company or government department is supposed to accomplish in the outside world—he is told that is not his job. But he still needs goals, purposes, values. He can't share those of his organization as a whole, so he tends to develop his own. One is personal career success: moving up the corporate ladder. Another, which is powerful even though most people aren't aware of it, is a tendency to see as *most important* those things which take *most of his time.*

Especially in a big company or a government department, where does most time go? Not into work directly concerned with the company's or department's purpose in the outside world, but into problems *inside* the firm or department. For people inside bureaucracies, most of their time goes into dealing with the office just above or just below them, with the division across the hall, with the competing program or assembly line or department. So, over time, a person inside a bureaucracy—if he is a "good" bureaucrat—comes to be much more interested in "keeping everybody happy" inside his organization than about whether his organization's *product* is useful and competitive in the outside world.

And, if he isn't a good bureaucrat, if he keeps saying, "Hey, this may make everybody here happy, but it just won't sell," or, "This is nice for us, but how will it help the public?" then he fails at his other goal, promotion. He is passed over or even fired in favor of someone who knows how to "play the game."

Conservatives have recognized for a long time what bureaucratic behavior does in government. Complaints have focused on the poor jobs these bureaucracies do in serving the public, and about the good job they do in serving themselves. If we understand how a bureaucracy works, we can see why. It isn't because of the people government bureaucracies employ. It is because of the *inherent nature* of bureaucracies.

What has happened to our private industry as more and more companies have become bureaucracies? The ability to compete has been lost. Our big automobile companies, e.g., have become more and more bureaucratic since Henry Ford's day, and what has happened? The cars are not designed or made as well as those coming from overseas so they no longer sell. We see the same thing in other big industries—industries we need for full employment. Steel, railroads, shipbuilding—all have lost the ability to compete as they have become more and more bureaucratic. Interestingly, our most competitive industry today is agriculture, where we still have individual farmers instead of bureaucrats in narrow jobs.

The problem has been made worse by the fact that all our industries and government departments must operate in a rapidly changing world. How does a bureaucracy adjust to change? Very poorly. Change upsets all the comfortable arrangements inside the company or department. It makes it hard to "slice up the pie" of the budget and of high-prestige responsibilities in the same old way. As they say in the military, it "upsets all the rice bowls." So change is very slow and difficult. Outside events move faster than change inside the institution. And the product becomes less and less relevant, less and less competitive.

The price of our declining ability to compete is very high. Billions of dollars of our tax money are wasted. Over 7 percent of our workers are now unemployed. But these are only two of the costs of bureaucracy. The other costs may be even higher.

What are they? One is the price paid by people who are trapped inside a bureaucracy. Today, more and more of us find ourselves in this situation. We go to work wanting to do a good job, to produce a good product, but the company or the union or the government department won't let us. When we see a problem or a mistake, the bureaucracy says to us, "Shut up about it. It's not your job to worry about that. Besides, it will make the supervisor or the department head or the local union boss mad if you mention it. It will make him look bad." Or, maybe we have an idea about how the product or the way the office runs can be improved. We are told, "Don't rock the boat. That's the way *they* want it. Go along to get along."

In government and in private business, in big organizations and even in small firms, we hear this more and more often. Most of us don't like it. We want to do a good job. We want to be allowed to be honest, to point out problems and mistakes. We want to use our intelligence and initiative to help the company be more competitive. We want to know we are all working together to make something we can be proud of. We know our country was built on quality work, on work and workmen determined that, whatever they built, it would be the best of its kind in the world.

And, now we are told we can't do that. We are told we will ruin our chances for promotion, or even get fired if we try. We are told to "play the game," and we sell our product and our country down the river in the process.

So we come to hate our job. We can't get any satisfaction from it, because the bureaucracy won't let us do it right. Whether we are auto workers or businessmen or military officers, we feel we are caught up in a system that has something horribly wrong with it. But we can't see any way out. So we go through the motions, play the game to the degree we must to keep our jobs and try not to care.

It's not much fun, is it?

Of course, some people come to like bureaucracy. We all know the type. He knows just how to flatter the boss and to project the right appearance to manipulate other people for his own gain. He knows how to sound like he knows what he's talking about, even though he usually doesn't. He knows how to dress, he uses just the right tone of voice and he is always in fashion and "in tune." He is incompetent at his work—but then that's why he likes bureaucracy. A bureaucracy doesn't care whether you can do the real job well—whether you can produce a good product. It only cares about the little games that go on inside itself, the games designed to "keep everybody happy." And the bureaucrat plays these games very well.

Recently, my friend Bill Lind sent me a very interesting article. It is about a special kind of bureaucrat we see more and more often these days—the "courtier." The article is titled, "The Military Courtier and the Illusion of Competence," and it was published in one of our Air Force magazines.

The author, Dr. Donald Chipman, describes the courtier as someone who "is entirely self-centered. He is a product of the 'me' generation and believes he is entitled to his share. He is an image maker who constantly manipulates other people and events, to ensure he is perceived as a competent person . . . He has read all the books on how to dress properly, exercise organization power, and play the assertiveness game. He admires everything and praises whatever he is expected to praise. The courtier knows that in these times of imitation food and imitation materials, appearance can be deceptive . . . accomplishing the job is not always important. In budget-based organizations, such as education and government, incompetence, indifference, and misdirection are often suspected but difficult to prove. To the courtier, making a decision is not as important as projecting the right image of a person who actually knows what he [is] doing."

Dr. Chipman points out that the rise of the courtier is not just "happening." It is being actively promoted. "Nationwide advice is available on how to avoid work and yet succeed. Books and magazines clearly present the message: Forget the job and concentrate on refining your social skills. If you want a bigger salary and control of others, then you must learn to grab for power." One such book offers these suggestions for the person who wants to be a courtier:

- To gain recognition, create an artificial catastrophe, then proceed to fix it.
- In offering your opinion, be silent, impassive, alert, visible until everyone else has spoken his piece, then fire away in complete safety.
- When accepting bad news, pretend that you could care less.
- When you are approached for a pay raise, make the person feel guilty and force him to apologize for being so obtuse. (A good technique: Ask the person to get you some aspirin because you are so sick.)
- Create a legend (for yourself) outside the organization by attending the right parties and conventions.
- On every paper make a minor correction telling the originator that you are just adding the finishing touch.
- To be promoted, pattern your style after a recently promoted worker and try to be dramatically different from the individual who was fired.
- Before retirement try to create an aura of an elder statesmen. Write no memos, enter no arguments, acquire a reputation as a peacemaker, and if possible smoke a pipe.
- To encourage another to retire, keep him involved in all decisions and make him feel uncomfortable by constantly referring to pop music, new dances, and posh restaurants.
- Women should learn that flirtation, flattery and seductive innuendos can be turned into a technique of control.

The preceding list is from one book. There are, however, several books written to take advantage of this crisis in competence. For the most part, they are filled with suggestions for promoting flattery, gestures, and passion into full-fledged courtier power plays.

These courtiers and other bureaucrats ruin the lives of honest workers. Even though they are destroying the company, they get ahead. They get the raises and promotions. They are the bosses' favorites. When we try to do something right, they mess it up, then get praised for what they've done while we get criticized. We see that the whole operation is falling apart, but there is nothing we can do, because our abilities no longer count for anything.

We are often the majority. But we are a silenced majority. The bureaucrats and courtiers have taken over.

There is still another price we pay for bureaucracy and bureaucrats. It is a price that goes beyond the company or government department and into our whole society. In fact, it is destroying an important part of our culture.

In the past, when a group of Americans got together to do something, they gave their attention to what they were trying to do—to the product. They were willing to disagree among themselves, to criticize each other and to tell the leader of the group he was wrong if that was necessary to build the product. No one became upset because someone else in the group said he was wrong, if the other person had a better idea. They were a team, and they had a purpose.

Today, this is changing. More and more often, when a group is formed for some kind of project, the people in it pay attention not to what they are supposed to produce, but to each other. Each member of the group tries to flatter everyone else. They all try to build personal connections rather than the product. We even hear a word for the process: "stroking." Everybody is supposed to "stroke" everyone else, and if doing that means building something that won't work, nobody much cares. Each person is out for personal gain. There is no common purpose, and there is no team.

This is a social or cultural problem, because it is springing up everywhere, not just in bureaucracies, and because it is becoming automatic. It is becoming "the way things are done," the way you are expected to behave if you are not to be thought rude or ill-educated. It is becoming a part of our culture.

It is clear to me where this will lead unless it is stopped. It will make bureaucratic behavior part of our culture. Bureaucracy will no longer just be a type of organization, it will be part of our behavior. This may be the most dangerous price we can pay for bureaucracy, because once we have paid it, there will be no escape. We will no longer be aware of what we are doing. The most important issues facing our nation are *moral* issues. I have been involved with a number of what I believe are the most important moral issues of our time: abortion, the right of our children to pray in schools, the right of parents to educate their children free of state interference. And in looking at bureaucracy, what is most striking is that it is *also* a moral issue. It is as much and possibly as important a moral issue as abortion or school prayer, because of the ways it affects the lives of so many of us.

Why is bureaucracy a moral issue? If we look at the kinds of actions a bureaucracy rewards with praise and promotions, we see that most if not all of them are those things traditional Western values define as immoral. First, the "good" bureaucrat must be a hypocrite. He must pretend to work at creating the product or service his company or government department is supposed to provide, while he is really working to keep his own little part of the company and his boss comfortable. He must practice the hypocrisy of talking about the good of his company and his country while sacrificing both for personal gain. Second, he must use the people around him—and sacrifice them, if necessary—for his personal advantage. One minister I respect very highly once said, "As Christians, we are commended to love people and use things. Yet too often we end up loving things and using people." The bureaucrat uses people as things, twisting them to his advantage, then throwing them away when they are of no more use to him. Third, the bureaucrat uses any means available to advance himself, including cheating, lying and betraying those who depend on him. The bureaucrat has only one commandment: Promote yourself. Any means is OK.

We see the inherent evil of bureaucracy most clearly if we look at life in Russia today. The Soviet Union is an enormous bureaucracy. What has the result been? Aleksandr Solzhenitsyn described it well in an article in *National Review*.[1] Soviet agriculture, he writes, "is controlled by a grotesquely bureaucratic central plan incapable of anticipating real-life circumstances or of giving thought to the future, striving only to plunder the earth, as if this same earth will not have to sustain us tomorrow. . . . The peasant is no longer devoted to the land and to his work as he was for centuries. What an achievement! Peasants have been numbed into indifference, obediently carrying out stupid orders, sowing and harvesting at the wrong times, irreparably turning the best meadowlands into unproductive plowed fields, cutting down forests until the rivers dry up, or draining good lakes to satisfy the formal requirements of 'land reclamation'. . . . During the past ten years imports of foodstuffs to the USSR have increased fortyfold, and there have been four poor harvests in a row—such is the worth of this system of agriculture. . . . The same type of absurdity besets the entire economy. . . . The party bureaucracy is unable to organize either production or commercial distribution; it knows only how to confiscate goods that have already been produced. It is a system that cannot tolerate independence. . . . The central plan controlling the economy does not take into account local circumstances or concrete events, yet it must be followed in rigid detail. The result is absurdity and chaos."

While the Soviet bureaucracy is the world's worst, many of these things—the rigid plan, the numbing effect on individuals of stupid orders that must be obeyed, the directors' interest in nothing but their own personal well-being—are common to all bureaucracies, including many of the ones here. What are the moral effects? Solzhenitsyn describes what they are in Russia:

"Local officials work-full-time devising ways of resisting or circumventing the plan, risking criminal charges at every step. . . . Bold men with initiative have here and there attempted to set up the finances at their factories so as to get around petty state regulations and to be able to pay according to the quality and quantity of work performed. The results have always been spectacular, but such managers are immediately reined in from above with new restrictions, cuts in budget allocations, and sometimes even with criminal proceedings. The emergence of free economic forces is seen as a threat to the bureaucracy's control of events. . . . To thousands of such examples one must add one other aspect of Communism: the mandatory system of lies. . . . Meanwhile, 12 percent of the state's income is derived from the sale of exorbitantly priced vodka (which brings the populace to the point of induced idiocy). . . . Children with living parents grow up like orphans: because the father's salary is invariably insufficient and the mother must work, millions of children begin their lives in overcrowded day care centers, in unhealthy and tension-filled surroundings. . . . From ancient times theft was looked upon as a deadly sin in Russia, but today stealing from the government has become a common, universally understood fact of life, an act necessary for survival. . . . Children of collective farmers learn to steal at an early age. No one has any desire to work honestly for the benefit of a dishonest regime. No one is paid a fair wage, but neither does anyone exert himself to the fullest. This is true of the workman at the lathe, of the government official, and even of the scientist in his research institute. . . . The harshness of life, the constant feeling of hunger, cramped living quarters, and lack of time all combine to deprive women of the strength to raise children, which leads to a large number of abortions. Among the Slavic peoples in the USSR, there are four abortions for every live birth."

Above all this live the top Soviet bureaucrats. "This is a caste supplied in abundance with every privilege—special stores (where the highest-quality goods are sold at low prices), secret payments of money untouched by taxes, the best houses and apartments, special medical facilities, free access to health resorts, a power over the population that has virtually no legal restraints—but a caste that pays for these benefits with unquestioning and obsequious service. A member of this caste must ignore the suffering of his own people, present, past and future: he maintains his position only so long as he is faithful to the system; he is expelled at the slightest hint of disloyalty."

Of course, many of these evils are due to communism. But one of the things communism does is let bureaucracy run rampant. And if we look at our own bureaucracies, do we not see some of the same things? The privileged top bureaucrats, who get away with things the rest of us would quickly be punished for, and who get special privileges in return for loyalty to "the system"? Honest people below them frustrated by having to put up with the inefficiency? Lies as a way of life, along with theft and other types of dishonesty?

Whether in Russia or in the United States, bureaucracy rewards immoral behavior and punishes the honest man. And so it works to turn the honest man into a liar and a cheat. That is not an accident. It is part of the soul of bureaucracy. Not only can it happen here. It *is* happening here. And it *is a moral issue.*

What can we do about it? Can anything *be* done? Does the complexity of modern life and the size of our economy mean bureaucracy is inevitable?

The answer is yes, we can do something. There is an alternative to bureaucracy, even for very large organizations. And it is an alternative that helps promote moral instead of immoral behavior.

The alternative is what is called a "corporative" institution. In a corporative institution, people have jobs, just like they do in a bureaucracy. But the job means something very different. The institution—it may be a business or a military service or a government department—works to get the people inside it to adopt its goals and purposes in the outside world as their *personal* goals and purposes. It sets values, not just production quotas, and it tries to convince all its employees to adopt those values. It expects all its people to do everything they can, not only in their jobs but beyond their jobs, to advance their common goals, purposes and values.

There are a number of corporative institutions in the world around us. Historically, the Catholic Church was one. The people in it—bishops, priests, deacons, the Pope himself—all had jobs. But being a Catholic clergyman was more than a job. It was a *calling*, a vocation. What is the difference? The clergyman was expected to work to accomplish the goals of the Church, to express and further its values, in everything he did. If he saw something going wrong, he did not say, "That is not my job." He called attention to it. A priest did not say, "That sermon was good enough to get by with." He always tried to do better. He shared the Church's beliefs, its goals and values, and because he believed in them himself, he always strove to do more and to do better.

Some businesses are set up this way. Many Japanese companies, including very large ones, are corporative institutions. The company works very hard to convince its employees to share its goals and values. That is why they have company songs, company uniforms and strong company loyalty built on lifetime employment. Management and labor do not see each other as opponents, but as partners, all working for the same goals. Employees not only do their jobs, they also look for ways to do their jobs better. Every person in the company is expected to search for ways to make a better product. When a worker finds a way to make a better product, management listens to him, appreciates his suggestion and rewards him well.

Another example of a corporative institution is the United States Marine Corps. A Marine doesn't just have a job. He *is* something. He is a *Marine.* Being a Marine means sharing certain values and goals. It means working in every possible way for the Marine Corps.

We see how well companies and other institutions that use this corporative approach compete. And we see it not only with Japanese companies. IBM is a corporative company in many ways, and it has been one of our most successful companies.

Why do corporative institutions compete better? If the people inside the institution share the same goals and values—goals and values that support the institution's purpose in the marketplace—there is a check on bureaucratic behavior. When someone starts to cut a deal that will help him or his little shop but hurt the company's or department's ability to compete, people throughout the organization object. And other people, including the bosses, recognize their right to object. They are just doing what the company wants them to: working for its goals and values. Bureaucratic games are cut short, and people are praised and promoted for helping the company instead of just helping themselves.

Some congressional observers, both liberals and conservatives, have pointed out that three of our military services—all of them except the Marine Corps—have adopted the bureaucratic instead of the corporative approach, and that this hurts our defense very badly. Among these commentators has been Senator Gary Hart (D-Colo.). In an article he wrote about our defense problems,[2] he told a story about how the corporative approach can help restore our ability to compete.

An American bank in San Francisco had not been doing very well. In fact, it was on the verge of failing. It was bought by a Japanese bank which sent in new, Japanese managers. The American employees said, "Fine, we are willing to work for Japanese. Just tell us what to do differently." They wanted specific instructions on how to do their jobs, just like they were used to in a typical bureaucracy. Instead, the Japanese said, "These are the goals and values of our company." The Americans replied, "That's nice, but tell us what to do." The Japanese again explained the company's goals and values.

At first, the Americans were confused. They had never been dealt with this way before. Productivity continued to fall. But the Japanese kept working to convince the employees to accept the firm's values and goals. The Americans began to realize they were expected not to follow a new set of tight, bureaucratic rules, but to do everything they could to advance the company's goals and values. They were expected to use their own imagination and initiative to do their jobs better and to suggest changes for running the bank better. Once they understood this, the bank's productivity began to rise swiftly. Its people became a team. Everyone used his abilities to do a better job. The bank ended up one of the most successful in the city.

And, I suspect, the employees were much happier in their jobs than they had been when the bank was a bureaucracy. They were rewarded for their ideas, and they probably enjoyed it. They were encouraged to do a better job, and I imagine they liked doing a better job. Most of us want to.

A Japanese automobile company, Nissan, has built a plant in the United States, in Tennessee. They are using the corporative approach. While the plant is not operating yet, many employees have been hired for training, and newspapers and magazines have interviewed some of them. One of them, Kathy Landry, said, "I am made to feel important here, like they want to hear what I have to say." Another, Larry Burks, said, "It's like having a good dream and I hope I never wake up."[3]

What about the moral issue? Of course, no approach to setting up an organization will eliminate immorality. Human nature does not change. But the corporative approach seems to reward moral behavior much better than a bureaucracy does. A corporative organization rewards sincerity, teamwork, and real competence in producing a better product instead of hypocrisy and narrow self-interest. It rewards people for helping each other instead of for stabbing each other in the back to get ahead. It rewards the real workman, instead of the courtier.

That is the real issue. We will always have evil with us in this world. The question is, do our institutions—our government, our companies, our military services, our schools, and so on—reward moral or immoral behavior? That is, in many ways, the real problem in the Soviet Union. Even there, people have the basic freedom God gave us all. Every man has the freedom to choose good or evil. But in Russia today, evil is rewarded and good is punished. The price of choosing good in the Soviet Union is great hardship and often prison or death, while corruption, lies and theft are rewarded with a high living standard.

What about us? Where does America stand? My fear is that we are becoming more and more like the Soviet Union—not because we are becoming communist, but because we are becoming bureaucratic, and bureaucracies everywhere tend to reward evil and punish good.

Abortion and school prayer are important moral issues. Abortion is the most important moral issue of our time. But there are other lessons as well and some of them are of great importance. It is time to do a better, more thoughtful job of defining moral issues. It is time to reach out to people everywhere and show them how important moral issues are in their lives, how moral problems are at the root of the growing dissatisfaction with life in the United States in the 1980s.

The question of how we should design our institutions to reward good and punish evil is only one such moral issue.

Notes

[1] Aleksandr Solzhenitsyn, "Communism at the End of the Brezhnev Era," *National Review* (January 21, 1983), p. 28.

[2] Senator Gary Hart, "What's Wrong With the Military," *New York Times Magazine* (February 14, 1982).

[3] "A Tale of Two Worlds in Tennessee," *U.S. News and World Report* (December 20, 1982), p. 84.

14

Judicial Reform: Improving the American System[1]
Patrick B. McGuigan

Until recently, only isolated conservative scholars and activists were concerned with the excesses of federal and state judges, or so it seemed. Now, however, many Americans are concerned about the amount of judicial power exercised—particularly by federal judges. More important, they seem more and more willing to do something to correct judicial abuses.

During the last four decades, activist judges have changed the very structure of our law without utilizing the constitutional amendment process ordained by the Founding Fathers. Scholars such as Professor Raoul Berger *(Government by Judiciary)*, Lino Graglia *(Disaster by Decree)* and Thomas Higgins *(Judicial Review Unmasked)* have laid bare the usurpations of congressional and state powers committed by federal judges seeking to impose their own policy views on all Americans.

The Free Congress Foundation's *Blueprint for Judicial Reform,* published in 1981, focused on the problems created by judicial activism in a sweeping, comprehensive manner. Besides the Free Congress efforts in this area, conservative organizations such as the National Legal Center for the Public Interest, the Center for Judicial Studies and the Washington Legal Foundation are offering specific ideas for improvement of the American legal structure.

Not surprisingly, defenders of the legal establishment have bitterly attacked even the most modest conservative proposals for judicial reform. Paul Weyrich, one of the leading strategists of the modern conservative movement, referred to this when he unveiled *Blueprint* in 1981:

> Conservatives have no quarrel with judges who conscientiously interpret the Constitution and our existing laws. What bothers us is the increasing

number of judges who impose their own liberal views on matters of policy through judicial fiat. Given the cumbersome nature of the impeachment process, the practical and frequently utilized mechanism for reining in the courts has been pointed criticism of judicial excesses. But recently liberals have sought to equate our criticism of the courts with a kind of unpatriotic questioning of our basic institutions. Nothing could be further from the truth.

Indeed, it is the genuine conservative desire to preserve what is best in our system that has led to all the recent activity—both legislative and scholarly. Given the American tradition for pointed criticism of judges, it is more than a little ironic to read the tortured reasoning of some liberals who contend that it is *conservatives* who are the radicals.

Chief Justice William Howard Taft—the only man to serve both as president and on the Supreme Court—once wrote: "Nothing tends more to render judges careful in their decision and anxiously solicitious to do exact justice than the consciousness that every act of theirs is to be subject to the intelligent scrutiny of their fellow men, and to their candid criticism."

The late Justice Felix Frankfurter once wrote, in a letter to Alexander Bickel, that "I can assure you that explicit analysis and criticism of the way the Court is doing its business really gets under their skin, just as the praise of their constituencies, the so-called liberal journals and well-known liberal approvers, only fortifies them in their result-oriented jurisprudence."

Judge Malcolm R. Wilkey, currently serving on the District of Columbia Circuit Court of Appeals, struck upon an important truth when he wrote: "When we judges act within our constitutional competence, we are supported; when we act outside that competence, then distrust, disrespect, and active dislike of the courts sets in, impairing our ability to perform with the confidence of the people even unquestioned judicial tasks."

The current criticisms of the courts have not occurred because of a desire to destroy the independence and integrity of the courts. Rather, these criticisms have arisen because federal courts—including this nation's highest court—have repeatedly undermined the processes of our representative democracy.

The Supreme Court is to police the bounds drawn by the Constitution, not read its own predilections into the document. To the degree the Supreme Court strays from this basic principle to the extent the Constitution becomes in the Court's hands irrelevant to constitutional law, the federal judiciary and its highest organ falls once again subject to questions about its ultimate authority and role in a democratic society.

The inventive nature of many recent High Court decisions has contributed to the disrespect many now have of the courts. In fact, there is a substantive base to the feelings many Americans have that judges do not reflect their views. In 1981, the *Connecticut Mutual Life Report on American Values in the 1980's* found a disturbing gap between typical Americans and their leaders. The *Report* focused on nine major leadership groups, including law and justice leaders (lawyers and judges). Law and justice leaders differed most from the general public on a number of religious, family and moral issues, and they ranked second only to scientists as the least religious leadership category.

Disenchantment with the judiciary has led to an increasingly popular willingness to support dramatic changes in our legal system. In a poll conducted for the Heritage Foundation in 1981, Sindlinger and Company of Media, Pennsylvania, found that 77.3 percent of the American people do not believe the federal judiciary reflects their views. Public disenchantment with the lifetime tenure of federal judges was demonstrated when nearly three out of four of those surveyed (73.7 percent) endorsed the concept that federal judges should undergo periodic reconfirmation during their time on the bench. More than two-thirds (68.3 percent) said they would support direct *election* of federal judges. On a wide range of other issues, those surveyed endorsed substantive proposals for judicial reform.

In no other area is popular concern about the legal system more manifest than in popular views toward the crime explosion. In a poll conducted early in 1982, the National Opinion Research Center found that 90 percent of those surveyed believe the courts are not harsh enough with criminals. In contrast, only 74 percent felt this way in 1972. One of the most dramatic changes the Research Center found was a jump in support of the death penalty for persons convicted of murder. In 1972, 57 percent supported imposition of capital punishment in such cases. In 1982, 78 percent supported the death penalty.

More recently, a Gallup Poll conducted January 28–31, 1983, found that the fear of crime has jumped in recent years. The poll found that 76 percent of women in urban areas feared walking alone at night in their neighborhoods. Overall, the poll found that 45 percent of Americans were afraid to go out alone at night within a mile of their homes, with 13 percent expressing the same fear even during the daytime.

Although the 1983 Gallup Poll found that the apparent incidence of crime and fear of crime had remained about the same in the last ten years, it found other evidence that the fear of crime is, simply put, widespread. This is neither necessary nor inevitable. Whatever economic or political explanations there may be for popular fear of crime, it is clear that part of the blame for increases in crime must be laid at the feet of judges who have removed the ability of society's peace officers to operate with efficiency and dispatch.

In the pages that follow, positive alternatives to the present state of affairs will be explored. The focus is on two areas: Judicial Reform in the broadest sense and, more specifically, criminal justice reform.

Judicial Reform: Reining in the Courts

The Judicial Reform Act. Realistic approaches to solving the legal crises engendered by judicial activism must approach the problem on two levels: statutory and constitutional. The most useful and comprehensive proposal to curb judicial abuse through legislation is the Judicial Reform Act, introduced by Senator John East (R-NC) as S.3018 on October 1, 1982. Senator East's proposal deals with a wide range of judicial excesses, including the exclusionary rule, habeas corpus, awards of attorneys fees, implied causes of action and oversight of the federal judiciary.

The key portion of Senator East's proposal, which was reintroduced in the 98th Congress, focuses on the question of the so-called "doctrine of incorporation." Senator East's legislation would specifically undo the so-called doctrine, which has allowed federal courts to destroy many aspects of genuine federalism.

The whole process of "merging" or "incorporating" the Bill of Rights into the due process clause of the Fourteenth Amendment has been *judicial.* In no sense has it been constitutional or legislative. Proponents of the incorporation doctrine maintain that all the restrictions on federal government power embodied in the first ten amendments—the Bill of Rights—now apply to state governments with the same force as they apply to the federal government.

No serious student of the Constitution can maintain that the framers intended the Bill of Rights to limit state government powers. Indeed, those first ten revisions in our basic document were passed precisely because the states insisted on protection of their rights vis-à-vis the federal government.

The dispute arises over whether the Fourteenth Amendment forever ended the rights of states—rights secured less than 100 years before passage of that amendment. Many historical events can illuminate the understanding of the Fourteenth Amendment, but the most useful may be that cited by Professor William Stanmeyer of the Lincoln Center for Legal Studies. Stanmeyer noted that in 1872, Congress, four years after passage of the Fourteenth Amendment, *declined* to pass the Blaine Amendment, a measure specifically stating that no state could provide funds for sectarian schools. As Stanmeyer put it, "This suggests that those who . . . wanted to adopt the Blaine Amendment in 1872 . . . did not believe the Bill of Rights was applied to the states."

As useful as such examples of congressional intent might be, it is probably more instructive to examine legal precedent itself. Proponents of the doctrine of incorporation usually admit that it is in fact a result of a judicial process, and not the result of any constitutional amendment or specific act of Congress. What, if anything, can or should the Congress do to reassert its own powers on the one hand, and the rights of states on the other?

The clear language of Article III, Section 2 of the Constitution provides for the appellate jurisdiction of the Supreme Court (and the inferior courts created by Congress itself) with such exceptions and regulations as Congress shall deem appropriate. This power of the Congress is broad indeed. In an insightful essay entitled "Congress and the Courts" (*National Review,* February 5, 1982), veteran attorney C. Dickerman Williams noted no less than seven occasions upon which the Supreme Court itself had admitted that restrictions on federal court jurisdiction may be imposed by Congress.

No less a luminary than Justice Oliver Wendell Holmes expressed concern about what he viewed as illegitimate expansion of federal court powers. In 1930, Holmes wrote in *Baldwin v. Missouri,* "I have not yet adequately expressed the more than anxiety I feel at the ever-increasing scope given to the Fourteenth Amendment in cutting down what I believe to be the constitutional rights of the states. As the decisions now stand, I see hardly any limit but the sky to the invalidating of those rights if they happen to strike a majority of this court as for any reason undesirable. I cannot believe that the amendment was intended to give us *carte blanche* to embody our economic or social beliefs in its prohibitions. . . ."

It is significant that Justice Holmes's comments came some 60 years after passage of the Fourteenth Amendment, at a time when the doctrine of incorporation was well on its way to acceptance in legal circles, but when it was not yet apparent just how far the courts would go to impose federal standards on virtually every state activity. The wise Holmes was a bit of a prophet. In recent years, we have witnessed the unfortunate spectacle of usurping judges involving themselves more and more in the matters the Founders—and the framers of the Fourteenth Amendment—clearly intended to be left to state and local jurisdiction. Edicts have been imposed in matters of prison facilities, the death penalty, school desegregation, zoning, school discipline, amateur athletics, affirmative action, local government organization and abortion.

Clear precedent exists to curb such judicial excess, including Supreme Court decisions and legislation such as the Norris-LaGuardia Act of 1932, which limited the federal courts' use of injunction in labor disputes. Yet, such steps to curb court jurisdiction and powers have seldom been used and there is reluctance, even among conservatives, to do anything meaningful to rein in the courts.

But a power seldom exercised still remains a legitimate power. The Judicial Reform Act would simply restore the original purpose of the Bill of Rights, by withdrawing from federal courts jurisdiction over cases claiming state abridgment of rights secured by the Bill of Rights. This jurisdiction would revert to state courts. Contrary to liberal assertions, this is not an assault on the Bill of Rights. State judges take the same oath to uphold the Constitution as do federal judges. Indeed, as Professor Jules Gerard of Washington University noted at Free Congress Foundation's Conference on Judicial Reform in June of 1982, "There is no evidence that state judges are more corrupt, more likely to be bought off, more likely to sell their souls to the devil than federal judges. There simply is no evidence of that at all."

Other than impeachment (seldom used) and constitutional amendment (cumbersome and, in most cases, unnecessary), restriction and limitation of court jurisdiction is the most direct and legitimate method for reining in the imperial judiciary. Senator East's Judicial Reform Act should be supported.

Abortion, Social Justice Issues and the Constitution. On a wide range of social justice issues—abortion, tuition tax credits, religious freedom, forced busing and others—usurping federal judges have taken away the rights of innocent minorities, parents, students and the states. When conservatives seek to reassert traditional interpretations of the constitution through legislation, such as Senator Jesse Helms' Human Life Statute and his various proposals to support neighborhood schools and end forced racial busing, they are accused of seeking to undermine the Constitution itself. It must be emphasized that in each of these substantive areas, there are appropriate *statutory* responses. Nevertheless, efforts to amend the Constitution to restore rights or legislative options precluded by court interpretation *are* in order when the alternative is inaction on major moral questions such as abortion or religious freedom.

The classic case of judicial legislation is the Warren Court's *Roe v. Wade* and *Doe v. Bolton*. These cases discovered within the Fourteenth Amendment a right to privacy broad enough to include the decision whether or not to destroy an unborn human being. The High Court read into the Constitution a right that does not exist in that Amendment's clear language and that was, as Justice William Rehnquist wrote, "completely unknown to the drafters of the Amendment."

The *Roe* decision was not an instance of the Court "discovering" or "interpreting" the Constitution or the law, but a case of judicial *creation* of law. By its 1973 decision, the Supreme Court—not pro-lifers—cut short an important moral and intellectual debate in this country, one which had scarcely begun.

The *Roe* case and its progeny have had a devastating impact on the integrity of our system of laws. It is the Supreme Court, not pro-lifers, which created law out of whole cloth. Through "creative" judicial pronouncements the Court has made it clear that virtually no law passed by the Congress or by the state legislatures—the institutions which are, after all, those closest to the people—is to be considered legitimate until it has passed federal court inspection. The Court legislated in *Roe* against the desires of the American people. It permitted abortions in instances where *no* state—not even those with the most "liberal" abortion statutes—would have allowed them before the decision. More than any modern legal controversy, the abortion decisions have undermined the very meaning of the term "representative government," in that these cases removed a political and moral issue from the realm of political discourse, consensus and compromise.

Abortion policy may be the central moral and political issue of our time, but responsible efforts to deal with abortion policy have been attacked by abortionists and supporters of judicial activism as threats to basic American liberties. In fact, the standard tactic of the supporters of most activist decisions is to claim that *they* are the guardians of the Constitution, while their opponents seek to deprive all the rest of us of freedom.

Unfortunately, this deliberate confusion on the part of supporters of judicial activism has had its effect in thwarting efforts to restore the meaning of the Constitution on a range of issues. Thus, it may be that the only way to approach this problem is to borrow from the judicial activists themselves. Supporters of the Constitution will probably not find among the activist judiciary sufficient support to reverse even the most outrageous decisions or to return these issues to the political arena. This means the solution probably lies in some sort of constitutional amendment.

As much as conservatives would like simply to remove the abortion cases from our history, it is important to remember that the term "right to abortion" has been used roughly 90 times in federal court decisions since 1973. The best way to remove *Roe* and its progeny is to amend the Constitution. Conservatives should continue, however, to support efforts such as Senator Jesse Helms' Human Life Statute and the recent efforts of Congressman Henry Hyde (R-Ill.) and Senator Roger Jepsen (R-Iowa) to restore respect for human life. But it is a reality that such legislation might itself be found unconstitutional by the federal courts.

On the other hand, many supporters of the Constitution who count themselves in the pro-life camp find themselves intrigued by a "Federalism Amendment" which does not deal with abortion *per se,* but rather addresses itself to the proper relationship between the federal government and the states.

The idea of a Federalism Amendment was explored by Professor Gary L. McDowell of Dickenson College in an article in the *Wall Street Journal* (January 26, 1983). McDowell's proposal seeks to accomplish many of the goals of Senator East's Judicial Reform Act, but would do so through an amendment to the Constitution itself. McDowell has not written language to accomplish this goal, but he explained the concept in his *Journal* article:

> The idea that the Bill of Rights is now a source of restraint on the states is the result of a creative and unrestrained judicial imagination, not constitutional provision. Thus what lies at the heart of the current problem is the deterioration of the principle of federalism as a source of restraint on the exercise of judicial power.
>
> Prayer in public schools is only one policy choice; the school prayer amendment seeks only to substitute one constitutional policy for another. It does not reach to the level of principle. Like the amendments dealing with abortion, busing, criminal justice and legislative apportionment, the school prayer amendment seeks only to treat symptoms at the expense of curing causes. But there is another way.
>
> By . . . advocating a federalism amendment, a stronger case can be made for achieving with one amendment the same results that the collection of amendments currently being tossed about are designed to secure.
>
> A federalism amendment would seek to nullify the judicially created notion of "incorporation" by clearly stating that the Bill of Rights applies only to the national government . . .
>
> It would also seek to limit the power of the federal judiciary from interfering with the *administration* of the domestic policies of a state by emphasizing that the demands of the 14th Amendment are directed only toward a fair administration of state laws toward the citizen of each state. Such an amendment would *constitutionally* obligate the federal judges to exercise what Justice Harlan Fiske Stone termed a "scrupulous regard for the rightful independence of state governments."

According to McDowell, his amendment could "restore somewhat the healthy federal balance that the doctrine of 'incorporation' has seriously undermined."

McDowell's concept is more than interesting, it points the way to possible tempering of many of the unfortunate results of judicial activism. The Federalism Amendment concept has merit because it would restore to states, local communities and the people themselves the power to deal with clearly local concerns *without* conceding that, for instance, the *Roe* decision and similar cases were legitimate interpretations of the Constitution.

Reasserting Religious Freedom. In this great nation, founded upon the Judeo-Christian tradition, it is sadly ironic that freedom of religious expression has been methodically undermined. Major factors in the decline of religious freedom have been extra-constitutional and non-constitutional decisions in the federal courts. Dr. James McClellan of the Center for Judicial Studies examined the history of religious freedom in his chapter "The Making and Unmaking of the Establishment Clause," in *A Blueprint for Judicial Reform.* McClellan and Professor Robert Cord, author of *Separation of Church and State,* are among the scholars who have demonstrated the utter lack of historical accuracy in judicial descriptions of a strict "wall of separation" between church and state.

Even though there is no textual basis for High Court rulings curbing freedom of religion and such activities as voluntary school prayer, supporters of the Constitution face the same difficulty in this area as in those discussed previously: On the one hand, if they seek legislative remedies to judicial usurpation in this area, they are accused of "undermining the Constitution." On the other hand, in seeking Constitutional amendments as solutions to judicial usurpation, supporters of the Constitution give the invalid judicial pronouncements a kind of legitimacy they do not deserve. Nevertheless, constitutional amendments have one overwhelming advantage: They are, by definition, constitutional.

On May 17, 1982, President Reagan sent to Congress a proposed constitutional amendment to "restore the simple freedom of our citizens to offer prayer in our public schools and institutions." The proposed Reagan Amendment would restore the freedom of individuals or groups to engage in private or public prayer in public settings, while preventing state or federal coercion forcing an individual to pray. In its legal analysis of the proposed amendment, the Justice Department contended that the Supreme Court decisions banning prayer and Bible reading "do not give adequate regard to our religious heritage and misinterpret the historical background of the First Amendment."

Support for voluntary school prayer regularly exceeds 75 percent in nationwide public opinion polls, yet the practice has been held to violate the Constitution on more than one occasion. Even *access to public facilities* for religious groups has been challenged by the American Civil Liberties Union (ACLU), the same organization that defends such access for communists and has defended the "right" of Nazis to march through a Jewish community. Despite outlandish judicial pronouncements curbing the freedom of religious expression, Americans continue to practice their religion even in a public setting. They will, undoubtedly, not change their beliefs to suit the whims of shifting majorities on the Supreme Court.

Some federal judges themselves are apparently willing to recognize that the judiciary itself has acted irresponsibly, and therein lies this nation's greatest hope for restoration of religious freedom and the rights of states and local communities. On January 14, 1983, Federal District Judge W. Brevard Hand of Alabama departed from recent judicial orthodoxy in his landmark ruling in *Jaffree v. School Commissioners of Mobile County*. Hand ruled that the "establishment clause" of the First Amendment was never meant to be applied to the states. Further, he ruled that the Fourteenth Amendment did not retroactively apply the Federal Bill of Rights to the states.

Eventually, Hand's view of the Constitution—which seems to coincide with the clear language of that document—will probably be overruled because it is a clear-headed challenge to those who now prevail in judicial circles. Nevertheless, his decision represents one of the most courageous and articulate federal court decisions of recent years.

Judge Hand made it clear that the purpose of the First Amendment was to preclude the *Congress* from imposing a national religion, and that the Fourteenth Amendment was never intended to forbid religious prayers in the schools. Hand did not avoid the heart of the larger issues raised by his decision. He wrote:

> The interpretation of the Constitution can be approached from two vantages. First, the court can attempt to ascertain the intent of the adopters, and after ascertaining that attempt [to] apply the Constitution as the adopters intended it to be applied. Second, the Court can treat the Constitution as a living document, chameleon-like in its complexion, which changes to suit the needs of the times and the whims of the interpreters. In the opinion of this Court, the only proper approach is to interpret the Constitution as its drafters and adopters intended . . . [later, Hand writes] in cases involving the federal constitution, where correction through legislative action is practically impossible, a court should be willing to examine earlier precedent and to overrule it if the court is persuaded that the earlier precedent was wrongly decided.

As Justice Frankfurter noted in a letter to his former clerk cited above, there exists a "network" of legal journals and other arms of the legal establishment that serve to ratify and sustain the fruits of judicial activism. Conservatives will probably never be able to match the influence of this legal network, but it is incumbent upon them to offer encouragement and support to those brave souls who stand for sound jurisprudence and strict constructionism. Simply put, when a judge does the right thing, he needs to know that it has been *noticed*.[2]

Judicial Accountability: The Heart of the Problem. Professor Jules Gerard of Washington University Law School in St. Louis, Missouri, has argued persuasively that conservatives might be misplacing their efforts by striving for constitutional amendments or even for proposals to limit or withdraw court jurisdiction. According to Professor Gerard, what is needed is "a mechanism to check judges who usurp power not rightfully theirs."

The articulate Professor Gerard argues that: "Lifetime tenure lies at the heart of the misbehavior of federal judges. It is the salient from which imperialist judges launch their attacks upon the democratic processes and the impregnable fortress which shields them from retribution for their misconduct. . . . Abolishing lifetime tenure is . . . the *sine qua non* of an effective system of ending judicial abuses of any variety."

Writing in *A Blueprint for Judicial Reform,* Professor Gerard went on to propose a comprehensive rewriting of Article III of the Constitution to require that federal judges be subjected to periodic retention votes of the people. Every few years, under his proposal, Supreme Court justices would stand for reconfirmation—a yes/no vote of the people—throughout the nation. Circuit judges would stand for reconfirmation within their circuits, and so forth. In addition, Professor Gerard's proposed amendment to the Constitution would grant Congress the power to remove, short of impeachment, judges for misbehavior or abuse of their offices. Finally, under the Amendment, Congress would have the power to recall judges, subject to a two-thirds vote of both houses.

For those interested in addressing the most significant problems of judicial abuse, Professor Gerard's proposal for popular reconfirmation holds a great deal of promise. To the extent that usurping judges also hold power at the state and local level, much of Professor Gerard's analysis still applies.

The selection and retention process for state judges is much more democratic than that for federal judges. Whereas federal judges are appointed by the president with the advice and consent of the U.S. Senate—and serve life terms during "good behavior"—state judges are selected in various matters and serve limited terms except in a few states.

In most states, there are three court levels: Supreme Court, intermediate appellate courts and various general jurisdiction courts. Some states do not have the appellate court level, and in others the levels are much more intricate. At the Supreme Court level, popular involvement in the selection and retention process is limited in many states. Generally, however, the further down in the state court system, the greater the degree of voter involvement in both selection of judges and decisions on their retention in office. The most common mechanisms for initial judicial appointments are: 1) partisan election, 2) non-partisan election, 3) executive appointment (gubernatorial appointment with legislative approval), 4) commission appointment (often this works in tandem with gubernatorial appointment) and 5) legislative appointment. Generally, these widely varied methods of judicial selection work well for the states in which they prevail. The real concern here is not with judicial selection—which is, under any of these mechanisms, still a subtly political process—but with procedures for judicial retention.

Retention methods vary widely, with lifetime tenure the exception rather than the rule. Essentially, the retention methods are variations on the initial appointment mechanisms described above. It is significant that the retention methods tend to be more democratic than the initial selection procedures. For instance, while a commission selects Supreme Court judges in Nebraska, those judges are retained by popular reconfirmation. The six mechanisms for retention of state judges are: 1) partisan election, 2) non-partisan election, 3) retention elections (popular reconfirmation), 4) reappointment by the executive, 5) reappointment by commission and 6) life tenure.

Only four states give life tenure to judges throughout the state court system: Massachusetts, New Hampshire, New Jersey and Rhode Island. In those states and in the others where a high degree of judicial insulation exists, some increased accountability might be worthy of consideration. This could take the form of either popular reconfirmation or the recall process. The recall is an aspect of direct democracy which is less known than the initiative and referendum process. The recall allows voters to circulate valid petitions seeking the names of registered voters to "recall" an elected official. If the required number of valid names can be gathered, the official must stand for reconfirmation in a special (or at the next general) election. For judges, the recall mechanism is not widely used.

Occasionally, however, it is utilized, as in the case of Circuit Judge William L. Reinecke of Lancaster, Wisconsin. In May of 1982, Judge Reinecke barely survived a recall election prompted by his comment, from the bench, that a five-year-old victim of sexual assault was "unusually promiscuous." Reinecke made the comments in December of 1981, when sentencing a 24-year-old farmhand he described as mildly retarded for the assault of the five-year-old daughter of the woman with whom he was, at the time, living. Reinecke sentenced the convicted man to a 90-day work release jail term and probation. A recall drive began almost immediately.

Interestingly enough, Judge Reinecke survived the recall with a 50.85 percent "yes" vote. At the time, he told reporters, "I hope I've learned by this. I'm a human being. I made a mistake, and I'll make another mistake. But I'm going to watch what I say." To the extent that Reinecke might also watch the sentences he hands down, the recall might have served its purpose.

The Reinecke case is typical in that, even in instances of widespread popular dissatisfaction with a judge, judges are normally retained in their posts. Still, the concepts of both recall and reconfirmation have great merit if we place store in a system which is more democratic than elitist. As Professor Gerard noted in his examination of a retention system for federal judges:

> As courts have entered, and come to dominate, areas which formerly were the exclusive province of the political branches, a backlash against the resolution of social problems by politically irresponsible judges has developed. Only at great peril can we ignore the wisdom embodied in Justice [Felix] Frankfurter's observation that a court's authority "ultimately rests on sustained public confidence in its moral sanction."

Conservatives should look for opportunities to increase popular involvement in a structured, responsible manner which will sustain popular support for the judiciary.

Criminal Justice: Possibilities for Reform

It is no wonder that Americans are more afraid of crime than ever before, as indicated in the January 1983 Gallup Poll noted above. Every year, the Federal Bureau of Investigation (FBI) in Washington, D.C., issues a lengthy report on crime in the United States. One of the more telling graphs contained in the report is the "Crime Clock" which illustrates in brief the frequency of crime in the United States. Either crime has been increasing during the last 10 years, or clocks are ticking slower. In 1971, Americans could expect a murder every 30 minutes, a rape every 13 minutes and another violent crime every 39 seconds. By 1981, the figures were even more disturbing. Murders were occuring every 23 minutes, a rape every 6 minutes, and another violent crime every 24 seconds!

Crime is affecting more and more Americans. The January 1983 Gallup Poll found that crime affected 25 percent of American households during 1982. The 1982 FBI Report on Crime in the U.S., which is based on the actual accumulation of all reported crimes in the country, found a slightly higher percentage: 25 million American households (30 percent of the total) were victims of crime. U.S. families are actually more liable to have a member attacked in a serious crime (rape, robbery or aggravated assault) than to have a residential fire or have a member injured in an automobile accident. Family members are more likely to be robbed than to be stricken by cancer or heart disease, this country's leading health problems.

There are some signs that improvement might be on the horizon. No doubt because of increased public awareness of crime and support for toughened criminal justice statutes at the state level, the incidence of crime held steady or even declined slightly in many communities during 1982.[3] But it is important to remember that even in those instances, the sheer *volume* of crime is much higher today than it was only a decade ago.

How has this state of affairs developed? Many sociologists and psychologists argue that somehow society is to blame for the increase in crime. Perhaps they are right, but not in the sense they intend. "Society"—all of us—may indeed be at fault for the increase in crime. We have tolerated increasing judicial interferences in day-to-day police work. We have allowed legislators to acquiesce in such judicial intervention and not assert the legislative power to remedy judicial excesses. Finally, too many Americans have allowed unbelievably tortured judicial reasoning to turn murderers and rapists loose on our communities.

Perhaps the classic case of judicial legislation in the criminal justice area was *Miranda v. Arizona* (1966). The *Miranda* case came from allegations of police misconduct during questioning of criminal suspects. Specifically, the Court held that voluntary confessions were not admissable as evidence unless the suspect were treated in a particular manner *invented* by the Court. For instance, if the accused had not been informed of his right to remain silent and his right to counsel, a completely voluntary confession was inadmissible evidence in court. In dictating the specific rules for police interrogation, the Court clearly extended its role from constitutional interpretation and review to legislating. As Alexander Bickel points out, the *Miranda* Court did not review congressional laws about interrogation but undertook "to promulgate on its own hook . . . a detailed set of rules—a veritable police manual—governing practices of interrogation." As Bickel asserts, the *Miranda* case clearly violates the important premise that the Court should work "not as a front line administrator, executive or legislator nor as an initial policy maker, but as a reviewing agency."

Such decisions do not exist in a vacuum. They have an effect on real situations, real neighborhoods, real victims of crime. Judicial expansion of the rights of criminals, at the expense of the rest of us, has played a major role in the growth of crime. In his essay "Making

Criminal Justice Work" in *Criminal Justice Reform,* Professor William Stanmeyer summarized in one devastating paragraph the reality of crime in modern America:

> Crime is a frightening problem. In 1980, almost one-third of all homes were victimized, a reported 23,000 Americans were killed by criminals; rapes and burglaries are so frequent that at least one of each will take place during the time it takes to read this essay. The perpetrators of the majority of crimes are under the age of 30; in roughly one-third of all crimes the perpetrator, of whatever age, is a repeat offender. Television police stories notwithstanding, in most cases nobody apprehends the offender; in many if not most cases where the police do indeed catch him, he does not stand trial for the original offense; even if so tried, he has a good chance of a "not guilty" verdict; if found guilty, he may well receive a light sentence. If sentenced, he will find himself in a prison where its long-term inmates will school him further in the arts of violence and deceit. We have far more crimes than convictions. Thus we have far more crime than punishment.

Crime is nothing new, and what to do about crime—in most cases—is no great mystery. In the Old Testament, the Preacher said, "Why do people commit crimes so readily? Because crime is not punished quickly enough. A sinner may commit a hundred crimes and still live." (Ecclesiastes 8:11–12)

In 1981, President Reagan touched upon these truths in a speech to the International Association of Chiefs of Police in New Orleans. The President said: "The war on crime will only be won when an attitude of mind and a change of heart take place in America—when certain truths take hold again . . . truths like: right and wrong matter; individuals are responsible for their actions; retribution should be swift and sure for those who prey on the innocent." Attorney General William French Smith, normally the most restrained and mild-mannered of men, reflected the quietly building anger which many Americans bring to criminal justice issues. He told a congressional subcommittee that it was time to stop wasting scarce resources in rehabilitation of criminals, when what is needed first is more thinking on "punishment, deterrence and protection of the public." Attorney General Smith, and most conservatives, would be the first to say that rehabilitation and genuine efforts to understand criminals are laudable. *But first,* we have to bring the epidemic of crime under control.

The Comprehensive Crime Control Act. In March of 1983, President Reagan presented a detailed crime fighting package to the Congress of the United States, identified as the Comprehensive Crime Control Act of 1983, or the Domestic Defense Act of 1983. For conservatives who had been extremely disappointed in many Administrative initiatives, the Crime Control Act was a breath of fresh air. Although portions of the package might actually be enacted into law during the

98th Congress (1983–1985), it is more likely that the package will serve largely to spark debate, with only some portions gaining approval in the near future.

The legislation consisted of 16 titles. Although it was not a comprehensive reform of the criminal code, it nevertheless was a comprehensive approach to reform of important criminal justice statutes. In the area of bail reform, the Reagan proposal would authorize pretrial detention of defendants shown to be dangerous to the community and reverse the presumption in favor of bail while appeals are being processed. Courts would be authorized to inquire into the sources of bail, and could refuse to accept money or property that might not assure a defendant's appearance at trial.

In the area of sentencing, earlier proposals were substantially toughened and parole could be abolished under the Administration proposal. Forfeiture of criminal property would be made easier, and labor racketeering would be easier to prosecute.

In two areas, the package was not perfect, but was still a substantial improvement over the present state of affairs. First, under the President's proposal the exclusionary rule would be modified to stop the suppression of evidence in criminal trials if a police officer had acted in reasonable good faith, in the belief that his or her actions were in accordance with the Constitution's protections against unreasonable search and seizure. As emphasized in the discussion that follows, it would be preferable to abolish the exclusionary rule outright. Second, under the President's proposal the use of the insanity defense in federal proceedings would be more restricted. However, pleas of "not guilty by reason of insanity" would still be permitted. Many conservatives, including this writer, prefer either abolition of the insanity defense, or creation of a new verdict of "guilty but insane." The case for a guilty but insane verdict was made succinctly by Senator Edward Zorinsky (D-Neb.) in *Criminal Justice Reform*. Although it could be better, the Administration's proposed toughening of the insanity defense is still quite good, and worthy of national support.

Other portions of the Administration crime package in its original form focused on reinstitution of capital punishment, toughening of drug enforcement provisions, mandatory penalties for use of a firearm during commission of a crime, Federal Tort Claims Act amendments, and many other issues. In particular, provisions to allow more frequent prosecution of child pornography should have unanimous conservative support.

The Comprehensive Crime Control Act of 1983 could, if actually enacted, constitute the most enduring legacy of the Reagan Administration. Americans have been eager for leadership on the crime issue for many years, and the emergence of Ronald Reagan and William French Smith on these issues can only be viewed positively. As long as these critical proposals remain as "pure" as they were when presented to the Congress, the Administration should be able to count on the support of conservatives around the country.[4]

Specific Criminal Justice Reforms. Three significant reforms in criminal procedure are needed as soon as possible to assist peace officers in their efforts to protect innocent, law-abiding citizens. These reforms are: abolition of the exclusionary rule, significant toughening of bail provisions and substantial reform of habeas corpus procedures. These last two are included in the President's comprehensive package outlined above. A fourth reform of the criminal justice system would be to assert the rights of victims with greater clarity. These four reforms are examined in turn in the following pages.

In his essay, "Excluding the Exclusionary Rule" in *Criminal Justice Reform,* Professor Steven Schlesinger makes a persuasive case for outright abolition of the exclusionary rule. The exclusionary rule, as the doctrine now operates, allows an individual, who may in fact have committed a crime, to be set free—not because he is innocent but because a judge finds that evidence necessary to establish his guilt was seized in violation of the Fourth Amendment's "reasonableness" standards for searches.

It is important to remember that the exclusionary rule is not in the Constitution. It is a court-made rule of evidence that was not applied to federal criminal trials until 1914 and state criminal trials until 1961. As Justice Benjamin Cardozo noted, the exclusionary rule is an inversion of logic: "The criminal is to go free because the constable has blundered." As Dean S. J. Wigmore wrote satirically in his *Treatise on the Anglo-American System of Evidence:*

> Titus, you have been found guilty of conducting a lottery; Flavius, you have confessedy violated the Constitution. Titus ought to suffer imprisonment for crime and Flavius for contempt. But no! We shall not punish Flavius directly, but shall do so by reversing Titus' conviction. This is our way of teaching people like Flavius to behave, and incidently of securing respect for the Constitution. Our way of upholding the Constitution is not to strike at the man who breaks it, but to let off somebody else who broke something else.

Professor Schlesinger and others have proposed intelligent and workable alternatives to the exclusionary rule, creation of independent review boards within police departments which could take disciplinary action against police officers who do violate search and seizure standards. In addition, Schlesinger would allow innocent victims of illegal searches to seek civil remedies as a curb to official misconduct.

These and other proposals for elimination of the exclusionary rule seek to uphold its stated purpose—curbing official misconduct—while fulfilling the larger goal of a rational criminal justice system: the determination of guilt and innocence.[5]

Studies of bail standards have built a convincing case for substantial revisions of federal bail policy. Nineteen studies over the last 15 years have documented the high incidence of crime committed by individuals free on bail.

In his essay, "Bailing Out a Failed Law" in *Criminal Justice Reform*, Randall R. Rader makes a convincing case, both from historical and rational perspectives, for the needed revisions. At present, judicial officers can only deny bail to criminal defendants on the basis of whether or not said defendants are likely to show up at their trails. Rader recommends changes in the Bail Reform Act of 1966 which would:

> ... (1) permit judicial officers to consider community safety when setting nonfinancial pretrial conditions of release, (2) allow the pretrial detention of defendants when no conceivable conditions for release are sufficient to ensure their appearance at trial or to ensure the safety of the community or of other persons, (3) authorize temporary detention of individuals arrested while free on some form of conditional release, and (4) provide procedures to revoke earlier release determinations for violations of the conditions of release.

The Constitution provides that: "The privilege of the writ of habeas corpus shall not be suspended, unless when in cases of rebellion or invasion the public safety may require it." The term *habeas corpus ad subjiciendum* refers to the right of prisoners to obtain a (judicial) writ as a protection against unjust or illegal imprisonment. The constitutional provision upholds rights to inquire into the lawfulness of imprisonment.

In recent American history, however, the writ of habeas corpus has been abused. In 1971, Supreme Court Justice John Marshall Harlan addressed himself to this legal doctrine which is frustrating the effective deterrence of crime: "No one, not criminal defendants, not the judicial system, not society as a whole is benefited by a judgment providing that a man shall tentatively go to jail today, but tomorrow and every day thereafter shall be subject to fresh litigation on issues already decided."

As long as criminal punishment is subject to endless appeals and legal maneuverings, as long as the defendant has no incentive to admit his mistake and begin constructive preparations to reenter society, the judicial system is burdened with unnecessary (and costly) proceedings, and society's objective of sending a clear deterrent message is eroded. In modern criminal practice, it has almost become grounds for a malpractice suit to fail to lodge numerous "collateral" habeas corpus attacks on a final decision of guilt. These collateral attacks often seek freedom for a convict on grounds ranging from the incompetence of a court-appointed attorney to undesirable prison conditions.

While the Constitution guarantees the writ of habeas corpus, no right for prisoners convicted in *state* courts to petition *federal* courts for release existed until 1867 when *Congress*—not the courts—created a statutory means for state prisoners to appeal to federal tribunals. It is clear, then, that Congress can refashion that statutory right to preclude abuses by state prisoners.

In his essay on "Proposals for Habeas Corpus Reform" in *Criminal Justice Reform,* Attorney General William French Smith argues:

> The most straightforward solution to tensions, burdens, and inefficiencies presently resulting from federal habeas corpus would be the simple abolition of federal habeas corpus for state criminal convicts. If this were done, state defendants would continue to have access to the various remedies and means of review provided in the state courts for the protection of their rights. Such a reform would, of course, have no effect on direct review of state judgments in the Supreme Court. Hence, the mechanism contemplated by the Constitution for the preservation of the uniformity and supremacy of federal law—direct review in the Supreme Court—would be in no way impaired.

Although the desirability of Attorney General Smith's suggested reform is clear, he does not believe such a sweeping revision of criminal procedure is achievable at the present time. Thus, the habeas corpus reform finally placed in the Crime Control Act of 1983 would require greater deference by federal courts to adjudication by state courts, as long as the state procedures were "full and fair." The Administration's suggested reforms would also limit "the time within which a person convicted of a state offense could seek to challenge that state conviction in federal court."

The three substantive changes in criminal procedure outlined above—abolition of the exclusionary rule, tightening of bail provisions and substantial reform of habeas corpus procedures—would do a great deal to support meaningful efforts to combat crime. The fourth suggested reform, reasserting the rights of victims, represents as much as anything a change in the focus of the criminal justice system.

Conservatives were heartened when the 97th Congress passed the Witness and Victim Assistance Act of 1982. The law requires that presentencing reports include a "Victim Impact Statement," a concept examined by Senator Paul Laxalt (R-Nev.) in *Criminal Justice Reform.* The Act also amended former law to permit the Attorney

General to obtain court orders prohibiting the intimidation or harassment of witnesses or victims by suspects.

However, as Senator Laxalt noted, aspects of the original legislation were lost in the give and take between the House and Senate. Among the key items dropped from the bill before final passage were provisions for witness security and relocation, and a provision "which would have held the Bureau of Prisons and the Parole Commission accountable for grossly negligent acts which resulted in the premature release of a dangerous felon." Senator Laxalt plans to focus on these matters in the 98th Congress.

In another essay on victims rights, Frank L. Carrington and Linda J. Duggan of the Victims Assistance Legal Organization (VALOR) examined a variety of ideas which could restore the victims to a more significant role in our system. One of these is compensation, governmental provision for financial reimbursement to victims for some of the losses they incur in crime. Many conservatives believe that compensation programs on a massive scale might result in the kind of financial drain which has contributed to present federal and state government deficits.

An additional area of expanding victim involvement in the criminal justice system seems more in line with conservative philosophy and justice. Restitution is defined by the National Symposium on Restitution as ". . . a sanction imposed by an official of the criminal justice system requiring the offender to make a payment of money or service to either the direct or substitute crime victim." Carrington and Duggan note the benefits of restitution:

1. It is at least a first step toward making the victim financially whole.
2. It may have a rehabilitative effect on the perpetrator in that, through the act of making payment, he must, of necessity, recognize that he has injured another.
3. It costs the taxpayers very little because, with the exception of administrative costs, repayment to the victim comes from the violator and not from the public coffers.
4. The release of some individuals conditioned upon restitution to their victims may alleviate, to a certain extent, overcrowding in prisons and jails.

As Carrington and Duggan point out, "Compensation and restitution concepts symbolize the desire of the system to come to grips with the rights and the needs of crime victims and do something about them."

Popular Involvement in Criminal Justice Reform. One of the most significant developments of the 1982 election was the emergence of a number of criminal justice ballot questions. In June, California voters approved the sweeping Gann Initiative, known popularly as the Victim's Bill of Rights. In September, citizens in the District of Columbia approved a mandatory sentencing initiative after an unusual alliance was forged between black neighborhood activists and the National Rifle Association.

On the November 2 ballots around the country, bail toughening provisions gained approval in Arizona, Colorado and Illinois. Florida voters approved two significant measures: one toughening up on search/seizure and one focusing on pretrial release and detention. In Missouri, the people voted to remove the requirement that the state Supreme Court review every term of life imprisonment. In Nevada and New Hampshire, voters chose to reaffirm the right to keep and bear arms, while the Death Penalty passed easily in Massachusetts. While the two proposals passed earlier in 1982 were both initiatives, all of the proposals on November 2, 1982, were referred—placed on the ballot by the state legislatures. Finally, also on November 2, voters handily rejected the Handgun Control Initiative in California.

Given what appears to be strongly conservative sentiment on crime/justice issues, there could be an opportunity for conservative activism, particularly in those states where the initiative device is available. However, it should also be kept in mind that *even* in those states where the initiative is not available, the lesson of the 1982 election is that it is possible to get right-leaning ballot propositions before the voters through legislative referral. Conservatives around the country should look carefully to see what appropriate opportunities exist for such activity in their states and communities.

Other examples of citizen impact on the criminal justice system can be cited. One of the most prominent is Mothers Against Drunk Driving (MADD), a grass roots organization formed by a California woman whose daughter was killed by a drunk driver. In March of 1983, this group was the focus of a made-for-television movie.

A well-publicized instance of popular influence on a criminal case occurred in the summer of 1982 in the case of Joseph (Jo-Jo) Giorgianni. Giorgianni, who weighed 560 pounds, was convicted of "carnally abusing and debauching the morals of a 14-year-old girl." New Jersey Superior Court Judge Richard J. S. Barlow, Jr. initially sentenced Giorgianni to 15 years in prison. But Giorgianni's counsel contended that prison life threatened the health of his client, who, it was contended, should not be imprisoned due to asthma and high blood pressure, among other ailments. Incredibly, the judge reduced the sex offender's sentence to three years of probation and a $2,000 fine. Giorgianni had served one week in jail. This particular judicial scandal touched off what might mildly be described as a nationwide public furor. As a result, the Mercer County prosecutor's office appealed the decision, and eventually a New Jersey appeals court allowed Judge Barlow to reimprison Giorgianni.

In Maryland, organizations such as the Stephanie Roper Committee and the Family Protection Lobby are working to strengthen the state's sentencing laws. The Roper case involved a 22-year-old Frostburg State College student who was murdered in 1982 outside of Washington, D.C. Two young men were apprehended, tried and convicted in the case, during which evidence emerged that they had beaten, raped, shot, maimed and then burned their victim. The two men were given "life" terms which would make them eligible for parole in 12 years. The prospect of these two men ever being able to walk the streets in freedom sparked creation of the Roper Committee.

As a direct result, several "Roper Bills" were introduced in the state, and as this was written the measures appeared to have excellent prospects for passage. Among those being pushed by the Family Protection Lobby was a measure to eliminate the state Parole Commission and replace it with a sentencing board, a major element of President Reagan's package at the federal level.

One of the most innovative approaches to judicial accountability—a crucial element in criminal justice reform—is the "Court Watch Project" of the Washington Legal Foundation (WLF). As explained by WLF Founder Dan Popeo, the Court Watch Project "is designed to promote public scrutiny and accountability of prosecutors, judges and parole boards who are too lenient with criminals at the expense of crime victims and the law-oriented public." The Court Watch Project is the sort of no-nonsense, action-oriented program that makes ACLU lawyers and activist judges extremely nervous. The Project has the great merit of existing in, and for, the real world, and not in the esoteric realms of legal theory.

As Popeo tells it, "The Project began as a result of numerous complaints received by WLF from its members across the country. The Foundation frequently receives reports either by telephone calls or letters, oftentimes accompanied by newspaper articles about criminal cases which seem to have been decided without due regard to the public interest." WLF has already investigated more than 500 local, state and federal judges, examining their decisions for legal correctness and philosophy. Most judges, of course, are simply doing their job. But some are making law, and this is where WLF comes in. In the most egregious cases, "WLF has initiated formal disciplinary review proceedings before state judicial conduct commissions and has assisted in initiating others."

Naturally, WLF has drawn bitter criticism for some of its activities. But most of the charges made have been, as Popeo puts it, "over-drawn, inaccurate and unfounded." Supreme Court Justice Hugo Black pointed out: "The assumption that respect for the judiciary can be won by shielding judges from . . . criticism wrongly appraises the character of American legal opinion. For it is a prized American privilege to speak one's mind . . . on all public institutions. And an enforced silence, however, limited solely in the name of preserving the dignity of the bench, would probably engender resentment, suspicion, and contempt much more than it would enhance respect."

Given the fact that we live in an era in which judges are deciding upon administrative, procedural and legislative matters which traditionally were not in their sphere, it is entirely appropriate to seek methods to bring judges back to responsible positions. In the absence of more direct methods of popular involvement in the system, the kind of simple scrutiny of judicial opinions and actions advocated by the Washington Legal Foundation is worthwhile indeed. Conservatives around the country should consider starting Court Watch Projects in their own communities. The "how to" is explained in WLF's *Court Watch Manual: A Citizen's Guide to Judicial Accountability*.

Conclusion

The authority of our legal system, and of the Supreme Court and other federal courts, rests on "sustained public confidence in its moral sanction," as Justice Felix Frankfurter wrote more than 20 years ago. This public confidence has declined in recent years, not because of any moral decline or shift in the citizenry, but because judges have assumed powers which simply do not belong to them. Perhaps this reality is nowhere clearer than in judicial efforts to pull this great nation away from its religious and ethical heritage. In a footnote near the end of his controversial opinion, Judge Brevard Hand of Alabama, although he was discussing school prayer *per se*, offered an admonition to his colleagues on the federal bench which has applicability beyond the particular issues of *Jaffree v. School Commissioners of Mobile County*. Hand wrote:

> The founding fathers were far wiser than we. They were content to allow the peoples of the various states to handle these matters as they saw fit and were patient in permitting the processes of change to develop orderly by established procedure. They were not impatient to bring about a change because we think today that it is the proper course or to set about to justify by misinterpretation the original intent of the framers of the Constitution. We must remember that "He, who reigns within Himself, and rules passions, desires, and fears, is more a king." Milton, *Paradise Regained*. If we who today rule, do not follow the teachings of history then surely the very weight of what we are about will bring down the house upon our head, and the public having rightly lost respect in the integrity of the institution, will ultimately bring about its change or even its demise.

As this nation conceived in liberty approaches the bicentennial of the Constitution, it is time to consider to what degree our institutions have wavered from the intent of the framers, and to what extent the federal courts have chosen to ignore the standard ratified and sustained by the popular will. To the extent either has occurred, it is the challenge of the 1980s to reorient our institutions and our leaders toward what former Senator Sam Ervin has called "the most precious instrument of government the world has ever known." In this democratic republic, it is the job of all of us to keep the system honest.

Notes

[1] Some portions of this chapter are adapted from "Judicial Oligarchy: Have the People Ceased to Be Their Own Rulers?" in *A Blueprint for Judicial Reform* (Washington, D.C.: Free Congress Foundation, 1981) and the first chapter of *Criminal Justice Reform* (Chicago: Regnery Gateway, Free Congress Foundation, 1983). Both were co-written with Randall R. Rader, Chief Counsel for the Senate Judiciary Committee's Subcommittee on the Constitution. The opinions expressed in this chapter of *Future 21* are mine.

[2] The Senate rejected the Reagan Voluntary School Prayer Amendment in March 1984 by a vote of 56–44. On May 15, 1984, a moderate "Equal Access" bill received majority support, 270–151, in the House of Representatives. However, the 270 affirmative votes were 11 short of the two-thirds majority needed to pass the legislation under the parliamentary tactic employed to secure a floor vote. Majority support for the pro-religious freedom measures in both houses of Congress indicated the saliency of school prayer and related issues, which were expected to play a vital role in the 1984 elections and future contests.

[3] This trend toward less crime accelerated dramatically in 1983.

[4] After this chapter was completed, events in Congress changed some of the particulars previously listed. Key elements of the President's original proposal were divided into separate legislation. On February 2, 1984, the Senate passed S. 1762, a worthy proposal which incorporates significant reforms in bail, sentencing, insanity defense, forfeiture provisions and other matters. The vote approving S. 1762 was 91–1. On February 6 the Senate voted 67–9 to support S. 1763, providing for habeas corpus (related to sentencing and incarceration appeals) reform. On February 7 the Senate backed S. 1764, providing for the "good faith" exception to the judicially-created exclusionary rule. On February 22 the Senate voted 62–32 in favor of S. 1765, designed to create a new federal Death Penalty. Although Congressman Peter Rodino (D-N.J.) pronounced bail, exclusionary rule, habeas corpus and death penalty reforms "Dead on Arrival" in the House of Representatives, clear sentiment

in favor of these and other reforms had led to some movement on the criminal justice reform measures in early summer 1984. Although I remain optimistic about long-term substantive reform, odds are it will not be enacted by the 98th Congress.

[5] Presidential Counselor and Attorney General-designate Edwin Meese II has supported a "reasonable good faith" exception to the exclusionary rule. Meese's standard would allow admission of evidence so long as the law enforcement officers were acting in a reasonable good faith belief that their actions were in accord with Supreme Court interpretations of the Fourth Amendment. On June 11, 1984, the Supreme Court established an "inevitable discovery" exception to the exclusionary rule. In essence, the Court's new standard will allow prosecutors to use evidence if they can prove that law enforcement officers would have eventually found it anyway.

15

The Reform of Democratic Institutions: The National Initiative

Paul M. Weyrich

In my travels around this great country, one of the saddest things I have encountered is the increasing sense among many voters that elections simply do not make a difference. After working in the political trenches for many years, I can understand why average, hard-working, patriotic Americans feel this way.

In election after election, politicians have campaigned as fiscally responsible conservatives who would come to Washington to cut the bureaucracy and reduce the size of government. Yet, when they arrived in the nation's capital, these same politicians found themselves surrounded by lobbyists demanding ever-increasing government appropriations for this or that boondoggle. All too many of our elected officials eventually succumb to the lobbyists.

As a result, little real change has occurred in Washington, despite a string of conservative victories in the late 1970s and early 1980s. With the election of President Ronald Reagan and a host of brand new conservatives to the Congress in 1980, the size of government has continued to expand, the real tax burden has continued to rise, and the bureaucracy has increased its powers. By early 1983, grassroots activists who worked their hearts out for conservatives in 1978, 1980 and 1982 were being offered the spectacle of one "conservative" tax increase after another, and serious discussion of the repeal of indexing of income tax tables.

In this context, it is not surprising that more and more Americans are looking with favor on the voter initiative, a process by which the people themselves can decide directly upon issues of vital importance. Shortly after the 1982 election, initiative expert Patrick B.

McGuigan described what is going on around the country in a "op-ed" piece for the *Christian Science Monitor.* McGuigan wrote: "[V]oters across the ideological spectrum have become more and more convinced that many of their most pressing concerns—ranging from tax relief to the safety of nuclear power—are not addressed by state legislatures, where well-organized groups manage to control what is debated. The initiative process is viewed by its supporters . . . as an important safety valve to supplement, not undermine, representative democracy."

The initiative is simply the most direct form of the referendum. In essence, any yes/no vote of the people on a ballot issue is a referendum. More specifically, there are three types of referenda. Initiatives are those ballot questions (referenda) that come to the ballot as a result of citizen petitioning. Such proposals can be either constitutional or statutory. On the other hand, referred measures are those ballot questions which come to the ballot as the result of legislative action, constitutional edict, or some other mandate of state government. Such proposals can be constitutional amendments, statutes, bond issues, advisory proposals or other types of measures.

Finally, there is the popular referendum, the rarest form of direct democracy. Those states which have the popular referendum allow citizens to circulate petitions calling for a vote of the people on legislation already passed by the legislature. When journalists refer to the whole process of voters deciding upon ballot measures, they simply call it initiative and referendum (I&R). In the discussion that follows, we will be most concerned with the initiative itself.

On June 6, 1978, California's Proposition 13—which dramatically reduced property tax assessments—became the most famous initiative in history. But for 80 years prior to that vote, conservatives enjoyed success with the voter initiative.

The process of passing or repealing legislation through petitions by the people and elections on the issues began in the United States in South Dakota in 1898. Twenty-three states at present allow for the initiative, while three others allow the popular referendum only.

An analysis of the historical results by the Congressional Research Service of 1,200 ballot propositions found that, by better than a 5 to 1 margin, voters have rejected regulatory boards and regulations and, by a 3½ to 1 margin, they have turned thumbs down on taxing and spending measures.

Of course, I do not agree with every I&R measure passed in every state, but neither do I agree with every law passed by the 50 state legislatures or by the U.S. Congress. In fact, the predominantly conservative outcome of the I&R proposals contrasts sharply with the liberal record of the Congress and many of the legislatures.

Since Proposition 13, conservatives have become even more active in utilizing the initiative. It would not be practical to list all of the recent success stories, but two cases deserve special mention.

In November 1980, Massachusetts—the home state of Tip O'Neill and Teddy Kennedy—voted 1,424,248 to 999,449 for Question 2, more commonly known as "Proposition 2½" because it limited property tax assessments to 2½ percent of appraised value.

The Citizens for Limited Taxation, a grass-roots organization, was able to defeat the combined power of the public employee unions, the Massachusetts Council of Churches, the League of Women Voters and the Massachusetts Teachers Association.

In September 1982, by a vote of 70,037 to 26,179, the residents of Washington, D.C., gave approval to an initiative proposal to require minimum sentences for crimes committed with a firearm. This new law reached the ballot through a petition of the people after the City Council voted overwhelmingly against it. This anti-crime measure was also opposed by the *Washington Post* and the American Civil Liberties Union (ACLU). Interestingly enough, the supporters of the mandatory sentencing initiative included black voters and the National Rifle Association (NRA), a coalition that must have nonplussed the liberal establishment.

Thus, in perhaps the two most liberal areas of the country, where left-wing politicians are regularly elected to office, the conservative position on major issues prevailed *only because of the initiative process.* The gap between the general public and elected politicians is not, of course, limited to only these issues.

One of the reasons for the disparity may be due to the nature of representative government itself. Congressional and legislative seats are not apportioned on the basis of voter turnout or even on the basis of registered voters. In fact, apportionment is not even based on the number of potential voters (those citizens over 18), but rather on total population. It would be theoretically possible for a district to have no registered voters at all!

Thus, low-voting, often liberal constituencies are awarded seats in Congress and the legislatures based on their population. But when an issue is placed on the ballot, the outcome is based on the total overall turnout and vote.

For instance, in 1980, 296,260 people voted in the conservative 7th District in Houston, Texas, while only 93,026 voted in the liberal 18th Congressional District in Houston. Both of these districts receive equal representation in Congress. But if the people had a chance to vote directly upon an issue, it is easy to see how conservative sentiment would often prevail.

Another reason why the legislative process frequently fails to reflect the will of the people is because of the power of well-organized interests with paid lobbyists. When governmental decisions are being made, the voices of these groups are always heard loud and clear. Unfortunately, often no one is around to speak up for the average citizen.

President John F. Kennedy, in his book *Profiles in Courage,* written while he was a U.S. senator from Massachusetts, pointed out that it is very difficult for public officials to know what the people are really thinking: "In Washington, I frequently find myself believing that forty or fifty letters, six visits from professional politicians and lobbyists, and three editorials in Massachusetts newspapers constitute public opinion on a given issue. Yet in truth I rarely know how the great majority of the voters feel, or even how much they know of the issues that seem so burning in Washington."

Kennedy also expressed his belief that a legislator should sometimes disregard the views of his or her constituents: "It is difficult to accept such a narrow view of the role of a U.S. Senator that assumes the people sent me to Washington to serve merely as a seismograph to record shifts in popular opinion . . . This may mean that we must on occasion lead, inform, correct and *sometimes even ignore constituent opinion* if we are to exercise fully the judgment for which we were elected." (Emphasis added.)

Although there is a kernel of truth in Kennedy's view, you can understand how this kind of attitude, which is typical of many elected officials, would lead to giving away the Panama Canal, for example, even though the American people were overwhelmingly against it. Likewise, if the voters had the right of initiative on a national level, there is little doubt that, despite the intransigence of Congress, legislation could be passed to prohibit deficit spending by the federal government, to restore voluntary school prayer and to prohibit forced busing, to name just a few.

I have always thought the initiative was a useful device at the state and local level. Originally I believed the process should not be considered at the national level but I have changed my mind.

In 1978 and 1982, the Gallup Poll surveyed Americans to find out their attitudes on the prospective use of the initiative on a national level. Both surveys found the concept was favored by a 2-1 majority (other polls have found equal or even greater support). Interestingly, nearly identical proportions of Republicans, Democrats and independents agreed, an unusual finding on any question of political significance.

There are several different ways the initiative could work on a national level. One group, Americans for the National Voter Initiative, headed by Edward A. Dent of Washington, D.C., has advocated a statutory initiative plan.

Dent's proposal, which has been introduced in Congress by Jack Kemp (R-N.Y.), would permit ordinary laws—but not constitutional amendments—to be passed through I&R. To get a proposal placed on the ballot, a petition would have to contain the signatures of registered voters equal to three percent of the number of people who voted in the last presidential election. Based on the 1980 election, this would amount to 2.5 million signatures. There would be a time limit of 18 months to gather these signatures. The referendum on the proposal would be held at the same time as the next scheduled congressional elections. If it received a majority of all of the votes cast, it would become law—just as if it had passed the Congress and been signed by the president.

This version of the national initiative would preclude conservative oriented constitutional amendments—such as a balanced budget requirement, school prayer, and so forth—but it would still be a starting point for direct citizen influence on national policy. The Kemp proposal would also exempt popular consideration of foreign policy and treaty issues. Still, there are many important proposals which could be passed on a statutory level.

Those who have advocated a national initiative for constitutional amendments would require voter approval of such amendments in each of at least three fourths of the states (38). The referendums could be scheduled by the state legislatures any time within seven years after the signatures had been gathered and certified.

Another variation would provide for an indirect system of national initiative, which exists in several states and has worked well. Under this plan, when the signatures on the petitions were obtained, Congress would then have an opportunity to consider the proposed measure. After public hearings and debates, if Congress passed the proposal in substantially the same form in which it was presented, no referendum would be necessary (unless this variation of I&R included constitutional amendments in which case referendums in each state would still be needed). But if Congress did not pass it, the measure would then be placed on the ballot for a vote of the people. In addition, Congress could propose alternatives to appear on the ballot, along with the proposal that originated through citizen petitions.

There may be other national initiative plans worthy of serious consideration. The specifics are not as important as the general concept of allowing the people to have a greater voice in their government. There are, of course, serious arguments against the initiative in any form. In sum, however, these arguments against expansion of the initiative at either the state or national level betray a general distrust of the people.

Some claim that the initiative is contrary to the intent of our Founding Fathers in establishing representative government. While it is true that the framers made no provision for direct democracy, this argument is somewhat simplistic. Most states have used referenda to ratify state constitutional amendments *from the very beginning of their establishment as states of the union.* Today, Delaware is the only state which does not *require* the consent of the people for enactment of constitutional amendments.

Initiative opponent Clifford D. Sharp admitted in a 1911 Fabian Society pamphlet that referenda have always been a part of Western government process:

> Historically the referendum is the offspring by unbroken descent of the primitive mass meeting of self-governing citizens. Both in Switzerland and the United States, the only countries where it flourishes today, the whole body of citizens were from the earliest times . . . accustomed to exercise all the functions of government for themselves in open assembly. This direct control over the affairs of State was never entirely surrendered, and when the assemblies of all the citizens became impracticable and more and more and more powers had to be delegated to representative councils, the referendum came into being gradually and naturally, not as an accession of popular power, but as a mere retention by the sovereign people of certain important powers in their own hands.

Gordon S. Wood, a professor of history at Brown University, writing in the book, *How Democratic Is the Constitution?*, states: "Americans in 1776 thought of democracy in a traditional classical manner. . . . It meant literally government by the people, referring in the strictest sense to political gatherings of the people in town meetings and the like."

In a review of the book, Art Kelly, writing in the January 1982 *Initiative and Referendum Report,* summarized this very well:

> Because travel and communications were extremely difficult in this time period, the representative system of government that was established in Congress was a good substitute for a more direct democracy. But in the current age of television, radio, newspapers, national wire services, and weekly news magazines, it is now realistically possible to effectively employ initiative and referendum as a form of nation-wide town meeting on those issues of major concern to the voters. To do so would be entirely consistent with the philosophy of a majority of the American people in the post-Revolutionary War period.

Another argument against the initiative is that clever advertising and public relations can trick the voters. Thus, the argument goes, ordinary citizens should not be allowed to vote on important matters, which are best left to the experts. This argument is elitist and anti-democratic. The concept of rule by the people is based on the premise that the voters will make the right decisions most of the time. The people are no more vulnerable to being deceived on referendum issues than they are on candidates for public office. In fact, if there has been any artificial political merchandising, it is in the election of candidates. The Joe McGinness book *The Selling of the President, 1968* and the Robert Redford movie *The Candidate* document in fact and fiction how candidates for public office are merchandised and sold to viewers.

Assuming the voters do occasionally make mistakes in their decisions on specific issues, it seems far better to decide incorrectly upon an issue than to make a collective mistake on a candidate. Once elected, the wrong person can do harm on a spectrum of issues for two, four or six years. And, as we have seen, he or she can commit these errors far removed from the voters' daily scrutiny, with the active encouragement of lobbyists and the establishment. In contrast, a bad piece of legislation voted into force through a referendum is limited to one subject. Bad legislation can be repealed through the same process by which it was instigated.

Opponents of the initiative claim that it produces poor legislation because it is not subject to the checks and balances of the legislative process. Of course, for the indirect initiative this criticism is not true. Even for the direct initiative, this criticism is not correct.

In the modern era, the legislative process itself leaves much to be desired. It has been correctly stated that the two things you should never watch being made are sausages and laws. Unfortunately, Congress and state legislatures rarely work in practice the way they are described in civics textbooks. Arrogant committee chairmen who refuse to give hearings to bills, unrepresentative committees, unfair rules, and enormous logjams of legislation are just a small part of the problem. The result is that bills and resolutions are frequently killed in the legislative process even when they have the overwhelming support of the people.

The other side of this same coin is that legislation proposed by initiative actually undergoes much more scrutiny than many measures that are considered in the hectic atmosphere of a legislative session. For instance, a few years ago, the Texas House of Representatives unwittingly passed a resolution praising the "Boston Strangler" for his efforts at population control. Regrettably, that kind of thing happens all too frequently in legislative bodies—but rarely through the initiative process.

Perhaps because of the conservative outcome in most I&R contests, the liberal National Education Association (NEA) and the AFL-CIO, along with their state affiliates, have opposed expansion of the initiative into those jurisdictions where the process does not already exist. In fairness, it should be noted that many highly principled liberals with whom I disagree on most issues are among the supporters of the initiative.

On the conservative side, the initiative attracts its share of opposition, particularly from some representatives of what some call "Big Business." One corporate lobbyist, testifying before a committee of the Texas State Senate, said he opposed the initiative because the business community would "not have the opportunity to educate Mr. Six Pack."

Despite this misguided historical distrust of the average voter, many conservatives have begun to reconsider their opposition to the initiative. This reconsideration comes in the wake of what Patrick Buchanan described as *Conservative Votes, Liberal Victories*—the process summarized at the beginning of this essay.

The efforts to expand the initiative to the 27 states that do not now have it—and the proposed national level initiative—are part of the struggle to implement democracy. This is a struggle which has persisted throughout human history. The initiative will be no panacea to the ills of our modern democracy, but it will help restore popular confidence in our system of government.

There will, of course, be intense opposition to expansion of the initiative process. But we live in a time when narrow, well-organized interests dominate the legislative process—both in popular perception and in fact. It is time to consider institutional changes that will improve the American system. It is time for changes that will once again empower voters themselves to shape the American agenda.

Conclusion

This is not the end. Of this book, yes. But of the search for new ideas, new approaches, new solutions which will comprise the conservative movement of the 21st century, this book is only a beginning. This is a book of ideas, explorations, theories. Reforms are suggested and some public policy positions are advocated, but it is with the humble realization that many of them may be time-bound. Events may overtake some of the suggestions, just as events may overtake some of the players on the political scene at the time the book was written. That does not reduce the validity of these or other ideas discussed in these pages. They are all the germs of ideas that will be on the agenda in the 21st century.

It should be clear by now that the authors of *Future 21* are proceeding from a set of premises that differ from those of established liberalism, or even, in some cases, of classical liberalism. They are premises upon which the political movement—variously called the New Right, the Religious Right, the traditional-values movement—has been built. It is our premise, for instance, that individuals should seek to achieve by every means possible their fullest potential, and should be responsible for their own needs and those of their families. That is not new. What is new is the second part of that premise: When individuals cannot provide, there exists the obligation on the part of other individuals to care for them. The extension of this care may be delegated to government when more personal expressions of it are unavailable, though personal charity is preferable to government compulsory welfare.

The United States is a great nation, and should continue to be one. It is our premise that the United States has first of all an obligation to its own citizens, and only secondarily an obligation to the rest of the world—hence, if serving national interests is frustrated by global commitments the prioritization seems clear to us.

We believe in growth, but not as 19th-century visionaries believed in it, as a panacea. We know that human nature is flawed. We know that mankind is not perfectible. We do not begin with that expectation for ourselves, so we will not be frustrated when we fail to achieve it. We begin with the belief that in order to change society people must change themselves. The liberalism of the Great Society mentality began with the opposite premise, and when the creation and expansion of a welfare state failed to produce a generation of angels in human form, liberals did not know what to do next. Our intense desire for education reform that will restore strong character to our citizens stems from this deep belief. In order that life in our society may improve, it is essential that the character of the young be formed in virtue; therefore we seek to deconsolidate and defederalize the education system in this country, and to maximize parental control. The family will be strong when it has functions to perform and educating children is a good place to start in returning functions to the family. Others need to follow.

Our strategies for making the criminal's lot a less happy one stem from the same fundamental premise: Crimes are going to be committed because there are going to be people who do evil. The correct strategy for a society to pursue is to minimize the harm its wrongdoers can perpetuate, and maximize the discomfort to them from doing wrong. Thus, our concern for victims' rights and for tougher criminal justice reforms. We believe politicians are as fallible as anybody else; hence, their personal power should be kept within limits. From that premise comes our conclusion that the length of a Congressman's or Senator's stay in office should be capped.

We have a fundamental belief in the basic soundness of the American people, too. Elitists often seem to proceed from the premise that the "people" need guidance in managing their own affairs. On the left, such thinking manifests itself in controlling people's choices—a paternalistic health care system, for instance. Elitists are afraid of what might happen if the people have too much taste of self-government. The suggestion of a national initiative as a serious proposal is a radical shift from this attitude. Not all the authors herein agree with each other on everything, of course—that is part of our diversity, and part of the reason that this book is only a beginning. The suggestion of a national initiative is made with confidence that the American people are fundamentally sound. Herein, perhaps, we differ from others who feel the people are too easily manipulated or cannot be trusted. We feel that our premises are shared by most Americans. Survey research supports that as well, in particular the 1981 Connecticut Mutual survey on values. This insurance company had expected to disprove the existence of majority adherence to traditional values in the country. Instead, their survey found a high level of religious intensity in the nation, with all the concomitant value preferences. More significantly, it also proved the existence of an immoral minority. Time after time, on issue after issue, the recognized leadership groups were far out of harmony with the populace at large. Teachers who don't think smoking marijuana is morally wrong are in charge of children whose parents do think it is morally wrong. Judges who don't think homosexuality is morally wrong are deciding cases for a citizenry who do feel its morally wrong. And so on it goes.

For discrepancies like that to continue is to perpetuate growing social disease, and the further shedding of the consensus that made possible our nation's greatness. The liberal fallacy of holding "society" largely responsible for everything that goes wrong is fast producing a nation of people who want no part of "society." The view of life, that people are responsible for what they do, gives incentive to achieve and to be good, and discourages the opposite. It makes life more challenging, true, but also more fulfilling. And what better remedy for an age that is burdened with a vast sense of minimal self-worth? What is the alternative to policies that encourage saving and investing of human as well as fiscal capital? Waste and overspending undermine individuals as well as institutions. The anti-poverty programs that have destroyed generations of those who were supposed to benefit by them are a good example of waste piled upon waste, problems producing more problems.

This book is a contribution to the idea of a conservative opportunity society. What does that mean? It means honest money, without inflation; it means jobs through economic growth; it means hastening creation of jobs through future-oriented technologies; it means balancing the budget by controlled spending; it means, as Lewis Lehrman advocates, a gold standard. The alternatives we already know: double-digit inflation; meaningless make-work jobs; continual transfusions to dying businesses; ever-increasing taxes with no control on spending to attempt, unsuccessfully, to balance a doomed budget.

Our conservatism would have decentralized and flexible government, giving local officials maximum discretion and leeway to govern their local communities. It would maximize the power of ordinary citizens to have an effect on affairs, to have their voices heard. Failed liberalism, in contrast, offers centralized, rigid government, and masses of regulations and procedures, which can never replace human judgment and are only a poor substitute for it. We believe in subsidization—the level of government closest to the problem is the best level at which it should be handled. Conservatism would stop criminals, and thus protect the innocent by making it less likely that crimes would be committed; liberals, instead, increase the police power of the state and overburden courts.

We want to stop the funding of terrorist groups with the supposed "peacemaking" money of the United Nations. We recognize that we must pursue the capability for unconventional war—only someone caught in a time warp pretends that conventional warfare is all we can expect ahead. To liberals, national health care is the next logical extension of the failed welfare state. Rather, prevention of disease, home health care and cost-control are more important. Looking toward the future and preparing for it are more important than lamenting the days gone by. Training our children in computers and exploiting the potential of computers for home-based employment are only two instances of this. Revivification of our processes of self-government is another. In everything, we are sensitive to the fundamental moral order. We consciously seek to formulate policies in harmony with human nature and which will contribute toward moral soundness and strength.

This book is about hope, about creating new frameworks for debate, about finding new solutions to old problems, about welcoming the future. Fear of the future, and preference for the old days when conservatives were only "aginners," spending their intellectual and political energies reacting to the creative ideas being generated by leftist circles, is the antithesis of what this book is about. Those who may feel threatened by the realization that new, vital forces are stirring on the political horizon should look closely, and understand that we offer hope, even if the context is unfamiliar. Of the development of political conservatism in America, the best is yet to come.

Contributors

Lewis E. Lehrman is founder of the Lehrman Institute, a public policy forum for the study of economics, foreign policy, and state and local government problems.

In 1982, Mr. Lehrman was the Republican and Conservative candidate for Governor of New York, losing to Mario Cuomo by only 180,000 votes of over five million cast. He has served the Republican Party of New York both as chairman of the 1978 Platform Committee and as chairman of the Economic Advisory Council. In 1980, he was chairman of Business for Reagan-Bush in New York State, and in 1981, he was appointed by Treasury Secretary Donald Regan as one of four "distinguished private citizens" to serve on the U.S. Gold Commission. From his work on the Gold Commission came the book *The Case for the Gold Standard,* co-authored by Congressman Ron Paul.

Mr. Lehrman is a graduate of Yale, where he was a Carnegie Teaching Fellow in history, and he received his masters degree from Harvard. He was the president of Rite Aid for nine years, and in 1977 he assumed the job of chairman of the executive committee to devote more time to public affairs. He resigned all positions with Rite Aid in January 1982.

He has in the past been a trustee and director of many educational and charitable institutions, including the American Enterprise Institute, the Heritage Foundation, the International Center for the Disabled, the Boys Club of New York, Eisenhower College of Seneca Falls, New York, and the American Jewish Forum.

Mr. Lehrman has written articles for such publications as *Harper's,* the *Washington Post,* the *New York Daily News,* and the *Wall Street Journal.*

* * *

Patrick J. Buchanan is a leading political analyst and syndicated columnist with the Tribune Company Syndicate. He appears weeknights on Cable News Network's "Crossfire," which he co-hosts with Los Angeles Times Syndicate columnist Tom Braden. The two also host a weekday talk show on WRC Radio (NBC) in Washington, D.C.

In January 1966 Mr. Buchanan became a full-time member of Richard Nixon's staff. During Mr. Nixon's ascent to the presidency, Mr. Buchanan was political strategist, press secretary, and speech writer. The day after Richard Nixon was sworn in as President, Mr. Buchanan was named Special Assistant. For the next six years, he served as speech writer for both the President and Vice President, as political strategist, and as publisher of the controversial Presidential News Summary. In 1972, he was a member of the official U.S. delegation to the People's Republic of China, and in 1974 he accompanied the President on his final summit at Moscow, Yalta, and Minsk. During the 18-month Watergate crisis, Mr. Buchanan's nationally televised testimony before the Ervin Committee was applauded by both Republican and Democrat members.

An honors graduate in English and Philosophy from Georgetown University, Mr. Buchanan holds a Master's Degree from the Graduate School of Journalism at Columbia.

His political column appears three times a week in 125 newspapers, and he has written articles for the *Nation, Rolling Stone, Conservative Digest,* and *Human Events.* Mr. Buchanan is the author of the books *The New Majority* (1973) and *Conservative Votes, Liberal Victories* (1975). In 1974 he was featured in a *Time* magazine cover story as one of the country's 200 future leaders.

* * *

Lt. Gen. Daniel O. Graham, USA (Ret.) is director of High Frontier, Inc. in Washington, D.C., an organization for the development of new policies for national defense. President Reagan's call for a space-based deterent against nuclear attack is closely aligned with the work issuing from High Frontier.

Gen. Graham is a graduate of the United States Military Academy at West Point. His distinguished miltary career includes serving his country in Germany, Korea, and Japan in various capacities, including Office of Assistant Chief of Staff, U.S. Army; Staff, Office of National Estimates, CIA; Commander 219th MI Bn, USARPAC/MACV; Director of Collections and Director of Estimates, DIA; Deputy Director CIA for Intelligence Community; and Director, DIA. He has been awarded the Distinguished Service Medal, the Distinguished Intelligence Medal, the Legion of Merit (two oak leaf clusters), and the National Armed Services Award of the Veterans of Foreign Wars, in 1980.

Gen. Graham was Research Professor, University of Miami, from 1976–1978, and served on the staff of the American Security Council and as co-chairman of Coalition for Peace Through Strength from 1978–1981. He was an adviser for Ronald Reagan's 1976 and 1980 campaigns.

He is the author of *New Strategy for the West* (1976), *Shall America*

Be Defended? SALT II and Beyond (1980), *High Frontier: A New National Strategy* (1982), and *A Defense That Defends: Blocking Nuclear Attack* (1984), with Gregory A. Fossedal.

* * *

Newt Gingrich was elected in 1978 as Georgia's only Republican congressman. He serves on the Public Works and Transportation Committee, the Aviation Committee, and the House Administration Committee. He has made a reputation as an innovator, a challenger of the status quo, and one who sees problems through to solutions.

Heading the list of Congressman Gingrich's legislative achievements are programs to fight inflation and wasteful government spending. As a member of the Military Reform Caucus, he is developing a defense posture for the nation's survival, with emphasis on bolstering the National Guard and bringing free market principles to Pentagon procurement.

Mr. Gingrich received his bachelor's degree from Emory University and his master's degree and his doctorate in modern European history from Tulane University. He was a professor of History and Environmental Studies at West Georgia College in Carrollton for seven years before winning election to Congress.

* * *

James A. M. Muncy is consultant to the White House Office of Science and Technology Policy, in which capacity he has authored or contributed to several papers and speeches on long-term goals for America's space program and space commercialization policy. He is founder and president of Using Space for America, a national pro-space civic league.

Mr. Muncy was an Echols Scholar at the University of Virginia. In 1981 he founded the Action Committee on Technology, a grass roots pro-technology lobby. That year he also served as Executive Director of the newly-formed Congressional Staff Space Group, and helped to found the Congressional Space Caucus. In 1982, he served as a staff aide to Congressman Newt Gingrich, before taking on his present position.

Mr. Muncy has written op-ed columns for *USA Today* and the *Washington Times,* and he has been quoted in *Newsweek* and the *Wall Street Journal.*

* * *

Burton Yale Pines is Vice President for Research at the Heritage Foundation in Washington, D.C., where he supervises the Foundation's domestic, foreign policy, defense, and United Nations studies; the lecture and seminar series; and *Policy Review.*

Mr. Pines was formerly Associate Editor of *Time* magazine, during which time he was chief of the magazine's East European bureau, deputy chief of the Chicago bureau, and served in the Saigon and Bonn bureaus. He is a three-time winner of the New York Newspaper Guild's "Page One" award for outstanding reporting on domestic and foreign affairs.

Mr. Pines received his B.A. and M.A. degrees from the University of Wisconsin, and he has completed his doctoral coursework in modern European history. He is the author of *Back to Basics,* a book analyzing the conservative resurgence in the United States.

* * *

Major General John Kirk Singlaub, USA (Ret.) is national chairman of the U.S. Council for World Freedom. He attracted the attention of the American public in 1977 when, as Chief of Staff of the United Nations Command in Korea, he openly took exception to the Carter Administration's order to cut back forces in that area. He was subsequently relieved of that command, and he retired the following year.

Gen. Singlaub is a graduate of the University of California at Los Angeles where he was Cadet Colonel of the ROTC. Commissioned as a second lieutenant of infantry on January 14, 1943, he immediately volunteered for parachute duty. During World War II his duties included a parachute mission into France to organize, train, and lead a French resistance unit to assist the Allied Invasion Forces. In 1945, he led Chinese guerrillas against the Japanese on the Indo-China/Chinese border; he also led a mission resulting in the rescue of 400 Allied prisoners of war held by the Japanese on Hainan Island.

In 1966, Gen. Singlaub was assigned to Vietnam as Commander of the Joint Unconventional Warfare Task Force. On July 1, 1976, he was made Chief of Staff, United Nations Command, United States Forces, Korea, and the Eighth U.S. Army in Seoul. In addition, he helped establish the Ranger Training Center at Ft. Benning, where he taught, and he was Deputy Assistant Secretary of Defense for Drug and Alcohol Abuse from 1971–73.

Gen. Singlaub has been the recipient of 33 military decorations, including the Distinguished Service Medal with oak leaf cluster, the Silver Star, the Legion of Merit (two oak leaf clusters), and the Purple Heart with oak leaf cluster.

Charles A. Moser is Professor of Slavic and Chairman of the Department of Slavic Languages and Literatures at George Washington University in Washington, D.C. He is at present treasurer of the Free Congress Foundation in Washington.

In the past, Dr. Moser actively worked to support the U.S. military commitment in Vietnam and to head off the congressional cut-off of funds to support U.S. military operations in Cambodia. He served as treasurer of the Committee for a Free China, and from 1981–1983 as treasurer of the Committee for a Free Afghanistan. He has visited almost all the communist bloc countries of Eastern Europe.

After receiving his undergraduate degree from Yale, Dr. Moser received his PhD from Columbia University, with a year's interval at Leningrad State University in 1958–59. He taught at Yale from 1960–67, and has been at George Washington University since.

He is the author of a number of articles and reviews in the fields of Russian literary history and Bulgarian literary and political history, as well as studies on public policy issues, including economic regulation, the federal budget, Social Security, and the election of the Speaker of the U.S. House of Representatives. Dr. Moser's books include *Antinihilism in the Russian Novel of the 1860's* (1964), *Pisemsky: A Provincial Realist* (1969), *A History of Bulgarian Literature 865–1944* (1972), *Denis Fonvizin* (1979), and *Dimitrov of Bulgaria: A Political Biography of Dr. Georgi M. Dimitrov* (1979).

* * *

Connaught Marshner is chairman of the National Pro-Family Coalition, a clearinghouse of some 100 local, state, and national pro-family organizations, founded in 1980 in opposition to Jimmy Carter's White House Conference on Families. In June 1980 Mrs. Marshner led the walkout of pro-family delegates from the Baltimore White House Conference.

Since 1979, Mrs. Marshner has served as editor of the *Family Protection Report,* a monthly newsletter of the Free Congress Research and Education Foundation. She is chairman of the bi-weekly Library Court Meetings, a coalition of 40 separate organizations concerned with education, family, moral, and traditional value issues.

During the 1980 Reagan-Bush campaign, she was named chairman of the Family Policy Board. In June 1982, President Reagan appointed Mrs. Marshner chairman of the Advisory Panel on Financing of Elementary and Secondary Education, and since February 1982, she has served as vice chairman of the American Society of Local Officials, a conservative organization.

Mrs. Marshner graduated in 1971 from the University of South

Carolina, where she was trained as a teacher. She is the author of *Blackboard Tyranny*, a critique of the public education establishment. She formerly worked with the Heritage Foundation, the Office of Economic Opportunity, and with the Committee for the Survival of a Free Congress.

* * *

Allan C. Carlson is Executive Vice President of The Rockford Institute and editor of *Persuasion at Work*. He holds his PhD in modern European history, and has received research grants from the American Scandinavian Foundation and the Institute for Educational Affairs.

In the past, Dr. Carlson served as Assistant to the President and Lecturer in History at Gettysburg College, MEH Fellow at the American Enterprise Institute for Public Policy Research, and Assistant Director of the Governmental Affairs office for the Lutheran Council in the U.S.A.

His articles on social, educational, and religious issues have appeared in *The Public Interest, Policy Review, This World, Chronicles of Culture, The American Spectator, Communio,* and other journals.

* * *

Ronald F. Docksai is Staff Director for the United States Senate Committee on Labor and Human Resources, chaired by Senator Orrin G. Hatch (R-Utah). He previously served with Senator Hatch from 1977–1982 as Majority Health Director for the Committee. In June 1982 he was appointed Special Assistant to the Director of the Office of Personnel Management, for Dr. Donald Devine, and he returned to the Committee in his present position in January 1983.

Dr. Docksai, considered a leading authority on health and education policy, authored the chapter blueprinting a new structure for the Department of Education in the Heritage Foundation's Mandate for Leadership study prepared for the Reagan Administration in 1980. He was highly instrumental in the formulation of drug regulatory policy, as well as legislation to expand provisions of home health care (S. 234), and longterm health care policies.

In addition, he has served as the U.S. representative to international conferences, sponsored by the International Communications Agency, in India and the Soviet Union. He was Captain in the U.S. Army Reserve, during which time he earned degrees in adjutant administration at the Army's Defense Analysis School.

Dr. Docksai received his B.A. degree from St. John's College in New York City, and his M.A. and M.P.A degrees in international relations and public administration respectively from New York University. He received his PhD in government from Georgetown University in Washington, D.C.

* * *

John C. Grunden is owner and president of The Jonathon, Risk & Insurance Consultants, Inc. and president of its affiliate company, Association Risk Management. As a special guest lecturer, he has taught classes on "Contractors' Risk Management" at Georgia Institute of Technology in Atlanta, and insurance courses for the Independent Insurance Agents Association of Georgia through their continuing education program.

Mr. Grunden served as finance chairman for Newt Gingrich's 1978 congressional campaign, and as campaign chairman in the 1980 race. He continues as a senior adviser to Congressman Gingrich and his campaigns. He has also been active in the establishment, filings, and funding of various political action committees. In 1982, he was a participant in the White House Conference on Voluntarism and the Private Sector Initiatives. His interest in the "new informational age" and the increasing impact of computer technology on society led him to organize Americans for Family Opportunity, an association to promote home earning and home learning via the computer.

Mr. Grunden graduated from Georgia State University with a B.B.A. degree, and from Continental National American Insurance Group Training Institute in Chicago. He received C.L.U. training at the Business School of Georgia State.

* * *

Paul M. Weyrich is Executive Director of the Committee for the Survival of a Free Congress, a bi-partisan conservative political action committee, and President of the Free Congress Research and Education Foundation, Inc., a public policy research organization.

Mr. Weyrich is also President of Coalitions for America, a nonpartisan organization to bring conservative, business, and single-issue groups together to coordinate their efforts in economics, social and educational issues, national defense, and foreign policy. In addition, he is founder and Chairman of the Board of the American Society of Local Officials, which works on public policy issues with mayors and county and local officials.

Following the 1966 elections Mr. Weyrich came to Washington as press secretary to Senator Gordon Allott of Colorado, a position he held for four years, and in which he assisted Mr. Allott in his work on the Transportation Appropriations Committee. From 1973–1977 Mr. Weyrich served as Special Assistant to Senator Carl Curtis of Nebraska. During that period he founded and became the first president of the Heritage Foundation, a position he left in 1974 to found the Committee for the Survival of a Free Congress.

In the last four elections Mr. Weyrich has helped direct a large volunteer operation of conservative congressional staffers to assist non-incumbent candidates with speech writing and issue development. He has been an advisor to such conservative religious groups as Moral Majority and Religious Roundtable.

Before coming to Washington, Mr. Weyrich was a broadcaster and journalist in Wisconsin and Denver, Colorado. He now writes a monthly column for *Conservative Digest.*

* * *

Patrick B. McGuigan is director of the Free Congress Foundation's Judicial Reform Project and editor of the *Initiative and Referendum Report.* His analysis of the initiative process has been quoted in *Time* magazine, *Congressional Quarterly,* and major newspapers.

Before coming to Washington, Mr. McGuigan taught history and education at Oklahoma State University, where he received his B.A. and M.A. degrees. He was a contributor to *Early Military Forts and Posts in Oklahoma.*

Mr. McGuigan has written numerous articles on participatory democracy, congressional races, family policy issues, and the American legal system which have appeared in such publications as the *Christian Science Monitor,* the *Washington Times,* the Dayton (Ohio) *Journal-Herald,* and the *Political Report.* In addition, he is editor (with Randall R. Rader) of *A Blueprint for Judicial Reform* (1981) and of *Criminal Justice Reform* (1983).

Index

ABMs, 56, 57
ABM Treaty, 56, 57
ACLU, 205–206, 224
AFL-CIO, 228
ASAT, 68
Abortion, vii, 124, 125, 140, 164, 190, 192, 195, 202–205
Accra, 38
Aesculapius, 123
Aerospace Corporation, 53
Afghanistan, 28, 43, 44, 78, 79, 90–91, 101, 103, 104, 107, 111–112, 114
Africa, 29–30, 39, 66, 91, 98, 102
African National Congress, 75–77, 87
African Development Bank, 38
Air Force, 55, 94, 188
airlines, 64
Air Mail, 64
Alaska, 30
Agrarian Age, 177
Algeria, 12
alpha-fetaprotein tests, 119
American Academy of Arts and Sciences, 141
Aluminum Co. of America, 65
American Enterprise Institute, 142
American Indians, 138
American Revolutionary War, 18
American (U.S.) health care, 167, 168, 169, 170, 175, 175n
American Medical Association, 119
Amin, Idi, 80
Angola, 91, 101, 114
Anscombe, G. E. M., 129
Anti-defamation League, 73
Apollo-Soyuz, 67
Aquarius, Age of, 152
Arabian crude, 29
Arabs, 29
Arafat, Yassir, 77
Aristotle, 130, 135
astronauts, U.S., 67
Argentina, 27, 30, 34, 37, 43, 67–68, 90–91
Army, 94
Army Air Corps, 64
Armenians, 80
Asia, 44, 98, 102
Asian, 142
Asian Development Bank, 38
Australia, 90

B-52, 54
balanced budget, 12, 21, 226

Baldwin vs Missouri, 201
Bangladesh, 61
Bank of America, 30, 34, 36
banks, private, 5
Barents Sea, 34
Barlow, Richard J. S., Jr., 217
barter economy, 7
Bateman, Newton, 136
Benelux Countries, 90
Bengalis, 80
Bentham, Jeremy, 127
Berger, Raoul, 197
Berlin, 44
Bible, 128, 136
Bickel, Alexander, 198
Bill of Rights, 200ff
Bismark, 43
Black, Hugo, 218–219
blacks, 131, 138, 140, 142, 160
Blaine Amendment, 200–201
Blueprint for Judicial Reform, 197, 207
Bohemian Grove, 32
bonds, 5ff
Born Again Christian (Cromwell), 40
Bolivia, 80
Boston, 138–141
Bowlby (John), 150
Bowman, Dr., 59
Brandt, Dr. Edward, 174
Brandt, Willy, 33
Brasilia, 29
Brazil, 27, 37
Brezhnev, 28, 111
Britain, 43, 75, 90, 92
British, 44
Bretton Woods, 19, 21, 24
Brown vs Board of Education, 138
Buchanan, Patrick, 229
Buddhism, 91
Buenos Aires, 30, 34
Bulgaria, 109
bureaucracy, 185ff
Burks, Larry, 195
Burundi, 80
Business Week, 65
Buthelese, Gaftsa, 78

C47, 100
CBO, 174
CIA, 37, 99
Caitlin, George, 26
California, 142, 162
California Medicine, 120–121, 123–124, 126

242

California Proposition 13, 223
Cambodia, 43, 79, 103–104, 106, 113
Canada, 90
Candidate, The, 228
Canton, 39
capital punishment, 119
Cardozo, Justice Benjamin, 213
Carlucci, 53
Carrington, Frank L., 216
Carrington, Lord, 105
Carter, President Jimmy, 12, 13, 30, 45–46, 49, 83, 96, 111, 113, 168
Cassandras, 30
Castro, 80
Catholics, 140
Catholics, Roman, 90, 137, 142, 193
Census Bureau (Bureau of the Census), 121–122, 162
Ceaucescu, 33–34
Chad, 43, 79, 91
Chamberlain, John, 35
Champion, George, 37
Chase Manhattan Bank, 28, 31, 32, 35–37, 169
Childs, John, 137
Chile, 72–73, 80, 87, 104, 113
China, 66, 107, 111, 112
Chipman, Donald, 188–189
Christ, 4
Christian, 91, 93, 130, 135, 142, 161, 191
Christian Science Monitor, 223
Christianity, 91, 136
Chrysler Corporation, 37
Churchill, Winston, 68, 108
Citibank, 29
Clausen, A. W. (Tommy), 39
coalition building, viii
Code of Restrictive Business Practices, 82
coin, 7
Colombia, 44
Colossus computer, 178
Columbus, Christopher, 62, 65–66
Comecon, 27
Commodity Credit Corporation, 36
common heritage, 84
Common Market, 27
Commoner, Barry, 59
communes, 150–151
Comprehensive Crime Control Act, 211ff
Computerland Corp., 179
computers, home, 176ff
Confucius, 66, 91
Congo River, 36
Congregationalists, 140
Congress, 7, 11, 23–24, 34, 36, 43, 96, 97, 164–165, 169, 170–171, 200–201, 203, 205, 211, 222, 223, 225
Congressional Record, 59
Connecticut Mutual Life Report on American Values in the 1980's, 199, 231
consequentialism, 125–128, 133

conservative(s), vii–viii, 46, 47, 60, 61–64, 96, 108, 134, 156, 161, 169, 179, 182, 185, 186–187, 194, 197–198, 209, 222–224
Conservative Votes, Liberal Victories, 229
Constantinople, 104–105
Constitution (U.S.), 6–7, 21, 23, 198, 200–207
Consumer Interpol, 85
convertible dollar, 23
Continental Army, 100
Cooper, C. C., 139
Cord, Robert, 205
Corps of Engineers (Army), 63
courtier, 188–189
Cranston, Senator Alan, 43–45
Crime Clock, 209
Criminal Justice Reform, 211ff
Cromwell, Oliver, 40, 152
Cuba, 43, 80, 86, 95, 101
Cubberly, Ellwood P., 137
Czechoslovakia, 93

Dar es Salaam, 38
Day of Truth, 31
DeBakey, Dr. Michael, 174
Declaration of Independence, 8, 129
deflation, 3ff
Defense Department, 50, 52–53, 95, 101
de Gaulle, Charles, 12
De La Madrid, 33
democracy, direct, viii
Democrats, 168, 171
Denmark, 90
dense pack, 49, 52, 95, 101
Deschooling Society, 141
detente, 28, 93
Department of Education, 143
Department of Health and Human Services, 11, 167–168, 170, 174
de Tocqueville, Alexis, 143
Dewey, John, 137, 139
diagnosis related groups, 175
Diderot, Denis, 139
Disaster by Decree, 197
Doctor's Declaration, 123
Doe vs Bolton, 202
Dole, Senator Robert, 170
domestic problem(s), 103ff
Douglas, Stephen, 63
DuBois, Cora, 137
Doyle, Denis, 142
Duggan, Linda J., 216
Durenberger (Senator), 170

East, Senator John, 200, 204
eccentric, vii
Ecclesiastes, 211
educational system, 134ff
Ehrlich, Paul, 121
Eisenhower, Dwight D., 50–51, 108

244 Index

Elementary and Secondary Education Act, 145
El Salvador, 44, 80, 96, 101, 105–106, 114
ENIAC, 178, 179
Enigma Code, 178
Ervin, Senator Sam, 220
England, 11, 19, 24, 92
ethics, traditional, vii
Ethiopia, 79
Eureka College, 45
Europe, 27, 29, 34, 39, 93, 99
Evangelicals, 140
Evans, Christopher, 177
Explorer I, 68
Exxon Oil, 47

F15 Wing, 100
Faber, Ed, 178
Falklands, (war), 34, 67
family, 148ff, 151–153, 154–157, 162, 164, 177–178
family allowances, 163
family, black, 153, 162
family, bourgeois, 148–149
family business, 149
family, ethos, 149
family farms, 149
family, nuclear, 128, 148, 149
family, traditional, 148, 156–157
father figure, 151
Fazal, Anwar, 85
Fed, 4–6, 9, 10–16, 24, 30
Federal Bureau of Investigation (FBI), 209
Federal Reserve notes, 7–8, 21
Federal Reserve (system), 4, 5, 8, 9, 10, 12–14, 23–24, 30, 31
FEHB, 171
financial disorder, 3
Ford, Gerald, 169
foreign currencies, 5
Fourteenth Amendment, 201
France, 12, 19, 90, 125
Frankfurter, Justice Felix, 198, 206, 219
Free Congress Foundation, 197, 202
French (the), 44
French Mirages, 33
Friedman, Milton, 12n
Fulda Gap, 100
full employment, 3ff

GAB, 42
GBMD I, 49, 51, 53–56
GNP, 167–168
Gallup Poll, 74, 199, 209–210, 225
Gann Initiative, 216
General Accounting Office (GAO), 174
Genesis, 6
General Agreement on Trade and Tariffs, 71
Geneva, 72, 76, 123

Gerard, Jules, 202, 207
German, 135, 136
Germany, 4, 12, 17, 19, 92, 101
Germany, East, 44
Germany, West, 4, 44, 90, 100
Gingrich, Congressman Newt, 180
Giorgianni, Joseph (Jo-Jo), 217
gold, gold standard, 13–14, 16–24
Government by Judiciary, 197
Graglia, Lino, 197
Graham, Lt. Gen. Daniel, 66–67
grain embargo, 113, 115
Grant, Gerald, 141
Graubard, Stephen, 141
Great Depression, the, 22, 30, 34
Great Society, 162, 230
Greece, 152–153
Grisez, *quoted,* 127–128
Guatemala, 80
Gulag(s), 44, 123

Hamburg banker, 34
Hamilton, Alexander, 18, 22, 62
Hand, W. Brevard, 206, 219
Harlan, John Marshall, 214
Hart, Senator Gary, 194
Harvard Mark I computer, 178, 179
Hatch, Senator Orrin, 170, 174
Hawkins, Senator Paula, 170
Health Action International and Pesticide Action Network, 85
health planning, 169
Heckler, Margaret, 170
Heritage Foundation, 75, 199
Helms, Senator Jesse, 202, 203
Helsinki Accords, 111
Herzlinger, Dr. Regina, 172–173
High Frontier, 46–60, 66
Higgins, Thomas, 197
Hippocrates, 121, 123, 125
Hippocratic oath, 123
Hispanics, 138, 142
Hitler, 4, 43, 44, 105
Hobbes, 127
Hobson's choice, 27
Holmes, Oliver Wendell, 98, 201
homosexual(s), 139, 157, 159, 163
Hong Kong, 90
Hoover, Herbert, 28, 62
House of Mirrors, 72
Human Life Statute, 202, 203
Hume, David, 139
Hutchins, Robert, 137
Hutus, 88
Hyde, Congressman Henry, 204

I & R (initiative and referendum), 223ff
IBM, 178, 194
IBOs, 80
ICBM, 50, 56, 68, 100
IMF (International Monetary Fund), 31–34, 35–38, 71–72

Index

Illich, Ivan, 141
India, 33, 39
in vitro fertilization, 119, 128, 132
Indonesia, 31, 91
Industrial Age, 177
Industrial Revolution, 24, 63
infanticide, 119
inflation, 3ff, 4, 11–12, 18, 19, 162, 168
information revolution, 177
Inkatha, 78
Institute for Security and Cooperation in Outer Space, 59
Institute of Policy Studies, 85
Inter-American Development Bank, 38
interest, 3ff, 4, 9, 12, 13, 18–20, 22–25
Interfaith Center of Corporate Responsibility, 85
Internal Revenue Service, 156
International Atomic Energy Agency, 71, 87
International Development Association 39
International Labor Organization, 72
International Organization of Consumers Unions (I.O.C.U.), 85
International Telecommunications Union, 71, 82, 87, 88
investment, long term, 10
Iran, 30, 43, 73, 78, 79, 80, 111
Iraq, 43, 78, 79
Irish, 135, 152
Irony of Early School Reform, The, 140
Isabella, Queen (of Spain), 66
Israel, 73, 77, 78, 79, 87, 104, 151
Italy, 44, 90
Ivory Coast, 89

Jamestown Colony, 65
Japan, 29, 31, 43, 54, 90
Jaruzelski, 36, 111
Jastram, Prof. Roy, 20
Jefferson, Thomas, 8, 38, 65
Jepsen, Senator Roger, 204
Jewish, 135, 206
Jews, 140
Johnson and Johnson, 64
Johnson, Samuel, 11
Jordan River, 71, 87
Journal of Medicine, 120
Journal of the National Education Association, 139
Judaism, 128
Judeo-Christian, 96, 128, 132, 135, 205
Judges, judicial, 197ff
Judicial Accountability, 207
Judicial Reform Act, 200–202
judicial reforms, states' actions, 216–218
Judicial Review Unmasked, 197

KGB, 45, 94, 101
Kadar, 34
Kagan, Jerome, 39

Kama River, 28
Kamal regime, 111
Kamenev, 28
Kampuchea, 78
Kant, Immanuel, 139
Katz, Michael, 140
Kelly, Art, 227
Kemp, Congressman Jack, 226
Kennedy Administration, 168
Kennedy, John F., 225
Kennedy, Senator Ted, 175, 224
Kenya, 89
Keynes, John Maynard, 12n
Keynesian(ism), 11, 13–15, 22
kibbutz, 150–151, 155
kidney machine, 131
King, Martin Luther, Jr., 138
Kinshasa, 33
Kirkpatrick, Jeane Jordan, (Ambassador to UN), 73, 80, 110
Kissinger, Henry, 28
Korea, North, 79
Korea, South, 89, 90
Korolev, Sergei, 67
Kosygin, 58
Kristol, Irving, 64, 86
Kurds, 80
Kurtz, 36
Kuwait, 75

LDCs, 31
LIBOR, 29
La Leche League, 155
Labor and Education, Senate Committee on, 174
Landry, Kathy, 195
Laos, 78, 79, 114
Las Vegas, 8
Latin America, 27, 34, 80, 91
Law of the Sea Treaty, 84
Laxalt, Senator Paul, 215–216
League of Women Voters (Mass.), 224
Lebanon, 43, 79, 104
lend-lease, 36
Lenin, 4, 70
Lewis and Clark, 65
liberals, 45–46, 47, 61–63, 134, 156, 169, 179, 181, 194, 198, 223–224
Libya, 43, 79
Life magazine, 121
Lincoln, Abraham, 63
Lind, Bill, 188
London, 29
London School of Economics, 38, 85
long-range ballistic missiles, 56
Louisiana Territory, 65
Luanda, 29
Lutherans, 136, 140

MAD, 46, 51–52, 57, 59, 106, 132
MADD, 217
M'Bow, Amadou-Mahtar, 82–83

MI rifle, 100–101
MX missiles, 45, 49, 54
Machiavelli, 127
Madison, 38
Malthusian, 61
Mann, Horace, 135–136, 137
Manny Hanny, 32, 36
Mansfield, E. D., 135
Manufacturers Hanover (bank), 31
Mao, 4
Marine(s) Corps, 194
Markham, Edwin, 34
Marshall, Plan(s), 27, 39, 97
Marx(ism, ist), 28, 30, 33, 38,76, 102, 108, 129
McClellan, James, 205
McDonnell-Douglas corporation, 64
McDowell, Gary L., 204–205
McGinness, Joe, 228
McGovern coalition, 59
McGuigan, Patrick, vii, 222–223
McNamara, Robert, 39
medical ethics, 119ff, 123–124, 125–127, 131
Medicare, Medicaid, 168, 173
Mellon, 38
Methodists, 140
Mexico, 27, 30–31, 33, 35, 37
Mexico City, 83
Military Courtier and the Illusion of Competence, The, 188
Micro Millennium, The, 177
Mill, John Stuart, 127
Ming Emperor, 66
mint act, the, 18
Minutemen(man), 54, 100
Miranda vs Arizona, 210
Miskitoe Indians, 80
Moakley, Congressman Joe, 59
Mobutu, Joe, 36
monetary standard, 3
monetarist 11–15, 12n
money, 3, 4ff
money, real, 6–11
"monotrophy," 150
Montessori, Maria, 181
Mormons, 140
Morocco, 43
Morris, Van Cleve, 137
Moscow, 28, 79
Moslem, 91
Moynihan, Senator Daniel Patrick, 72, 84–85, 110
Mozambique, 114
multinational corporations, 81–82, 85ff
Mutual Assured Destruction (*see* MAD)
Mutual Assured Survival, 57

NASA, 63–65
NATO, 70–72, 101
Nagel, Thomas, 139
Namibia, 76, 78

Napoleon, 19
Nast, Thomas, vii
Nation At Risk, A, 144
National Center for Education Statistics, 143
National Center for Health Statistics, 122
National Council of Churches, 85, 140
National Education Association, 138, 143, 228
National Institute of Education, 143
National Liberation Movement(s), 76, 114
National Opinion Research Center, 199
National Review, 191, 201
National Rifle Association, 217, 224
national security, 44
Navy, 50–51, 94, 178, 254
Nazis, 205
Nazi regime, 123
Nedbailo, Pyotr E., 80
Neuhaus, Richard, 144
neutron bomb, 107
New Deal, 62
New International Economic Order (NIEO), 26, 32, 74, 81–84, 87–89
New Republic, 27
New World Information Order, 83
New York, 111
New York Post, 31
New Zealand, 90
Nicaragua, 44, 80, 101, 105, 106, 114
Nigeria, 31, 80
Nissan, 195
Nixon, President Richard, 4, 12, 21, 28, 107, 111
Non-Government Organizations (NGO), 85
Norris-La Guardia Act, 202
North Pacific Fur Seal Commission, 70
North Sea, 30
Norway, 90
Novak, Michael, 144
nuclear freeze, weapons, 44, 46–48, 107
Nyerere, Julius, 33

OPEC, 29, 30, 31
Ogden, William, 31
Office of Bilingual Education, 143
Office of Education (U.S.), 136
Office of Personnel Management, 171
Olympic boycott, 111
Olympics, Munich, 79
O'Neill, Tip, 224
Oregon, 176
Organization of American States, 72
Ortho Division (of Johnson & Johnson), 64

PhD candidate, 131
PLO (Palestine Liberation Organization), 43–44, 72, 73, 75–79, 87
POSSLQS, 161

Pacific, 54, 65, 93, 100
Pakistan, 33, 80
Pan-African Congress, 75
Panama Canal, 62–63, 225
Parade, 149
Parsons, Talcott, 140, 153–155
Peking, 39, 107
Pemex, 33
Pentagon, 53, 56, 59
Pentecostals, 140
People's Republic of China, 39, 105, 111, 124, 131
Percy, Senator Charles, 96
Persian Gulf, 29
Peru, 44
Piccione, 163
Pike, John, 59
Pill, the, 122
Planned Parenthood, 159
Poland, 27, 33, 44, 79, 111
Polaris (missile[s], submarine), 50, 54, 58
Politburo, 39
Politics, 135
Popeo, Dan, 218
Population Bomb, 121
Populist New Right, 35
pornography, 159, 164
Portillo, Lopez, 31
Post Office, 4
President, 23–24, 33
President's power, 24
Presbyterian, 140
Pretoria regime, 78
Princeton (New Jersey), 65
Profiles in Courage, 225
Prussia, Leland, 30

Quirk, William, 27, 29

race track, 49, 52, 54
Rader, Randall R., 214
Radio Bulgaria, Service of, 109
Radio Free Europe, 109
Radio Liberty, 109
railroads, 63, 135
Raskin, Marcus, 141
Reagan Administration, 12, 15–16, 39, 106, 108, 110, 168
Reagan, President, 4, 13, 14–15, 26–27, 59, 68, 205, 211
Reagan revolution, 12, 39
Reagan, Ronald (W.), 13–14, 21, 26, 33, 35–36, 38–40, 45, 50, 52, 168, 170, 185, 222
Reaganomics, 32
Rechtin, Dr. Eberhardt, 228
Redford, Robert, 228
Regan, Donald, 27, 32, 39
Rehnquist, Justice William, 203
Reinecke, William L., 208–209
Republic of China, 111
Republican Party, 32

Republicans, 171
revolution, 4ff
revolution, technological, 176
Rhodesia, 113
Roberts, Paul Craig, 37
Rockefeller, David, 28, 29, 32
Rockefeller Family Fund, 59
Roe vs Wade, 202–203
Rolls Royce, 179
Roosevelt, Franklin D., 21
Roosevelt, Theodore, 63
Roper Poll, 74
Roper, Stephanie, Committee, bills, 218
Rubik's Cube, 167
Rueff, Jacques, 12
Rumania, 27, 33
Russia, 4, 43, 191–193, 195
SALT II, 46, 51, 52, 58
SR-71, 54
START, 51–52
SWAPO, 73, 76, 77, 78, 87
Salyut (space stations, Salyut 6, 7), 67
Sandinista, 114
satellites, 49, 54–56, 67–68
Satellites, Direct Broadcast, 63
San Francisco, 34
Saudi Arabia, 30, 43, 75
savings, 9–10
Scandinavian, 135
Schlesinger, Steven, 213
Schmidt, Helmut, 4
Schurmann, Carl W. A., 73
Schweiker, Richard, 170
Scylla and Charybdis, 35
seabed mining, 84
Selling of the President, 1968, The, 228
Senate, 32, 74, 185
Senate Foreign Relations Committee, 96
Separation of Church and State, 215
Shamanism, 91
Shanghai, 39
Sharp, Clifford, 227
Shultz, George, 32
Siberia, Gulags, 44
Signal Corps, 55
Sindlinger & Co., 199
Singapore, 84, 89
situationism, 125ff, 128, 133
Slavic, 135
Smith, Adam, 30
Smith, William French, 211, 215
Social Security, 121–122, 168, 171
Solzhenitsyn, Alexander (Aleksandr), 109, 191–192
South Africa, 17–18, 72, 73, 77–78, 79, 90, 113
South Atlantic, 67
Soviet Bloc, 30, 37, 56, 90, 102, 109
Soviet cosmonauts, 67
Soviet Empire, 29, 38
Soviet Institute of International Relations, 94

Soviet MIGS, 33
Soviet Military Power, 67
Soviet Union, 17, 44–46, 50, 60, 75, 79, 99, 104, 105, 106, 108, 109, 112, 115, 195
Soviets, vii, 46, 49, 55–58, 66–68, 93, 94–95, 101, 106
Space Shuttle, 47, 63, 64, 67
Space Studies Institute, 65
Spain, 66, 75
Spencer, Herbert, 11
Spetsnaz Troops, 101
Spitz, Rene, 150
Sprinkel, Beryl, 32
Sputnik, 68
Stalin, 36
Stanmeyer, William, 200–201, 211
"Star Wars" speech (Reagan's), 52
State Department, 35, 52, 70, 99
Stone, Justice Harlan Fiske, 204
submarine, nuclear-powered, 50
subsidy, subsidies, 11
Sudan, 79
Supreme Court, 144, 145, 198
Swiss bank, 33
Syria, 79, 101

Taft, William Howard, 198
Taiwan, 84, 89, 90, 98, 107
Tanzania, 33, 84
tax credits, 145
Ten Commandments, the, 140
Tennessee, 195
Thatcher, Margaret, 11, 111
Theobold, Thomas, 29
third wave, 61, 179
Third Wave, The, 177
Third World, 14, 25–29, 33, 35–36, 78, 81–89, 90–102
Toffler, Alvin, 61, 177, 179
Tokyo, 29
Toronto, 31–32
trading companies, British, 64
Transcontinental Railroad, 63
transnationals, 81
Trilateral Commission, 32
Triple Entente, 36
Trojan Horse, 172
Tsaio-ping, Deng, 39
Turks, 104

UN (United Nations), vii, 34, 37, 38, 40, 71, 72–89, 110, 232
UNCTAD, 83
UNESCO, 71, 72, 74, 76–78, 82–83, 87–88
U.S. Treasury, treasury, vii, 10, 20, 31, 37, 39
USA Today, 43

USSR, 56–57, 92, 93, 96, 104
Ugandans, 80
Ukraine, 80
Uncle Gringo, 34
unemployment, 3ff, 4–5, 10, 11, 12–15
United States Information Agency, 109

VALOR, 216
Venezuela, 31
video games, 177ff
Vietnam (Viet Nam), 43, 72, 79, 101, 106, 113–114, 141
Viking, 65
Vienna, 72, 76
vocational education, 139
Voice of America, 45, 109
Volcker, Paul, 12–15
Voltaire, 35
von Steuben, General, 100
vouchers, 145, 172
Voyager, 65

WCTU (Women's Christian Temperance Union), 52
Wall Street Journal, 29, 204
Warsaw Pact, 27, 36
Washington (DC), 49, 52, 59, 79, 86–88, 96, 114, 168
Washington, George, 70–71, 100
Washington Legal Foundation, 218–219
Washington Post, 224
Weil, Simone, 125
Weinberger, Caspar, 59
West Europe, 27
Western Electric Co., 65
Weyrich, Paul, 197
Wigmore, Dean S. J., 213
Wilkey, Malcolm R., 198
Williams, C. Dickerman, 201
Wilson, Woodrow, 34–35, 71
window of vulnerability, 46
women's liberation, 160
Wood, Gordon S., 228
Wood, Robert, 141
World Bank, 39, 72
World Council of Churches, 85
World Health Organization (WHO), 71, 72, 77, 80–82, 87, 88
World Medical Association, 123
Wyoming, 100

Yom Kippur War, 28
Young, Andrew, 83
Yugoslavia(n), 27, 32, 33, 172

zero population growth, 152
Zeus, 157
Zhukov, General, 108
Zorinsky, Senator Edward, 212
Zulu nation, 78